Robert Westall was nine when the war broke out. He studied Fine Art at Durham University, and Sculpture at the Slade in London, before teaching art in schools in the north of England. He was also a Branch Director of the Samaritans, a journalist and an antique dealer. Between 1985 and his death in 1993, he retired to devote himself to his writing.

His first novel for children, *The Machine-Gunners*, published by Macmillan in 1975, won the Carnegie Medal. He won it again in 1982 for *The Scarecrows* (the first writer to win the medal twice), the Smarties Prize in 1989 for *Blitzcat*, and the Guardian Award in 1991 for *The Kingdom by the Sea.*

'A writer who managed to combine literary excellence with an immense talent for capturing the imagination and interest of child and, in particular, young adult readers.'
The *Independent*

Other books by Robert Westall

The Promise
Fearful Lovers
Yaxley's Cat
A Place For Me
A Time of Fire
The Witness (picture book)
Fathom Five
The Cats of Seroster
Blitzcat
The Wind Eye
Rachel and the Angel
The Machine-Gunners
The Watch House
The Devil on the Road
The Haunting of Chas McGill
Ghosts and Journeys

CHILDREN OF THE BLITZ

MEMORIES OF WARTIME CHILDHOOD

ROBERT WESTALL

MACMILLAN
CHILDREN'S BOOKS

For John Geer, a Child of the Blitz

First published 1985 by Penguin Books Ltd, Harmondsworth, Middlesex

This revised edition published 1995 by Macmillan Children's Books
a division of Macmillan Publishers Limited
Cavaye Place London SW10 9PG
and Basingstoke

Associated companies throughout the world

ISBN 0330 33485 9

9 8 7 6 5 4 3 2 1

A CIP catalogue record for this book is available from the British Library.

Designed by Design 23
Printed by Cox & Wyman Ltd. Reading, Berkshire

CONTENTS

CONTRIBUTORS

AT THE RISK OF SEEMING INVIDIOUS, I must single out some people; because they contributed not just incidents, but whole ways of life.

First 'Boy, London' – the incomparable John Geer, to whom this book is dedicated; crawling down a foot-wide tunnel to damp down a phosphorus bomb at the age of fourteen; crawling under collapsed houses to separate the living from the dead at the age of seventeen – 'because I was the smallest'. Whenever I read in *The Times* that some notable 'had a good war' I think of John Geer.

'Girl, London', his doughty six-year-old counterpart, was Jean Underhill. I'm glad girls figure largely. Bessie Shea was my Orkney correspondent, who opened my eyes to a much livelier 'Phoney War' than most of us knew, round the British naval base of Scapa Flow. A mixture of Heinkel seaplanes and Sunday School outings; dead men washed ashore, salvaged kegs of butter and Bible classes.

Then there was my adorable communist grammar-school evacuee, Doreen Manwaring, battering away at the English class system in Folkestone, and hoping that the German bomber overhead will get away; though I couldn't resist showing her change of attitude as a Cambridge student, once Russia had entered the war. And lastly, A. C. Wilson, actually under the Nazi jackboot in Holland.

The boys, though, were after adventure. "Boy, Tyneside", in hot pursuit of bowler-hatted spies and German POW's was Aidan Harrison. Leading the real-life 'machine-gunners' of Withernsea was Reg Tomes. Cycling round blitzed Coventry with a bomb on his crossbar was Len Nugent, now of Barrack Heights, New South Wales. Michael Hyde collected his arsenal of weapons in Northamptonshire; John Houghton was the armigerous 'Boy, Edinburgh'.

And there were gentler souls. Alex Hastie in Northumberland

discovered his abiding 'love of country life'. The thoughtful 'Boy, Manchester' was Keith Mottram. I'll leave you to guess who the other 'Boy, Tyneside' was . . .

Otherwise, I'd like to thank, for their memories:
S. Balmforth; Emma Bell; R. Bennet; B. E. Bleckly; C. Board; J. M. Bowen; Chris Brazier; Lillian Cheeseman; Alan Campbell Cooke; H. S. Cousins; Alan Cross; Mary Davies; Janet Diamond; Miss I. Drennan; Betty Dutton; Paddy Easton; Richard Elliot; Ronnie Gaffery; Sarah Goodman; T. Gordon; Joan Henry; Irene Hosking; H. Jones; J. Jones; Mrs Lamb; Colin Lynch; G. J. McEntaggart; Mrs McEntaggart; Mr Morison; S. Peake; A. E. Prior; Rosemary Ralph; M. A. Read; Hazel Reddy; Mr Ringstead; M. Roberts; Mrs Robertson; Jill Rodwell; Peter Rutter; Richard Eyan; George Saven; Margaret Smith; N. Stead; Mr Stead; S. Thomas; Michael Towey; John Charles West; A. Williams; C. Winrow; P. Woolley; Mrs E. Woolley.

Next I must thank Mrs Caroline Aherne, Deputy Head of Ellesmere Port Catholic High School, and her intrepid team of young researchers who opened up for me 'the war on Merseyside'. Their names are: S. Balmforth; Kay Colligan; Debby Cook; Aidan Daly; Catharine Ellison; Tracey Fielding; P. Harris; Martha Jones; Robert Keir; M. McEntaggart; Sandra Morison; Colin Murphy; Michael Omar; Angela Pacetta; William Peake; Christopher Reddy; Rachel Reed; Joanne Ringstead; Andrew Roberts; Emma Robertson; Kerry Ryan; Andrew L. Simcott; Carol Smyth; Karen Swarbrick; Delia Sworm; Anthony Thompson; Gerard Tran; John A. West; Gordon Wilson; Michelle Winrow; Stephen J. Woolley.

Lastly, I must thank the Imperial War Museum's Department of Printed Records, and especially Ms Valerie France, and the Librarian of the Royal Marines' Regimental Museum, Portsmouth.

ROBERT WESTALL

FOREWORD

IT ALL STARTED with an old copy of the *Sunday Express* dated 20 February 1944.

THREE BOYS AND A PLATOON OF MARINES

With three rifles and 400 rounds of 0.22 ammunition, three boys aged twelve to fourteen defied a platoon of marines thirty-six strong, led by two subalterns, in the Welsh Mountains round Cader Idris.

For two days and nights they carried out their own guerrilla warfare, only surrendering under the protection of a white flag when reduced to two rounds of ammunition.

On Thursday the boys broke into the armoury of a camp at Barmouth. Three rifles and all the ammunition were taken. Soon the theft was discovered and a hue and cry started.

The lieutenant-quartermaster was recalled from leave, and the brigadier's batman sent after the young desperadoes.

When bullets started whizzing round his head, he decided that reinforcements were needed and went back for the regimental police.

They in turn retired in the face of superior enemy fire and the National Fire Service were called out. They gave up.

The boys were all night on the mountain and shot two fowls belonging to a local poultry-keeper. They then went to a disused mine in the mountains and dug themselves in.

On Friday, a platoon of marines, thirty-six strong with two subalterns, set out on the chase. They tracked the boys down and the bullets began flying again. The platoon got under cover and prepared to attack. Firing blank cartridges, they made a frontal assault on the boys' position, but had to retreat. Reinforcements were sent for, and a captain came to supervise.

Ammunition was running low and the boys flew the white flag. Out they came, with just two rounds, but without the rifles, which have not been found yet.

 The three were marched back to their home town, under the

escort of eight marines.

The boys were placed 'under restriction' at their homes, but last night went to the local cinema, fêted by all the boys in the neighbourhood.

Of course, I wanted to know more. The Royal Marines Museum put the thing in perspective.

Barmouth has fine sands, and a lot of empty hillside behind. As D-Day approached, the whole area became one massive armed camp, a training-ground for D-Day 'rear-echelon' like landing-craft crews, beach-masters and also officer cadets. We had two camps, 'Iceland' and 'Crete'. There was also an airfield, an aircraft strafing and bombing range, street-fighting training areas and an ordnance factory. The town of Barmouth was engulfed in this mass of military, but not evacuated of civilians. With civilians inside the camp, security does not seem to have been taken seriously. There could well have been some ill-feeling in the community as part of 'Crete' camp was made up of requisitioned houses at the north end of the river bridge.

Crete camp was where the trouble started.

What is also clear, from the account of the *Express* reporter who attended the boys' trial, is the panic among both civil and military authorities as the boys changed from mere thieves into children who had run amuck with deadly weapons and might do *anything*. Little wonder the two subalterns were replaced by a captain for the last battle. Had either a child or a marine been killed or wounded in that traditionally Welsh Nationalist area, the results would have been appalling. Yet captured they must be. Not only were they making idiots of the British Army, but their fusillades of rifle-fire coming down the hillside had convinced the inhabitants of Barmouth that German paratroops had landed and the town was on the verge of panic.

There must have been a court of inquiry, and several courts martial, as well as the civilian trial, but the Marines state the records were destroyed. But they sent me War Cabinet correspondence between the Prime Minister and Home Secretary.

Winston Churchill, angry about 'this extraordinary affair' wrote, 'The point is, did the boys fire with bullets on the Marines? If they did, the case is grave and they should be charged with attempted murder. We really cannot have the young hooligans setting upon the Marines with bullets.'

After extensive enquiries, Herbert Morrison managed to placate the fierce old lion.

'There is no evidence that the boys shot intentionally at the Marines or anybody else. The only living things among the various targets selected by the high-spirited youngsters were some chickens.'

I tried to contact the boys concerned, through a letter in the local Welsh newspaper. This resulted in a lot of sly Welsh postcards, saying, 'If you want to know the truth, why don't you ask old so-and-so.' And several very angry Welsh phonecalls, threatening all manner of things if I dared to publish a word. But eventually, with the help of reporter David Jack of *The Sunday People*, I managed to get the boys' side of the story.

We were resentful. Barmouth had been a peaceful little town before the War. Then we had two invasions – evacuees from Liverpool, then English soldiers, making us talk English instead of our own language.

We watched; we knew everything that moved – the ammunition trains from the ordnance factory. If we'd been – known – a Fifth Columnist, we could have told him everything.

We had nothing to do all day but watch them. By the end we knew how to use, fire and strip a sixteen-pounder gun, let alone a rifle.

We'd been inside the street-fighting area's buildings, while grenade-throwing and machine-gunning were actually going on. We'd gone in there looking for dud and spent cartridges. It's amazing we weren't blown up – it's amazing I'm talking to you now. We were on the aircraft-strafing ranges too, when aircraft were practising . . .

 Security? What security? We sat and played inside the cockpits

of the airplanes on the aerodrome.

We watched the Marines – they had Dinky Toys – *our* Dinky Toys by rights – for planning their war-games. They'd taken our toys – why shouldn't we take theirs?

We'd walked off the rifle-range with a Bren gun before then. We had it hidden. The officer-cadets had been firing it, but they went off for a brew-up in their billy-cans and left it. Then we saw the cadet who'd left it getting into trouble, so we went and told the sergeant where we'd put it. It was only a joke, like, a bit of a prank.

We had a grenade and took the pin out. It went off and singed us pretty badly. Luckily the explosion went the other way and blew our fireplace in.

We'd had our eye on those 0.22 rifles for quite a while. There were guns lying about everywhere. What else was there for us to do? We saw it as a challenge, I suppose . . .

We knew where the guns were – we'd been watching that armoury for ages – it was only an ordinary house in the village street. We knew they always left the window open in hot weather. The armoury was well-guarded – but we waited till the guard was being changed and they were all out on parade out front. (We knew their every move.) Then we nipped in the window and got the rifles and ammo. They reckoned we took 400 rounds, but it was 5,000 rounds. The authorities were trying to play it down because they were embarrassed about their lack of security, I suppose.

We fired and fired for hours on end, but we never hurt anybody. It was the poultry-keeper who started off the alarm.

We had about 2,000 soldiers out looking for us, for thirty-eight hours – officer cadets, Marines, police, fire-brigade, the lot. The Marines didn't know what they were looking for, because our cover was so good. From the hills we had a view right over the town and we could see them coming for miles. We even strolled back to the beach and watched them combing the hills for us. What a laugh! They fired off blank cartridges to try and scare us out into the open. When they caught us they gave us a whole Swiss Roll each to eat.

They marched us through Barmouth with fixed bayonets – we

were led by four armed captains, and surrounded by three more, and all the troops marching behind. I don't know why they were allowed to march with fixed bayonets – surely soldiers can only do that if their regiment's been given the Freedom of Barmouth?

My employer threw rotten tomatoes at the soldiers escorting us.

We were locked up for a week in an approved school.

They marched us into court, and sitting up with the Judges were officers in red hats – brigadiers, field-marshals, I don't know. The court was surrounded by troops with fixed bayonets. I suppose they were making a show – the brass hats were upset.

It was all a childish escapade, but boys will be boys.

It was a strange generation of kids who went to War. Their respect for adult authority will never be seen on this earth again. They always stood to attention when the National Anthem was being played, even in the privacy of their own home. They regarded policemen as God. If an old lady told them to stop mucking about in the street they obeyed immediately without arguing. Because that old lady might well know their own grandmother, and if their dad got to hear of it they'd probably get a larruping with his belt. They got caned at school, even for spelling-mistakes, and spat on their throbbing hands and took it philosophically.

All the boys wore caps, and raised them to every lady they knew. They believed that God was watching them personally from above, and might well cast them down into Hell if they didn't mend their ways. So by and large they were scrupulously honest. If they found a pound note in the street, they took it straight to the police-station. They *almost* believed that if they told a lie their tongue would turn black . . .

But they also had a pride in being British that will never be seen again. They knew Britain was greatest and best; the British Empire on which the sun never set. They celebrated their Empire with earnest poems, songs and plays on Empire Day; and got a half-holiday as a reward afterwards. A quarter of the
 earth's surface was ruled by Britain, and they had the biggest

navy in the world. Seventeen huge battleships, seven aircraft-carriers and hundreds of destroyers, lurking in their legendary base at Scapa Flow.

Britain was best at everything, from building ships, cars, bridges, to playing soccer to winning the Schneider Trophy for high-speed flight. British children *pitied* all foreigners.

They had no fear of strangers in the street. The world was utterly safe for children. They played out till all hours and very far from home, even after dark. They always had to walk to and from school, even if it was four miles away, even in blizzards. The boys wore shorts and the girls very short skirts and their legs bled from the cold in winter. Posh kids wore shoes, less posh kids wore great clumping boots with studs and heelplates so they could kick sparks from the road like horses. Poor kids went barefoot, especially in summer.

At school, they got a vast respect from their friends if they were top of the class; even more if they were good at games.

Quite a lot of them were chronically hungry, which meant they got rickets. This bowed their legs and gave them spectacular hollows in their ribcages. Quite a lot of them died young, from diseases that have almost vanished; scarlet fever, diphtheria, pneumonia and tuberculosis. Yet they were on the go from morning till night, playing long-lost games like hopscotch and five-stones, tig and blind man's bluff. They had toys that are now precious antiques; huge model steam-trains, huger steam-boats on the park lakes, flying model aircraft with petrol-engines. But they had very simple toys too; hoops and rubber tyres, tops-and-whips and bull's-eye lanterns with candles inside.

Few had radios. TVs were even fewer, only found in the houses of the wealthy round London, and the screens were flickering six-inch grey squares in a huge piece of mahogany like a chest of drawers. One programme only, for a few hours each evening. Instead, they read thick hardback books, and comics that were nearly as stuffed with words.

Boys and girls hardly spoke, between the ages of eleven and sixteen; mute with a giant blushing embarrassment. If a young girl got pregnant, she had to have the baby. Often her family threw her out; sometimes she was sent to a lunatic asylum for the rest of her life.

The young were always in bed by nine-thirty. After the nine o'clock news. Unluckier ones were in bed by eight.

They were brave, and hard as nails and it was not their style to moan or grumble. They were little monkeys, into everything, and they passionately wanted to help Britain, and their hero, Mr Churchill, to win the war.

I think most of them found the War was the best game for kids ever invented.

A very strange generation, more alien to you than the modern Chinese?

They became your grandparents. Still with you, most of them. Probably full to bursting with the things they got up to in the War.

Why don't you ask them?

So how did three of these good law-abiding children end up fighting a pitched gun-battle with the Royal Marines?

They have since led blameless lives; two of them are ambulancemen, that most compassionate of professions. One of them still bears the nickname of 'Chicago' from that crazy weekend, but they have never touched a gun since.

So what got into them?

Children are born apprentices. They learn from the adults round them, and if those adults are soldiers, the children become apprentice soldiers. And in 1944, Britain was more full of weapons than an egg is full of yolk. Just before the D-Day landings, there were tanks behind every hedgerow. And everyone was so pent-up, waiting for the day when we finally gave the Germans what-for, after four years of defeats and hunger and darkness and death raining down from the sky. The whole nation was explosive; the air was full of it. As Shakespeare said 'Cry havoc, and let slip the dogs of war'.

 And these three dogs slipped too early; boiled over. Only

they couldn't get at the new enemy, the Nazis. So they chose the old enemy, the English. But the fact that 5,000 rounds having been fired, only two chickens came to grief is a tribute to that basic respect for law and order and their marksmanship. To drive Royal Marines back again and again, without harming a hair of their heads . . . an incredible achievement.

Such things probably happened in a dozen places, as May turned into June, 1944. And nearly happened in a hundred more.

The adults were busy, up to their eyebrows, often working twelve-hour shifts; the adults were weary to death. Nobody wondered what the children were up to. So the children fought their own war, largely unnoticed by the grown-ups.

After researching the Battle of Barmouth, I just went round asking everybody who seemed to be the right age just what they got up to in the War. At first they shrugged and said, 'Nothing much'. And then their eyes would light up, and it would all come tumbling out.

Are all the stories true? I had to use my own judgement. I too was a Child of the Blitz. I too was bombed; I too had an insatiable hunger for weapons. For many years I had a Smith and Wesson revolver, picked up by my cousin on the Normandy beachhead on D-Day plus Three. I think I have a feel for the real truth. I threw a lot out. I suspected anybody who was on an ego-trip to make themselves seem brave or grand. The best stories were always comic, or crazy, or beyond belief.

Of course, I have only scratched the surface; for every story of mine, there must be a thousand, a million, to be uncovered. And these children who were so brave and crazy, these grandparents, are starting to die off. There is not much time left, if the truth is to be known.

Perhaps it is up to you?

ROBERT WESTALL
1992

'I would rather be bombed to fragments than leave England.'
Boy's letter to the press

'It's just as dangerous here as in Southampton. Now I can get my own souvenirs.'
Boy evacuee (Dorset) rejoicing in watching air battles

CHAPTER 1
LAST DAYS OF PEACE

26 AUGUST 1939
THE LAST NIGHT OF PEACE

I CAN'T SLEEP BECAUSE there's a torch and three large toy pistols under my pillow and they keep working down under my shoulders.

Is there going to be a war? That's why the torch and pistols are there. I think about the Germans; the situation is perfectly simple.

The Germans are the bullies of the European classroom. Lots of little countries have been getting their arms twisted behind their backs. But in the corner of that classroom, Britain is sitting, best fighter in the school, captain of football, popular hero. Britain has got her feet up on the windowsill at present, reading a book, because the bully hasn't gone too far. Yet! But when the little kids squeal too loud, Britain will get up and give the bully a bloody nose. The bully will crumple up, snivelling snots in the corner, and then we'll have peace.

Simple. Happened before, in 1918. Look at the map; half the world is coloured red, for British. Germany is a pathetic little green postage stamp; there is hardly room to print the word 'Berlin'.

I have one or two doubts. My father says the Germans are good engineers; he will buy me German toys; the rest are 'foreign rubbish'. My father respects German gunnery, after the Battle of Jutland, in the Last Lot. German captains keep clean ships; when they are in port, all their sailors march to the Seamen's Mission to worship in immaculate uniforms. The Germans, unlike the Latin races, are 'clean-living men'.

My mother is mortally afraid the U-boats will starve Britain to death. In the Last Lot she queued up four hours for a piece of suet, but when she got to the front of the queue, it had all gone.

But U-boats are just another example of sneaky German cowardice, attacking unarmed merchant ships; when our destroyers get there, they always depth-charge them into soup!

German bombers have evil names like Dornier and Heinkel and Stuka. They have evil shapes, long, thin and pointed, like snakes and dragons, praying mantises and sting-rays. They are always painted black and carry the crooked cross. They only bomb women and children.

British planes are honest brown and green, and look like faithful dogs, with friendly names like Hurricane and Wellington and Hampden.

Suddenly I am stricken with doubts. Will our faithful dogs be able to cope with the poisonous dragons? Then I remember about the Supermarine Spitfire. I don't know anything about the Spitfire; I've only seen it on a cigarette card, and the artist didn't know much about the Spitfire either, because he's painted it coming out of the sun, with no details. But that Spitfire is black too, and looks even more shark-like and poisonous than the Germans.

Reassured, I remember about 'ersatz'. Everything the Germans have is 'ersatz'. They make 'ersatz' coffee by stealing acorns off their pigs and roasting them, and it tastes yuk, but they can't afford real coffee. Their soldiers' boots have 'ersatz' cardboard soles that fall apart as soon as it rains. They're trying to make petrol out of potatoes because they haven't got any oil. (That's why they still pull their field-guns with horses.) All the oil and tin and rubber in the world comes from Malaya, which is part of the great British Empire. If a war comes, our Navy will starve them out. Like the Last Lot.

And the Germans have the hopeless burden of Hitler – a total nutter, worse than Happy Ralph. If he can't get his own way, he falls down foaming at the mouth and chews the carpet. Every kid you meet is pulling a lock of hair down over his forehead, sticking his finger under his nose and screaming fake German till his throat conks out or somebody kicks him. We do the goose-step till we fall over laughing. And there are songs . . .

Ven der Führer says
Ve iss der Master Race,
Ve vart, vart
Right in der Führer's face . . .

Too many bravissimo performances of this epic have greatly increased our mothers' burden of underpants washing. Then that other song, to the tune of Colonel Bogie,

Adolf . . . has only got one ball
Goering . . . he has none at all . . .

(We would be enthralled, in 1945, when a Russian post-mortem on the Führer's body actually proved the first line to be true. We waited with avidity for the disappointing results of the inquest on Goering . . .)

So, did I want a war? Well, I'd spent a long time collecting two sets of cigarette cards – 'Air-raid precautions' and 'Aircraft of the RAF'. And I didn't want to have wasted my time. I didn't want to waste the lovely Spitfires either. And the goodies *always* won – every film and book said so.

Yes, I wanted a war.

Mind made up, I rolled over and slept.

Boy, aged nine, Tyneside

1939 INDOCTRINATION

MY ANTI-GERMAN indoctrination began before I started school. Dad had a set of illustrated 'Great War' books, and on Saturday nights I was put to bed with one of these whilst Mum and Dad went shopping. I studied the pictures in the books avidly and grew up to Kaiser Bill and his murdering legions.

At junior school assembly, we always saluted the Roll of Honour which listed those boys who grew to manhood, only to be killed in France 1914–18. On occasions our headmaster would regale us with stories. I vividly remember his wife standing on the school steps on Empire Day, singing 'Land of Hope and Glory' with all the fervour of the last night of the Proms! To me, all these stories were a continuation of the goodie-baddie theme of Saturday morning movies, the cowboys and Indians.

Boy, aged ten, London

We scrounged cigarette cards off men taking their wives and girlfriends to the cinema. Some bought us whole bundles. We swapped those we had two of for those we had none of, stuck them in albums we sent away for, and used series such as 'Air Raid Precautions' and 'Aircraft of the RAF' as our guide-books to the war.

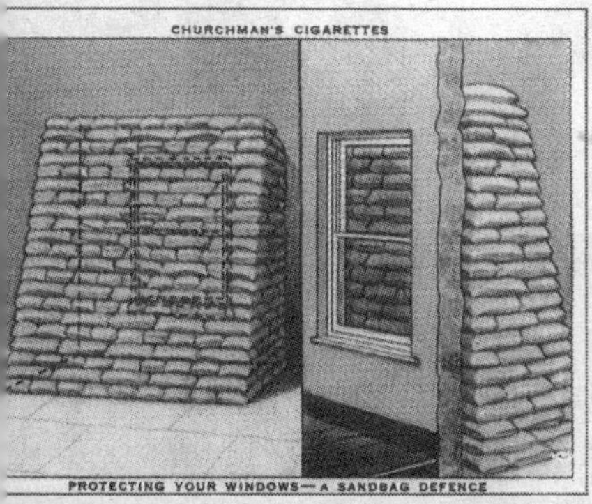

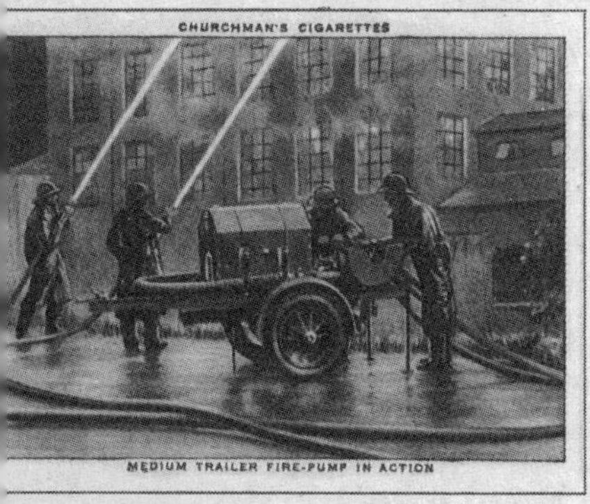

CHAPTER

2 FIRST DAYS OF WAR

3 Sept. 1939 DAY WAR BROKE OUT

MR CHAMBERLAIN'S broadcast was not impressive. I remembered him from the newsreels, coming out of his aeroplane after Munich, waving his little piece of paper and promising 'peace in our time'. I thought he looked like a sheep, and now he bleated like a sheep. He talked about notes being sent and replies not being received. He *regretted* that a state of war now existed between Great Britain and

Germany. He sounded really *hurt*, like Hitler was some shiftless council tenant who had failed to pay his rent after faithfully promising to do so.

That wasn't the way to talk to Hitler; he should be threatening to kick his teeth in . . . I knew there'd be trouble . . .

There was. The sirens went immediately. We didn't know what to do. We had no shelters; nothing but little gasmasks in

Mr Chamberlain, on his return from Munich in 1938, displaying the piece of paper carrying Hitler's signature guaranteeing peace.

cardboard boxes. We went to the front windows and stared out. Everything was peaceful and sunny. Old Charlie Brown, who hadn't worked for years with his bad chest, after being gassed on the Somme, was marching round the square, sticking his chest out. Wearing his best suit and medals from the Last Lot. He looked determined, but ridiculous. Mam said he had volunteered to be a warden yesterday, and obviously felt he should do *something*.

Dad said 'If he sounds his rattle, that means poison gas – put your gasmask on.'

I said 'He hasn't *got* a rattle.'

The world seemed broken in half. The earth, the houses, roses, sunlit trees were still England. But the air was suddenly German; there wasn't a Spitfire or a Hurricane, or even a Gloster Gladiator in sight. Soon, like on the newsreels from Spain, the air would fill with the orderly black crosses of German bombers, with endless strings of tiny bombs falling from their bellies. And only Charlie Brown to stop them. I couldn't stand still – I went into my bedroom and considered trying to pray, a thing I hadn't done for years. It didn't seem much use against Nazi bombers. The Spaniards must have been great prayers, being Catholics, and it hadn't done them much good . . . I decided to keep my eyes wide open instead.

My old teddy-bear was sitting in the corner; I hadn't spared him a glance in years, but now he looked at me, appealingly.

I put him under my bed for safety.

Then the all-clear sounded.

Charlie Brown headed straight for the Cannon Inn and downed several pints double-quick.

Boy, aged nine, Tyneside

1939 FALSE ALARM

IT WAS THE FIRST DAY of the war, when the siren went off in Newcastle. It was a false alarm, but it was received by the local coal mine. My brother-in-law, who was working as a roadman, was warned by the pit that there would probably be a gas attack and was told to go and inform his family to take gas precautions.

Most people thought gas would be Hitler's 'secret weapon' – but it was the only thing he failed to use, for fear of reprisals.

I was at their home at the time and we all set to, barred and sealed all the doors and windows, pushed pillows up the chimneys, stocked the food and water into the bedroom. My sister's baby was only a few months old, and we had to install her in a gasproof cot. This had to be pumped with air. My sister was new to the device and we were all terrified in case the baby should get too much or too little air. My sister's face was like death. We were all gathered together in the bedroom, terrified, waiting for news over two hours, before we learnt it was all a false alarm. We were ill for days after. Then we had to replace the food, etc., back down a long flight of stairs, haul down the soot-stained pillows from the chimney and clean them ready for bedtime. Our legs were worn out tracking up and down the stairs.

Girl, aged fifteen, Hexham

3 SEPT 1939 BUILDING A DUG-OUT

MY FATHER EXCAVATED a hole in the tennis court for a dug-out, covered with tree-trunks supporting corrugated iron and topped with several feet of earth.

Boy, aged ten, London

1939 THE SINKING OF THE *ATHENIA*

WE WERE SITTING ON A HATCH feeling sick when we were blown up into the air. I wasn't hurt but mother hurt her shoulder. After we were blown in the air we were put in a lifeboat. I climbed into it myself. Then we were out on the ocean all night. Nobody said very much, and there was no singing or laughing or crying. We saw a battleship and climbed on to it up a ladder. The sailors were very kind to us and we were taken to Greenock in Scotland. Mother was in hospital for eight days with her shoulder but I was up and around.

Rosie Ralph, aged ten

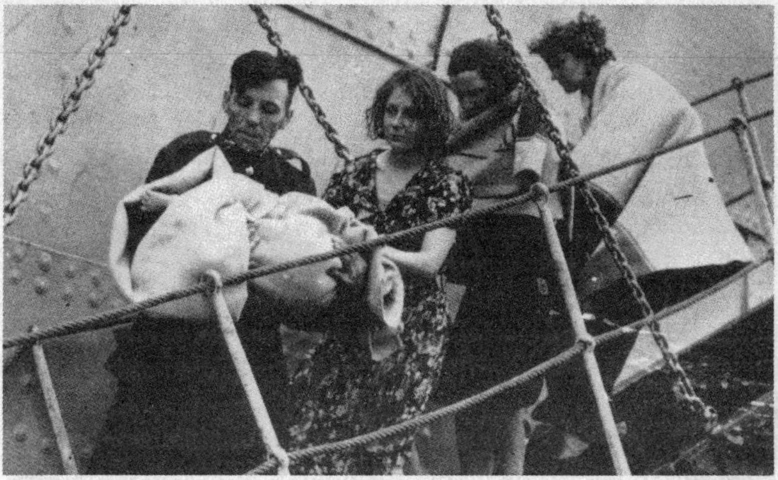

Survivors rescued from the torpedoed *Athenia*. This sinking of an unarmed liner, within hours of the outbreak of war, confirmed the war in our minds as a crusade against slinking cowards. Throughout the war, the U-boats were thought 'cowardly', as opposed to our 'heroic' British submarines, though by 1940 both were following exactly the same 'sink on sight' tactics.

SEPT–DEC 1939 LOOKING FOR THE WAR

THEY CANCELLED SCHOOL immediately 'for the Duration of the Emergency.' Handy; I had a lot to do. There was the map of Europe, given away free with the first copy of *War Weekly*, to pin on my bedroom wall; lots of little flags to cut out: British, French, German and, bafflingly, Russian. I also hung up score-charts for German ships sunk, planes shot down, tanks destroyed.

Then me and Stanley set off on our bikes to look for the war. Somebody said they were desperate for people to fill sandbags at Preston Hospital, to protect the windows, so we dashed down there. Unfortunately, the hospital porter turned out to be old Jack Dawson, our bossy neighbour. He turned us back at the gate, saying he didn't want a lot of bloody kids hanging about the place. We considered reporting him to the police, for sabotaging the War Effort.

We worked out ways of fooling German bombers. If they machine-gunned us from the air, we'd pretend to fall down dead, then get up and run again, then pretend to die again. This would ruin their estimate of civilian casualties.

We lived on our bikes, looking for Defences, which seemed in perilously short supply. Every little bit of barbed wire went down in our notebooks, even the thin strands round farmers' fields, which didn't really count but we put them down just the same. Then *real* Defences appeared – single pom-poms on the Bank Top; armed trawlers. We inspected them daily, looking for improvements, and making sure the crews knew their job. Best were the barrage balloons. We spent hours at Dockwray Square, staring through the railings; the balloon was like a great silver elephant, whose sides crinkled with every breeze. In the evenings, the RAF crew played football with us, till the girls came, then they lost all interest in football. We thought of reporting them to the police, for neglecting the War Effort. Playing football with us kept them fit; but daft giggling girls were sure to ruin their morale . . .

Then they restarted school, mornings only. We still couldn't actually *go* to school, because they hadn't built its air-raid shelters yet. Our class, only, met in the old winding-house of Preston Colliery; a huge dank brick underground arch that smelt evilly of cats. That winding-house was also our air-raid shelter. Later in the war, it sustained a near-miss from a very small bomb, and collapsed, killing forty. On fine days, we wandered round the town in a crocodile, looking for a place to sit down together. We usually ended up in Preston Cemetery, sitting on the tombstones, doing sums. Stanley reckoned this was so that if there was an air raid, and we got killed by bombs, we could be buried immediately, without being taken home first.

Later, our school was flattened by a land-mine, also the Rex Cinema next door. The Rex manager, a good bloke who told us jokes and made us laugh at Saturday morning matinees, was killed outright. The headmaster and the nastiest teacher in the school, Miss Townsend, were buried for hours in the wreckage, but dug out unharmed. We were outraged. We all wished *they'd* been killed, instead of the Rex manager, because they were both terrible caners and complete Nazi sadists. Miss Townsend actually had blonde hair coiled in plaits round her head and thick muscular legs just like the Hitler Youth Mädchen. My mother wondered what they'd been up to, fire-watching in the school on their own . . .

Unfortunately we were transferred to Spring Gardens School immediately, all classes having to sit together in the hall, with the Spring Gardens kids peering in at us and laughing, like we were something in a zoo.

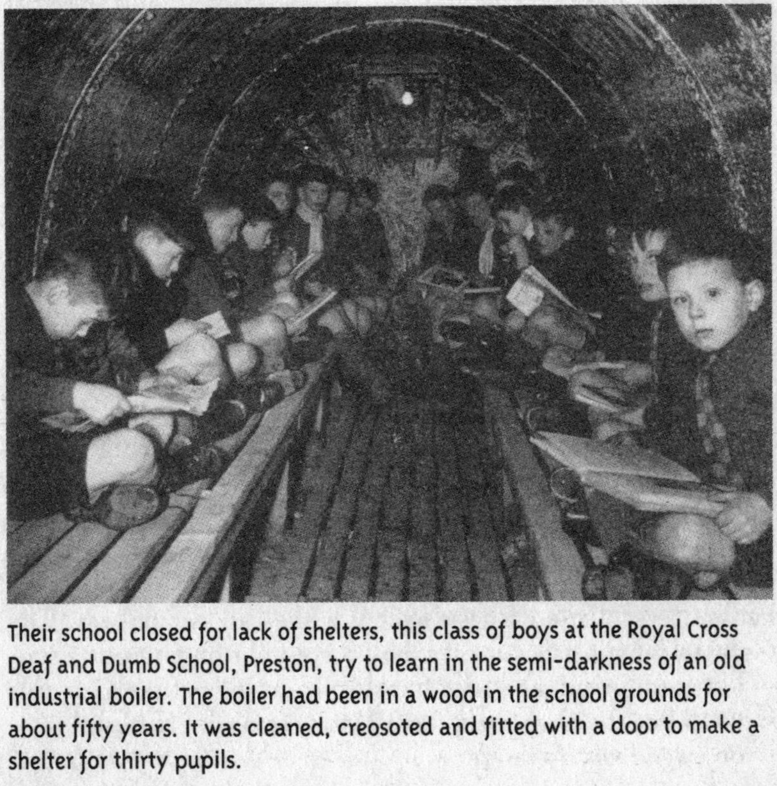

Their school closed for lack of shelters, this class of boys at the Royal Cross Deaf and Dumb School, Preston, try to learn in the semi-darkness of an old industrial boiler. The boiler had been in a wood in the school grounds for about fifty years. It was cleaned, creosoted and fitted with a door to make a shelter for thirty pupils.

Stanley was evacuated to Hexham, but returned after a fortnight. Some Hexham kids pushed him backwards into a cowpat. The woman he was billeted with didn't wash his blazer, and he had to go to school with the dry cowpat stuck to him, and she didn't clean his shoes or make his bed or anything. And the teacher kept remarking how scruffy town kids were. So he came home; he said it was all cows and cowpats and *boring*.

It was becoming increasingly hard to find any way of beating Hitler. We even volunteered to help knit comforts for the troops. We would hold the hanks of wool before us, on outstretched hands, while the girls wound it into balls. They were very bossy, constantly shouting at us 'Hold your hands *up*, can't you?' Then the vicar's wife got sarky about the quality of our mums' knitting, announcing 'We are trying to knit *comforts* for the troops, my dears, not *discomforts*.' So most of the mums gave it up in a huff. My mum gave me the Balaclava helmet instead.

Dad joined the wardens. They had one interesting night in our square, practising putting out real incendiary bombs with sand. They had to summon the ambulance; the wardens were so enthusiastic, everyone got their eyes full of sand, and they took the bomb-fins away, so we couldn't have them for souvenirs. All that the wardens did otherwise was hold a Saturday night whist-drive-and-dance for their funds. I was put in charge of lemonade selling. I sold an incredible amount of lemonade, ginger pop and American ice cream soda; I learnt to play whist and won the booby prize, and I learnt ballroom-dancing. But it didn't seem to have a lot to do with beating Hitler.

Perhaps Hitler was already beaten. The German pocket-battleship *Graf Spee* ran away from three very small British cruisers, and scuttled herself in Montevideo harbour, though she had suffered little damage except a shell in her bakery. The German captain said his crew could not fight on without a supply of fresh bread, and shot himself. To us kids, if the Germans were all like the *Graf Spee*, there didn't seem a lot to beat.

 Boy, aged ten, Tyneside

CHAPTER 3

EVACUATION

1939 GREY SQUIRRELS

WHEN WE WERE EVACUATED, we went to a massive manor owned by Lady Bibby. She was a fantastic woman, but she hated grey squirrels. She kept a gun under the window and every time she saw one she shot it dead.

Boy, aged eight, Liverpool

1939 EVACUEE'S FIRST POSTCARD HOME

DEAR MUM, I hope you are well. I don't like the man's face much. Perhaps it will look better in daylight. I like the dog's face best.

1939 EVACUATION – WORKING CLASS

WE LEFT HOME EARLY in the morning, with our gasmasks hanging round our necks. It was very dark. We got to the school and all the mothers looked very grim. They were trying not to cry but one or two of them did. We didn't cry because we didn't really know what was happening to us.

When we reached the end of our journey we all climbed out and went to a church hall. Then we found out that we'd come to the wrong place . . . we'd gone to where the boys should have been. But no one could be bothered to change us over. We were taken to a nice place with a very, very old couple. The house was old and stood by a lake, which was full of rotting conkers that smelt terrible. I was lucky because I was with my friend Mavis. In the evening we told each other creepy stories so that we were very frightened. We soon discovered a room that was full of apples. When everybody was asleep, we crept along the

A bag of sweets was some consolation . . .

passage and got some. But we didn't always succeed. The floorboards creaked and we thought someone would hear. When we did get apples, we took them back to eat in bed.

A few weeks later, the old man died. Then we were moved to different houses. I went to a house with people who went on organized stealing-trips into Redhill, and they tried to make me go with them.

After a while I got rheumatic fever. I was quite ill but I didn't like to tell anybody. One morning I went to school and collapsed in class and was taken to Earlswood Common Hospital. When I got there I was put straight into a hot bed – it had an electric blanket – which I'd never heard of. At the hospital they had a [wind-up] gramophone. They kept playing songs like 'Any Umbrellas' and 'Hang out the washing on the Siegfried Line'.

In a bed next to me was a poor Jewish girl who had escaped from Vienna. She was very upset because she didn't know what had happened to her parents.

Then our army had to retreat at Dunkirk. All the hospitals were preparing for that, so they sent me home in an ambulance.

I'd only been at home a few days when I picked up the paper and saw the big black letters saying PARIS HAS FALLEN and I couldn't really believe it.

And then came the bombing of London.

Girl, Surrey

IN THE CASE OF THIS GROUP there were no tearful farewells. They were already many miles from their parents, and they were with their friends. They travelled in two charabancs, taking with them a few members of staff and one of the joint headmistresses. They were bound for Woolacombe, a holiday resort in North Devon, which was an idyllic situation. They had lessons in the morning and in the afternoon they were free to do

Evacuation – middle class – was a great adventure. Used to being away from home, they revelled in what seemed a year-long holiday in West Country hotels.

as they liked. They could go anywhere in threes – one to have an accident, one to stay with her and one to run for help. There are three miles of sand at Woolacombe and swimming was much more interesting than it had been in the swimming pool at Reigate.

The countryside held exciting walks, either along the coast or inland up the donkey-track which was the old smugglers' path, used for carrying their brandy and rum.

In September, the rest of the school was evacuated; they took over four hotels.

Girl, aged twelve, Devon

1940 ROMANCE

WE WERE QUITE WELL-OFF during the war. We lived in a bigger house than all the other kids. But we weren't rich or anything. I was a spoilt child and got nearly everything I asked for.

We lived in Warrington; there were a lot of factories there, so the town was bombed quite a lot. Because of this, my mother sent me to live with my hard-up aunty in Yorkshire.

At first I was very unsettled – it was so different; in Warrington I'd had lots of friends. It was just like being born again. I missed my mother a lot, because we were very close. I cried a lot. My aunt called me a soppy spoilt little baby.

I had to do a lot of work, so hard that when I lay down in her bed at night I fell asleep almost straight away. I never had time to read the books I brought with me. I was also made to go to Mass, though I wasn't a Catholic.

I did not meet any children my own age, till I'd been at the cottage a year, and it was a boy. I did not like boys, especially dirty, smelly, scruffy ones like this Mark. He used to live in Weymouth, but his father had bought a little farm down the lane just past the shops.

Every time I went to the shops for my aunty, I used always to see Mark. After a few weeks he used to come round with his father. Because my uncle and his father were good friends, we too became good friends after a bit. Somehow I did not seem to mind the smelliness of Mark. When he came for Sunday dinner, I always went for a walk with him in the woods nearby.

But the war ended. I was a much older woman by then. I did not want to leave the village, not because of my aunty, but because of Mark. I think I was in love with him.

I must remain anonymous; my husband must not find out.

1939 BEING AMONG THE CHOSEN

WHEN WE ARRIVED IN PORTMADOC we were taken to the Town Hall – where people chose which children they would look after. My sister Pat was very attractive, whereas I was rather plain. An old man noticed Pat and asked a teacher if he could take her. She told him that she had a sister, and if he wanted her he must take me too. He went home to ask his wife if she could have two children. She agreed, so he returned to collect us. When he arrived I started to cry and refused to go. The old man went to the nearest florist and bought an enormous bunch of flowers for me. We finally arrived at the old man's house seated in a chauffeur-driven car. At the house there was a big library. Pat used to spend hours upon hours in the library. Then I caught chicken-pox and we had to go to another house.

At the second house was a very strict woman. Now I really liked ginger and one day this woman made some ginger-cakes. When the woman went to have her afternoon sleep I sneaked into the kitchen and picked round one of the cakes. When I looked at the cakes, I saw the one I'd picked stood out like a sore thumb. So I picked round all the cakes to make them look the same. When the woman woke up and saw the cakes she sat all the children on the floor and looked for the child with the guilty-looking face. When she caught me she took me off and locked me in a dark attic.

Pat had written to our mum a few days before. She said in our letter that we both wanted to go home. My mum came to collect us while I was still in the attic. When the woman explained why I was in the attic, my mum went mad. She took us straight away.

Girl, aged four, Liverpool

Complete with labels, the children were sorted like parcels, before going to the evacuation centre.

1939 A LONDON EVACUEE SEES HIS FIRST COW

THE COW IS A MAMAL. It has six sides, right, left, an upper and below. At the back is a tail, on which hangs a brush. With this it sends the flies away so they do not fall into the milk. The head is for the purpose of growing horns and so that the mouth can

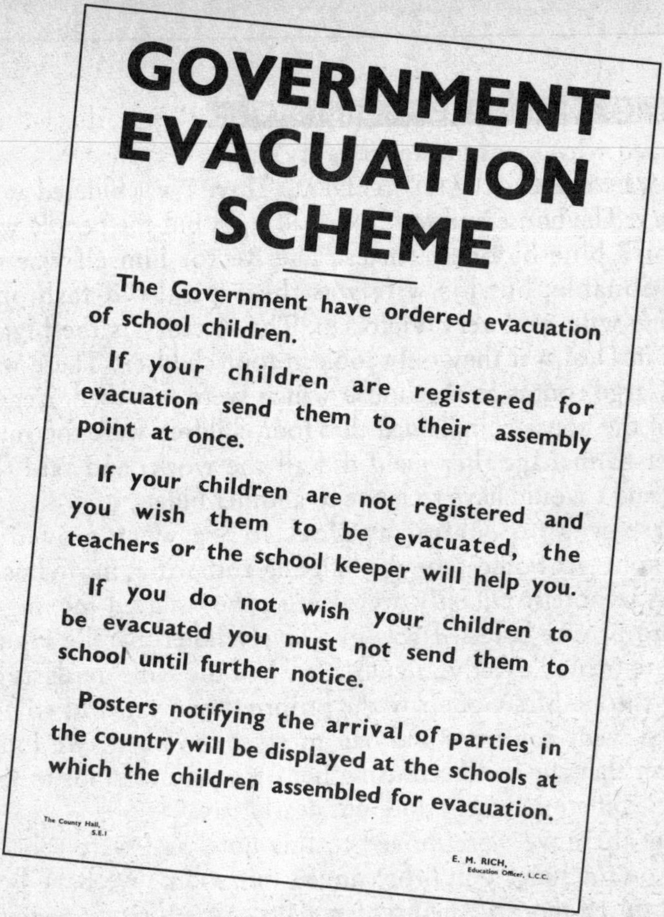
GOVERNMENT EVACUATION SCHEME

The Government have ordered evacuation of school children.

If your children are registered for evacuation send them to their assembly point at once.

If your children are not registered and you wish them to be evacuated, the teachers or the school keeper will help you.

If you do not wish your children to be evacuated you must not send them to school until further notice.

Posters notifying the arrival of parties in the country will be displayed at the schools at which the children assembled for evacuation.

The County Hall,
S.E.1

E. M. RICH,
Education Officer, L.C.C.

be somewhere. The horns are to butt with, and the mouth is to moo with. Under the cow hangs the milk. It is arranged for milking. When people milk, the milk comes and there is never an end to the supply. How the cow does it I have not realized but it makes more and more. The cow has a fine sense of smell; one can smell it far away. This is the reason for the fresh air in the country.

The man cow is called an ox. It is not a mamal. The cow does not eat much but what it eats, it eats twice so that it gets enough. When it is hungry it moos and when it says nothing it is because all its inside is full up with grass.

BBC news, 29 October 1939

1939 EVACUATION TO FOLKESTONE

First we were evacuated to Deal. There I was billeted at the Rectory. The house and food were all right but the people were snobbish blue-blooded Tories. The Rector himself was not objectionable, but his wife was the typical old-fashioned Rector's wife, and very Victorian. The Rectory is the biggest house in Deal, yet they only took in four children. There were seven large rooms in the house which were not used. Yet the lady of the house complained that four children were too much for her to manage (her maid did all the work) and said that Sheila and I would have to move to another billet.

There was no school at Deal so we were moved to Folkestone. At Folkestone the billeting authorities moved us all into large hotels. Directly we were in they started moving us out into private billets. I was in a lovely hotel, Barelle House. We were treated exactly as guests; we had the same meals as the hotel visitors. Mrs Godefroy the proprietress treated us so well that she went bankrupt and had to close the hotel. We found out later that she had been using her own private funds to feed us as the billeting money does not nearly pay.

From there we were moved to this hotel and were told, 'It won't be for long, you'll be moved out soon.' We have been here almost a month. The first few days at the Victoria were the worst I have ever experienced. I never knew what it is like to feel hungry before. We were reduced to eating anything, lumps of dry bread, cake crumbs, etc. (Mrs Godefroy used to let us come back to Barelle House for food; she used to give us cups of tea, plates of chips, apples and all manner of good things.)

We told our mistresses we had not enough to eat. As a result the hotel people called us liars and other things not fit to write. We protested so strongly that now our food is quite good. I feel

In spite of this poster, most children were back in the big cities in time for the Blitz.

TAKE THEM BACK!
TAKE THEM BACK!
TAKE THEM BACK!..
DON'T do it, Mother—
LEAVE THE CHILDREN WHERE THEY ARE
ISSUED BY THE MINISTRY OF HEALTH

certain that the hotel people must make a profit out of us, though. We have no milk except in powdered form, then it is a very little in our tea. We have no eggs or fresh food; it is all tinned. One day we did have eggs but they were pickled ones and nearly all rotten.

They are gradually moving us out; of course, the older ones will be moved last so I have a long time to wait. I am thoroughly sick of so much uncertainty; we will not be really settled down till Christmas. As they move us out, they move elementary children in. Of course, these are younger and not old enough to complain about food etc. The evacuation scheme in Folkstone is rotten. Over 1,000 children have gone home.

We are a long way from school here, over two miles. We first climb about 150 steps to the top of the cliff, and then uphill to school. We cannot get back to the hotel for dinner; they do not keep us any hot at the hotel so we must have it at school. This costs 10*d.* each. We have had continuous rain here this week and have had to ride to school. The fares are 2*d.* each way, so you can guess how difficult it is for mother to keep up with all the expenses.

When we got up this morning, the kitchen was flooded out – eight inches of water, so we went to school with very little breakfast. During the day the rain continued and the water rose. The men were wading about in water past their knees. We could have no cooked dinner as the gas stove was partly under water. You see we are right at the foot of a very steep cliff which the water simply pours down. In some of the hotels along the front the tables and chairs were floating about.

Another trouble in this hotel is infection. One girl caught a cold and practically the whole house went down with colds. A girl got impetigo, then a boy caught it. Both went to hospital.

I have got past the stage of caring what food we have, etc. now though.

I console myself with talking Communism, reading Communism and thinking Communism all the time.

 Girl, aged sixteen

1941 PERKS

DURING LIVERPOOL'S heaviest bombing, my two brothers and I were evacuated to a small town in Wales. Since I was the oldest, I took charge. A lady asked us if we had any pyjamas or slippers. Since we did not, I ordered two sets of pyjamas for my brothers and two nightdresses for myself, thinking I was getting them free off the government.

At the end of the war, when we returned home, my Mum gave me a big walloping because every week till the end of the war she had to pay bills for socks, underwear, pyjamas, shirts and jumpers. As well as paying for our things my Mum also paid for everyone else's in our school, because I was also ordering things for my friends and then swapping them for sweets.

Girl, aged twelve, Liverpool

1940–41 A LOVE OF COUNTRY LIFE

WE MARCHED FROM our schools to the station, complete with gasmask and lapel labels. The streets were lined with our families. Going down Nile Street, my grandmother ran into the roadway to say farewell. The police lining the route tried to stop her, but though she was tiny she bulldozed her way through and marched with us to the station. We had one teacher in each compartment in charge of twelve pupils. When the train departed, the wailing and tears echoed up and down the train.

At Morpeth, Joyce and myself were last to be housed. At nine p.m., feeling hungry and dejected, Miss Holmes took us and bought chips. After a short time, Joyce was moved to Wooler and I went to Alnham, a hamlet consisting of a pele tower, Anglo-Saxon church, school, Memorial Hall, a few houses and ancient earthworks. We lived in the Memorial Hall; part was curtained off to make a sleeping area and the rest was a common-room. Thirty children lived there, with a resident matron and cook. We attended the school, where I first encountered

Miss Black, the schoolmistress. The schoolhouse garden followed the road down to the Memorial Hall; there was a cucumber-frame. In one of our gardening periods, an Alnham lad demolished it, and unfortunately I carried the blame, and was punished. This started the feud between Miss Black and myself.

After the Memorial Hall closed, I went to the Wilson family at Scrainwood. Mrs Wilson was a first-class cook and had a huge pile of awards from country shows. Mr Wilson was a bedridden invalid, from a stroke. The living-room had a black-leaded stove and boiler with tap; a high-backed settle kept draughts off you when sitting at the fire. Paraffin lamps for light were mounted on the wall. Cooking was done by a paraffin oven which left the smell of burnt paraffin every time it was used. Sticky fly-papers hung everywhere.

Scrainwood was a backwater, consisting of the Big House surrounded by barns, byre, stores, hay-shed and workshop. The most impressive waterwheel was in a section normally kept locked for safety. Within ten feet of the wheel the noise was deafening. The wheel turned continually but I have no recollection of it having any end-product. Next was the stables – four shire-horses worked the farm. At right-angles were two cottages. Two brothers called Snaith lived in one, typical hill-shepherds, able to cook, knit, doing all the tasks to survive country life. One kept ferrets for hunting rabbits. When going rabbiting he would shout to me 'Eck, 'ere!' At this call he expected me to join him. He never spoke to me till the work started, then I joined in learning to ferret, snare, net and drive the rabbits out of the warrens. After he killed them, I would gut them and nick their back legs together, and pair them for carrying. A butcher called once a week and took the catch to sell.

Our water was carried from a tap in buckets. Washing-water was drawn from the burn that passed by the house. At the rear were the outhouses; first the pigsty: each family had at least one fattening-pig. Second the woodshed, used for cutting and storing logs, storing paraffin, pig-feed, hen-feed, tools. Last the netty, or earth-closet, which tipped on to the open ash-pit behind. Every spring the men would dig out the ash-pits and spread them on the fields before ploughing.

When the time arrived for killing the pig, a tripod of three poles was erected at the end of the cottages. This hung the carcass for scraping and butchering. The pig's head was hung on the back door, as was the custom. The joints were cut and salted, then hung in the larder for use in the following months. Sausage was made from the offal, using the intestine for skins. Other winter preparations included bottling eggs and fruit, making jam and digging the potato-pit.

The 1941 winter was very bad; we were unable to attend school for six weeks because of the snow. At one time it totally covered the cottage. Work was restricted to the farmyard, the animals having been brought in before the snow fell. Winter entertainment was considerable; the Wilsons were into country dance music. The two eldest lads played accordions, Tom the drums. Many a good night was had with their friends, Mrs Wilson providing the food and all playing till the early hours.

It was winter when we had ice-cream. Ice was taken off the rain-barrels, crushed and mixed with milk, sugar, cornflour, served on dishes in front of the fire.

During the summer we helped with the harvest, threshing corn with the steam-engines and thresher. Pulling turnips gave us the reward of riding the farm-horses from the field with loads of turnips.

The big event of the week was meeting the weekly bus. It arrived every Saturday at nine a.m. en route for Rothbury. When it returned at eight, the locals met it; long discussions were had with the passengers, relaying news of the area. I often wondered what time the driver finished! It was also a parcel-delivery service.

We walked to school each day, taking sandwiches for lunch. Miss Black taught five-year-olds to fourteen-year-olds, all in the same room. In winter it was heated by a pot-bellied stove in the front. The evacuees sat at the back, far away from it. My mother sent me a corduroy jacket to wear. It had a strong smell and

Miss Black made me hang it outside to get rid of the smell. I protested bitterly because of the cold, but it fell on deaf ears. I put up with this a few days, then decided to give up school. I used to go up into the fields, passing the time with the ploughmen. Eventually, Mrs Wilson found out. First her lads tried to take me to school, but I escaped. Then Mrs Wilson tried, with the same results. The final result was a letter home, and the end of evacuation, aged eight. Living at Scrainwood gave me a love of country life which has had a profound influence ever since.

Boy, aged six, North Shields

1939–40 THE END OF EVACUATION

I BEGAN TO GET BORED – here we were at war and nothing was happening. The standard of eating in the country was lower than I was used to at home. Mum and Dad visited me at weekends, bringing food parcels; the thought of returning home with them was very provoking. In London were hundreds of barrage balloons, shelters were being built, sandbags were everywhere. The pace was what I was missing, as well as my home.

My twelfth birthday was spent in West Peckham and the following Sunday, heartily homesick, I asked my parents to take me back with them.

London was, for me, like a return from exile. My pet cat met me at the gate, the neighbours welcomed me and the sun shone. Even my brother did not seem to find me so objectionable.

There were no schools open, but the local vicar arranged a class in his house, using local retired people with some teaching experience to help out. I joined this class which at least kept us off the streets. We learnt odd subjects such as Esperanto and Monopoly, all very enjoyable! The classes were ten to fifteen in number, and at least ensured there was a sprinkling of youngsters in the congregation on Sundays.

Boy, aged ten, London

CHAPTER 4
THE PHONEY WAR

1939 THE FIRST RAID

THE FIRST RAID CAME as we were sitting down to dinner. When the sirens went we left everything and ran down to the shelter.

I sat at the shelter door and stared at the sunlit path only inches from my nose, thinking 'In here it's safe, but out there is Danger.' I couldn't resist putting a finger out into Danger, like it was a bowl of hot water. Nothing happened, so I put my whole hand out, whereupon Mam clouted me for mucking about. I saw a beetle crawling on the path, in Danger. It seemed quite unworried. I imagined a huge piece of shrapnel coming down and squashing it flat. But the beetle would never know if was in Danger, and it still wouldn't know when it was squashed flat. So for the beetle, war didn't exist. And the birds were singing as well, and I felt stupid cowering in this hole, and wondered why wars were only for People.

Then Mam started worrying about the meal getting cold on the table, worrying the dog might eat it. So she nipped out and fetched the sausage and chips and we ate them. Then she went back for the bread and butter, and finally the prunes and custard, and then to make a cup of tea. The whole shelter was full of dirty washing-up and it was embarrassing because Mrs Spedding and Brian hadn't had their dinner yet, and there wasn't enough for them. But Mam gave them a cup of tea.

Mam was just thinking about nipping out to do the washing-up, and worrying about her two o'clock appointment at the hairdressers when the guns started, out to sea. The guns got nearer, like thunder, then worse than thunder. Like the sky was cracking in half.

Then we heard people shouting. Not screaming, but shouting like a football crowd, only scattered over the whole district.

Then the people in the next shelter.

'Kill the begger – get him – get him.' They were outside their shelter, so I nipped out, and there was the German bomber streaking up the river, so long and thin you could tell it was Dornier Flying Pencil. And bursts of anti-aircraft fire, like grey balls of cotton wool growing in the sky, in clumps of four, but all miles behind the bomber.

The man next door was jumping up and down on top of his shelter, screaming his head off. 'Get yer eyes chaarked, ye stupid beggers,' he was shouting at the gunners. 'What ye think ye're paid for?' Like they were the referee at a football match . . .

'Mind yer language in front o' that bairn, Jack!' said his wife, but he took no notice.

When the gunners missed again, you could hear the whole district groaning, like a football crowd. The man next door began pulling his plants up, he was so mad. Then when there was another set of bangs he would look up, then cover up his eyes, saying he couldn't bear to look.

Just as the bomber seemed to be getting away, it flew right into a cluster of grey cotton wool, and came out the other side as a mass of bits. God, you should've heard the cheering. Like Newcastle United had scored the winning goal for the FA Cup. It echoed and echoed.

Then the man next door said: 'They were brave lads for Germans. They flew in a straight line and didn't run away.' There were tears in his eyes. And everybody else began saying how brave the German airmen had been, and what a terrible thing war was.

But you could tell they were thoroughly enjoying themselves, really.

Boy, aged nine, Tyneside

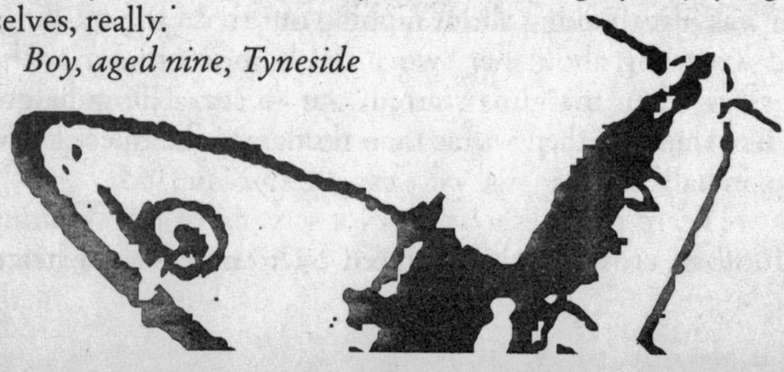

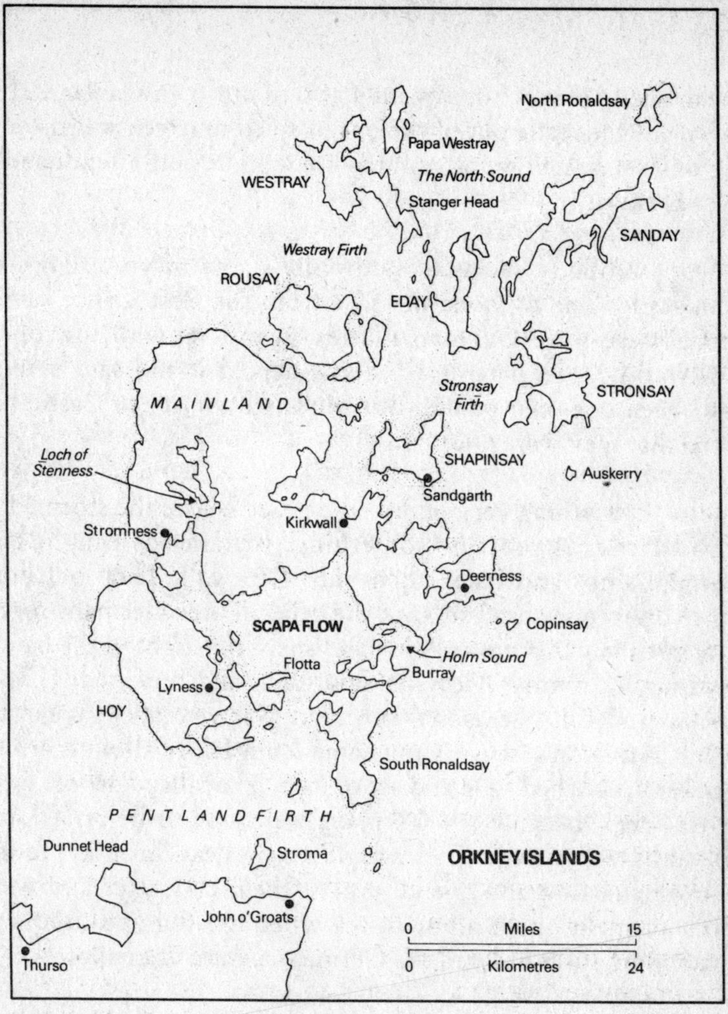

1939–40 WAR AT SCAPA FLOW

5 Sept. There was a German submarine in Scapa Flow before we declared war, but as it had done no damage they could do nothing about it. Three spies were caught on Mainland.

6 Sept. There's excitement enough now! This morning we heard the drone of planes but saw only two of our own seaplanes. Just as we got the cattle out of the byre I spied nineteen weird-looking objects, which we afterwards knew to be anti-aircraft shells, over Kirkwall.

7 Sept. Nobody seems to know the rights of yesterday's air raid. Astley had a phone-message from the Post Office saying there were nine German planes over Kirkwall Harbour. Kirkwall people, here at a funeral, denied it and said it must have been our own planes. But Miss Balfour at the Castle had word that they were Germans . . .

8 Sept. Everything very quiet – the peace before the storm? I'm afraid Hitler is plotting something. Britain has caught two German ships and taken them into Kirkwall. They put both crews on to one ship and sank the other. Three Germans somehow got away in a motor boat, and spent the night in the bay of Sandgarth. Tommy Nicolson saw them and reported it. Tom Sinclair and Bill Nicolson (both First War veterans) gave chase in Bill Nicolson's boat. A tug came from Kirkwall with armed men on it, touched here and set off too. The village people went into a 'steer' because the Germans were said to be armed and Bill and Tom weren't. They caught them, near Stronsay; found them unresisting and friendly; gave them cigarettes and were about to make them a pot of tea when the tug appeared and unceremoniously ordered the Germans aboard at gunpoint.

10 Oct. There is too little doing for my peace of mind! Hitler says he wants peace, but Britain won't give him peace, not on his terms! He is threatening to bomb every civilian town in Britain, sink every ship, and win the war! But he is NOT GOING to win. He is sure to try to bomb Kirkwall; Orkney is a dangerous place to live in. The King was in Scapa Flow and Kirkwall last week; Churchill the week before. There are rumours that Churchill said Orkney was not half-fortified – with the result that we are to have more coastal guns – one on this island too.

The summer is away and I don't know where it went. I enjoyed that summer, but I don't expect I'll enjoy another for a while. I *have* enjoyed it – the concert dance, the football dance, the Bible Class trip to Stromness . . . I have a strange unrest tonight. It's raining and blowing all it can. Oh, if I could only wander, to far-away places! This wind gives me unrest. Ruby is going to be a parlour-maid at the Castle.

I don't envy the Territorials on Stanger Head, this weather.

14 Oct. Two air raids over Kirkwall while I was in town. The *Royal Oak* was blown up in Scapa Flow and about 800 lives lost – many young boys in training.

14 Nov. There is a report that German planes were over Shetland again yesterday and dropped bombs. There is also a rumour that a spy was captured on Flotta, who had been poisoning the water supply. As there has been sickness among the troops, this is not impossible . . .

The siren sounded half an hour ago. Howe's flag is up; only it's not a flag, but a square sack of chaff!

There had been three Germans, adrift in an open boat, here in Orkney, trying to get back to Germany; they had apparently escaped from this area. They were caught near Fife, where the wind had blown them, exhausted, having gone without food for several days. The Chief Constable came out to the Castle and told Miss Balfour that they might land here – another false alarm.

20 Nov. Germans were expected last night, as there had been a North Sea battle. I'm sure I heard Germans this morning when the siren went. The clack-clack-clack of their engines is distinctly different from the steady drone of our planes.

I ordered shoes from Kirkwall; the shop sent three pairs on approval. I kept a plain black lacing pair, although I didn't like them. There was a brown pair, rather fancy, price 7s., but Daddy says such cheap leather is no earthly use.

Black Saturday: 14 October 1939. On that infamous day a surprise U-boat attack sank the 29,000 ton *Royal Oak*, one of the country's mightiest battleships – 809 men went down with the ship in Scapa Flow.

22 Nov. Clack-clack-clack-brrr-clack!

'German!' we said, and ran out with the binoculars. It was a broad-winged monoplane, with tapering body and wide tail. When it came nearer I saw a cross on the wings – a black cross in a blue circle – with a white or yellow circle outside that. It clacked away southwards, then came back again, not very high, and circled right over us. Then it came lower, rose again, and faded into the clouds towards Kirkwall. As no warning was sounded, we wondered if it could be one of our planes after all, though it looked 'uncan' and we went in to study the flag-book to make sure.

Rumble, rumble! Bang-bang! The clacking engine was coming nearer, over Kirkwall. The guns from Holm and Kirkwall opened fire. The siren wailed, and I think I heard machine-gun fire. The clacking engine stopped momentarily and we thought they'd got it, but it started again, more loudly. A destroyer came round Harcosness, stopped, turned, and went out again. More shell-fire, then off went the plane into the SSE and we heard it no more. The 'Raiders Past' has not yet sounded. Probably they are too dumbfounded. The thing has foxed them this morning, by coming much lower than the Germans usually do.

Rumour has it that a U-boat was seen in Mell Bay the other night.

27 Nov. Severe westerly gale yesterday. The sea reeked through the reef, and right out through the String past Harcosness, like white smoke. I went down to the shore early in the morning and again in the afternoon, and found a good box, some oddments, and a small plank.

There are no poles left on Wideford Hill now, and only three and three-quarters on Holm. They were there yesterday afternoon, so they must have gone down in the night; they are said to be listening-posts for planes . . .

3 Dec. The Germans are not all bad. A U-boat sank a British ship and the crew took to the boats. The submarine came up and stood by. Some of the British were soaked and shivering, and the Germans served up hot food and drinks to them, and waited till a British vessel arrived to pick up survivors. Then the U-boat commander shouted, 'Tell Churchill that there's some humanity!'

Girl, aged sixteen

1940 THE YOUNG COMMUNIST

I AM HAVING SOME DIFFICULTY in writing this letter as the guns are going off all round. At each explosion the windows shake and everything vibrates. I am sitting in a window overlooking the sea; it is a brilliant sunny day, it does not seem possible that somewhere, quite near, enemy planes are attempting to enter over the land. A few planes often enter the Channel on sunny days, but we have had no air raids here yet.

Once a German plane flew right above our hotel – anti-aircraft guns opened fire and we could see the shells bursting all round. The plane escaped over the Channel – somehow we were all glad when we saw that it had escaped; we dreaded seeing it crash into the sea. We did see the Norwegian ship [neutral] that was mined opposite here, burst into flames and sink. It was a terrible sight.

As far as I can see, the working class of England are not enthusiastic about this war. The government are issuing their propaganda frantically; everywhere there are posters – 'Freedom is in peril, defend it with all your might!' and 'Your courage, your cheerfulness, your resolution will bring us victory!', etc. The dance-bands play patriotic songs over the radio all day, but the people are not impressed. They are dissatisfied with the falling wages and higher prices and with ever-growing conscription.

Yesterday at the cinema the organist played 'There'll always be an England' and asked the audience to join in. A few voices started but died away after the first bars. The audience merely looked bored.

In August I joined the Young Communist League, which is part of the Communist Party. There is no YCL here in Folkestone but I still keep in touch with the Lewisham Party. The secretary sends me all the papers and leaflets. There are no political meetings held here but on Sundays I go to Spiritualist Meetings which are quite interesting; though as far as I can see, Spiritualism is all faked.

I spend my evenings writing to school friends and other friends, about the war, the causes of war and what we must do for peace. I sometimes get the rudest letters in reply, but some of the girls show an interest and I feel that some of them are seeing events more clearly now. I expect you know that the Communist Party is advocating 'peace now'. Our YCL at home hold a meeting practically every night.

Girl, aged sixteen, Kent

1940 'WHAT IF HITLER WINS? HE *CAN'T!*'

22 Jan. I hear that the Kirkwall schoolkids are to be evacuated to the Highlands. There is also a wild report that all the women and children in Orkney are to be evacuated, but this I do not believe.

23 Jan. Went to the Guild meeting last night. We're having a bring and buy sale on 21 Feb.; each member brings a friend. I heard at the Guild that Kirkwall, Stromness and Flotta children *at least* are to be evacuated to Caithness and Sutherland. Some say all Orcadians will get orders to take up their beds and walk! I wouldn't mind going a bit further afield, but not on someone else's orders!

That smelly tanker that is sinking in Inganess Bay had been torpedoed after all. They have got the torpedo in Kirkwall – so much for their 'internal explosion'.

 This is a lovely day – a lot of snow on the ground, hardly any wind, clear and sunny. On heavenly days like this one can't realize that there is a war.

27 Jan. The evacuation scare was all tommy-rot! Such a scheme has never been mentioned! The *Orcadian* newspaper officially denied that any such thing had ever been spoken of.

Now we are to be livened up! Two AA guns are coming to Shapinsay, and 100 men with two officers.

Wednesday was to have been our Burns' supper, but it was postponed until next Monday. The snow is all away. Oh, it's cold!

31 Jan. There was a dance last night. Some of our Territorials were coming home from Flotta, but because of bad weather they couldn't get home. The dance went on without them. We had quite a good evening.

I have found a lot of wood on the shore lately. Three ships have been sunk near here; two destroyers somewhere between Copinsay and Auskerry, and a patrol boat at Deerness. Very few lives saved. Jock Irving found a body near Sandgarth.

An anti-aircraft gun is to be put at Stromberry, and a searchlight. A 'heavy' is to be put at the Galt.

5 Feb. Three bodies have come ashore here, two in Sands and one near Hillside. Finding the bodies has rather scared the Sands people. Bill Nicolson (coastguard), going past the place where the bodies had lain, one dark night, nearly jumped sky-high when something gripped his trouser-leg! It was only a wee white dog!

A German plane came over on Saturday morning. It bombed the *Rota* but didn't hurt her; then off the east side of Shapinsay it machine-gunned an armed trawler. The trawler was not damaged but one man had bullets in his arm. The plane circled for a time then went off. Our patrols got up in full force after it was away. They said on the wireless this morning that three of our bombers chased it off! Utter nonsense! It went off at its own leisure. Not only the Germans tell fibs, it appears!

Only John Kirkness and I turned up for Bible Class this evening. Rev. J. Alan Robertson took us into the Manse for supper, and it was past ten before I got home. Daddy was just about to come and look for me. I wish he wouldn't get the wind up every time I'm late – it's so horribly silly.

10 Feb. Found a keg of Danish butter yesterday at Steiro – quite good, though a bit dirty on the outside, and the keg will fall to pieces if it gets too much handling. Seawater ran out when I hauled it up. It weighs 100lb. Reckoning it at 1s. a pound, it's worth £5. I'm going to report it. I also found an empty cask at the noust, in excellent condition.

Germany lost two U-boats yesterday.

22 Feb. Reported my butter and got a form to fill in. The butter is in Kirkwall now, and I'll get salvage according to what it sells for.

A destroyer was lost off Westray, on Sunday I think. She was one of a convoy.

16 Mar. Why did the Minister invite me to dance Strip-the-willow? I got into such a mix-up! I'm still sleepy after the dance.

Evening Another visit from Jerry! What an evening! I was up at Astley shop when Jim Stewart shouted 'Come out and see the firing!'

We all ran out, but thought it was a practice till Jim said 'I hear Germans!' It looked like fireworks and was really lovely. Gigantic sparklers going up, and great flashes from the Fleet in the Flow. About a dozen planes overhead, all lighted up, and making a noise like nothing holy. There was machine-gun fire coming down, and shells bursting above us. Suddenly a great fire burst out near Kirkwall, and we all yelled 'The oil tanks! The aerodrome!' But it went out again suddenly. I'm sure it was a ship.

 More fire came down, just at the Holm searchlights. A lull,

then nine planes with lights on went hell for leather northwards. Just as I was leaving, they got an air-raid warning! As I stepped outside I counted eight planes in the north and a roar of Germans in the distance. Very little firing, just a shot at a time, as I made for home. When I reached Newhouse it started again, fiercer than ever. Sixteen searchlights on. A great flash from Stromness, lighting up the west Mainland hills brilliantly. Shells burst right overhead, more firing seemed directly beside me. I was nearly gassed with gunpowder; the whole place reeked of it. Planes roaring overhead; the firing fiercer than ever. Did I run? The shells were right above me and the flashes at my very nose. Shrapnel falling, so I went hell for leather too!

There wasn't much firing after I got home. Honestly, I was not frightened, but I was excited, and I'm always chasing after excitement. All quiet now, the planes are down and the searchlights off. We'll have rain tomorrow . . .

17 Mar. The Germans hit a battleship last night, and killed seven on board her. She was only damaged. We got one German plane; it went off, blazing. Seven cottages in Stenness were hit, seven civilians injured and one killed. The Bridge of Waithe is blown up.

Lord Haw-Haw says they have accomplished what they wanted to do in Orkney and all their planes came safely home. He said some time ago they were going to bomb Orkney on 15 March. He was only one day out.

Jim says there are a number of the Fleet in Scapa, plus a good many 'dummies'.

There was a lot of confusion during the raid. The pilots who went up were young, practically untrained men, the rumour runs. Also we heard the guns were not quite quick enough off the mark. At Holm an officer phoned to the guns: 'There's a squadron of Germans overhead – open fire!' The planes were out of range before they fired . . .

There are ten Territorials here on Shapinsay, preparing for a big squad that comes next week. Two went past here yesterday and waved to me; I waved back.

22 Mar. The last convoy that went out past here was attacked off the east coast by eight Germans. Three ships were damaged, one had to be abandoned.

Forty Territorials were to have arrived here yesterday; don't know if they have come or not, but I'll find out when I go to the village for provisions. Our dress-rehearsal for the concert went not too badly. John Kirkness won't speak out properly – says that's because he has to have a 'lady's voice' (six feet tall and pretending to be a girl indeed!). Aggie has measles, so Lydia has to take her place in the duet with Barry.

The Territorials are coming to the dance!

The rain seems eternal – very mild soft rain, but naturally it wets you! Jean Gray has been in Stromness and says she saw the bombed cottages, and the Bridge of Waithe isn't demolished, only damaged. Some people in Birsay never knew the raid was on.

23 Mar. The concert went off OK, far better than the rehearsal. Our sketch wasn't bad. People say my recitation was good.

25 Mar. The Territorials have got their searchlight in Elwickbank Park. I believe the big thing they took into the Fort is a gun after all. Their enormous lorry got through the iron gate without knocking the pillars down! The lorry went past here a little while ago with men and a big trailer behind. The men were singing and they all waved. Mother lectured me for waving back, and when they returned she wouldn't let me go out in case I waved to them again! The men are planning to have a dance on Wednesday night, but I won't be allowed to go.

27 Mar. The 'thing' at the Fort is a generator after all, and the searchlight quite a small apparatus. The other large object is a new kind of detector – the very latest device.

We hear Miss Balfour is making the private soldiers billeted with her eat their food outside in the cold. She even refused to let them put their cooking stoves in the yard outside the kitchen door – the stoves are in the tennis court, and the men must eat there in the rain! And the lieutenant is treated like a gentleman, while he would prefer to be out with his men. They must take their boots off before coming indoors . . .

There's a rumour we are to have fifty Gordons, with guns. The Lancashire men are nice, though we have difficulty in understanding their speech, and they have the same difficulty with us, unless we speak English. (I don't like the Orcadian dialect anyhow.)

Evening Rattle-bang. 'It's Jerry! Come out and see the fireworks!' Twilight was beginning. Tracer bullets climbed upwards. A pale searchlight appeared over Kirkwall. Searchlight beams were all around, from Liviness, Cot-on-Hill, Stromberry and a lot from Holm and the south-west. Then everything as silent as the grave.

Suddenly, firing again, and a big display lit up the world. It was magnificent, beautiful. Our Shapinsay searchlights swept the sky, and Mainland was alive with sweeping lights and twinkling bullets and shells, and flashes of big guns to the south. I stood yelling encouragement at our searchlight batteries. I counted thirty-seven searchlights up at one time. Then the noise died away, and a voice from Liviness called through a megaphone 'Out!' The light shut off. I marched around for some time, whistling 'Run, rabbit, run' not very tunefully, I'm afraid, for I was a bit excited. Every raid we get, I long to be at the guns! These raids seem to rouse the Viking in me.

Jim Stewart says the whole German fleet is out – 100 or more. Norway is not objecting to our mining her waters. It's all a bit confusing . . .

9 April. Two German planes brought down last night – another won't get home.

America reports that Germany has invaded Denmark, and that German soldiers are parading in Danish towns. Norway is at war with Germany over Britain mining their waters. The 100

German ships are mainly armed trawlers, minesweepers and a few battleships, and they are heading for Norway.

About 8.30 Uncle Andrew came in. 'You'll hear something in a little while,' he prophesied. The siren wailed just as he spoke. A great noise of our planes rising . . . shells burst in an enormous barrage – a great black line in the sky. Great flashes from Lyness – whole batteries opening up at once. Our lighted planes scoured about, high above the shell barrage. As it grew darker, the firing increased.

'Look, a German machine-gunning!' An empty plane, going like smoke, was rat-tatting with his tail-gun, over Kirkwall. A shell crashed right behind him. He went off, then. Suddenly, the west side searchlight swept across the sky – and in the beam was an enormous plane! A great bomber, flying for its life, so low that one could easily have hit it with a shotgun! Four great engines under the wings; and red fire shooting down from the tail-gun, right between Hannatoft and the Old Manse. We lost sight of it then. Our four Shapinsay searchlights met and crossed overhead. An armed trawler, in the bay below us, fired. A faint red light appeared at the aerodrome. A pom-pom went crack, crack. We heard the men on the Elwickbank light shouting. The officer's car went past again. More bullets, flashes, searchlights. The lapwings were crying, and above it all a pale crescent moon looked down. It was weirdly beautiful.

10 May Norway is almost gone – and Germany has invaded Holland and Belgium simultaneously, dropping hundreds of men by parachute. We still have Narvik, but that's all of Norway.

There have been great ructions in Parliament, Churchill versus Chamberlain. They think Chamberlain is too slack and we must adopt some of Germany's tactics, or we'll never win the war. There was a vote. Chamberlain is still Prime Minister, but Churchill has almost supreme power now.

 15 May Jim Hayworth (searchlight battery) came here last

evening and said there was a submarine in here in the bay last night at two o'clock! A searchlight crew in Tankerness spied it cruising unconcernedly on the surface. They phoned Kirkwall, and all the men got orders to stand to. 'L' section from Liviness came out, watched for a minute, then went to bed again. There's a scare on that German parachutists may try to make a landing on Orkney. There were planes with parachutists on their way here on Sunday but our fighters drove them off. All the soldiers are to have more rifles, and four men are to be on guard together at night.

20 May The war gets more serious. Holland gave in last week. The Germans are half-way through Belgium, and this is one of the decisive battles of the war. 'L' section got orders to leave on Saturday; word came in the morning to pack up and be away by one o'clock. I hear heavy firing in the east, but cannot see anything.

21 May All last night I dreamed of quarries and water – very vivid dreams. This morning a case of suicide or accidental drowning occurred in Sands.

There was a great deal of firing last night – the Holm battery made a mistake – fired sixteen rounds with a twelve-pounder at a British ship and sent her to the bottom. The Germans have broken through the French lines and are some way in through France. Last night the news was bad – they had captured Arras.

25 May The Germans are right through the French lines now – they've reached Boulogne. I didn't hear the nine o'clock news last night but the news is getting worse and worse. What if Hitler wins? He *can't*. In all human reason he can't.

Girl, aged sixteen

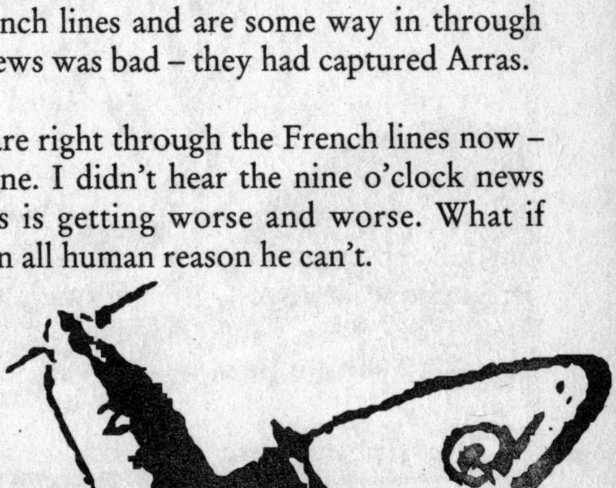

CHAPTER

5

THE FALL OF FRANCE

1940 THE FALL OF FRANCE

THERE WAS A SORT OF TINGLE in the air when I got up that morning; a sinking feeling in the gut, if you thought too much about it, and yet a heady excitement as well. Our radio was on all day, and they kept playing a fierce trumpet record, called 'Trumpet Voluntary', between the

"VERY WELL, ALONE"

announcements. Whoever thought of that was a genius; it keyed you up. I'd never realized why armies used trumpets before. It was harsh and bitter, and made you feel braver.

I couldn't understand why the French had surrendered. According to my war-map, they still had nine-tenths of their country left. In the Last Lot, the Germans had nearly got to Paris, had bombarded Paris with bloody huge guns like Big Bertha, and the French hadn't given in, and won in the end. What was the *matter* with them?

Of course, they had old-fashioned weapons. Daft old-fashioned helmets with a ridge along the top, and pale blue uniforms and puttees same as in the last war, instead of our new battledress. Their bombers tended to have three engines, and their fighters were always ten miles slower than ours, and their tanks had absurd round turrets and their submarines had huge guns instead of sensible torpedoes. But that was no reason for giving *up*.

I went for a walk, I was so worried. Met a kid on a building-site who said the French had only *pretended* to surrender; they'd waved a white flag, and when the Germans got out of their trenches, the French had shot them

I had this picture on my bedroom wall, and I always had the feeling that David Low, the artist, was actually a personal friend of Winnie's, and possibly a member of the Government. Only Churchill excelled him in capturing our moods. He probably did more to win the war than the whole Ministry of Information.

down like dogs . . . this was the first sensible suggestion I'd heard all day. I ran home to tell Dad the good news; he was not impressed.

People kept saying the French were *decadent*. Hints of black underwear and too much ooh-la-la in Paris. Till somebody said not in front of the child. My mother thought that lack of decent flush-toilets had sapped their morale. They drank wine instead

This magical cartoon marked the formation of an all-party war cabinet – hardly a very exciting occasion for a working-class boy.

The awesome thing is the rolling-up of sleeves. Working men really did roll up their sleeves in 1940, very slowly and methodically, almost meditatively, before starting a job or fight. You spat on the palms of your hands, too; surely a remnant of the old magic.

But here, glory be, it's not just socialist Morrison and docker Bevin . . . but near-aristocrats and gentlemen like Anthony Eden. *They* had grasped the reality at last, and joined us workers. And behind, the endless trailing line of all of us – including me and my dad, rolling our sleeves up too. In this cartoon are the seeds not only of Churchill's 1945 victory, but also of his 1945 defeat, at the hands of the Labour Party. Anthony Eden was much admired by working men, for his pre-war anti-appeasement resignation. But he was admired even more by working-class women – he shared 'star quality' with the British Hollywood greats Ronald Colman and Douglas Fairbanks Jr., whom he rather resembled.

of tea, *every day*! My father was pretty quiet. He said the French had stood up to Jerry pretty well in the Last Lot. Then Mr Churchill broadcast and said 'The Battle of France is over; the Battle of Britain is about to begin.'

I felt better, and went out on my bike to look for signs of the Battle of Britain.

Boy, aged ten, Tyneside

CHAPTER 6
SHELTERS, GAS MASKS AND BARRAGE BALLOONS

1939 ANDERSON SHELTER

THE GOVERNMENT didn't *build* shelters for you. Council workmen just came with a lorry and dumped the bits on your front lawn and left you to get on with it. We didn't think much of the bits, lying out in the rain, gathering rainwater. Just thin bits of corrugated iron, like some old shed. People felt they'd be safer in their houses, solid bricks and mortar. They weren't going out in the middle of the night to bury themselves in a *grave*.

Then my father saw an Anderson that had received a direct hit; he said there was quite a lot of it left; the house it had belonged to was just a heap of bricks.

So he and our neighbour Frank Spedding got cracking. They put me in charge of sorting and counting the bits and pieces, while they dug, but I soon got down into the hole. It had vertical sides, like a grave. Bits of worm kept poking out, then the worm would fall out altogether. It all smelt *good*, like gardening. People were calling out to each other, from hole to hole, and handing round tea. I got my pistol, and dreamt I was in the Trenches, in the Last Lot, and just about to lead my men Over the Top against the Germans, who were dug-in in Delaval Avenue. We found old clay pipes and blackened pennies, but only from 1935. Dad said he must have had a hole in his pocket, gardening.

Two foot six down, we came across an earthenware pipe running right across the hole. Mr Spedding, who was a builder, said it was a field-drain, from the time when our houses were fields. If

Gas masks were given out from house to house in 1939. These children are not only playing in their masks but have the boxes tied to their wrists or around their necks!

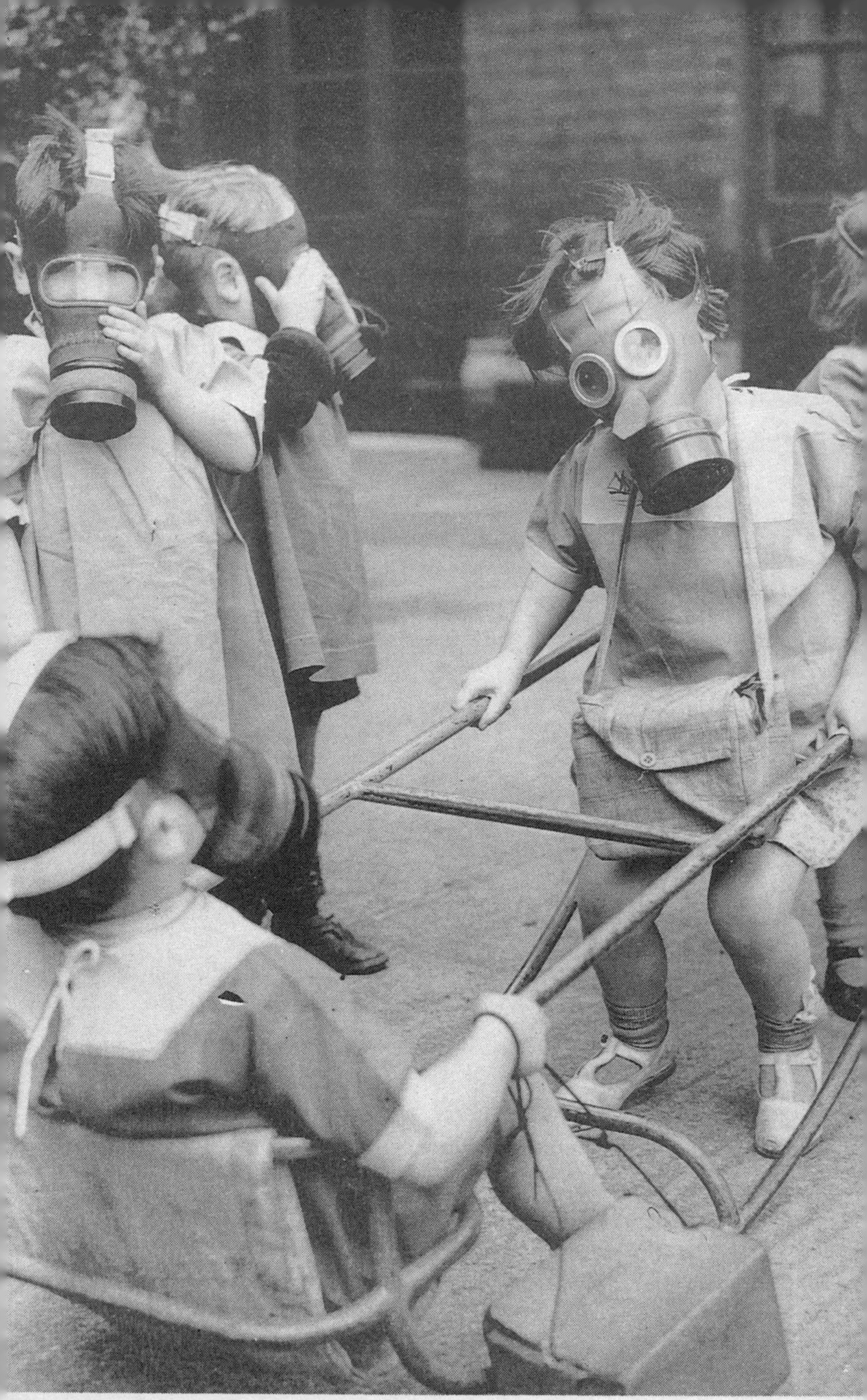

Anderson shelters going up.

we dug down through it, all the water in the field when it rained would end up in our shelter. So they decided to stop digging.

Mr Spedding, being a builder, got all sorts of bits and pieces,

A whole family survived in this one. The bomb, falling deeply into soft soil, has sent most of its blast harmlessly upwards . . . hence slates are intact on nearby roofs. Note the essential thumbs-up sign – solely used for the benefit of newspaper photographers.

and we made that shelter a real home from home. The floor was made of old maroon front doors, bought for a bob. The inside walls were painted white, and Mr Spedding threw handfuls of little bits of cork at the wet paint, so they stuck on; he said this would absorb the moisture from our breath, so condensation wouldn't run down the walls in winter. (Later, picking those bits of cork off the walls stopped me screaming while the bombs were dropping.) Mr Spedding also 'acquired' a lot of sandbags from somewhere, and soaked them in creosote, to stop the wet earth rotting them. I got really hooked on creosote, which I'd never smelt before; kept on going back to sniff them. We made them into a fine wall, all round the shelter, to keep the earth from falling off it. We also used them to make a porch, to keep rain off the shelter door. By the time we put the stout wood door on, and Mr Spedding had run electric cable out from the house, we were as snug as a bug in a rug. Electric light, electric fire, and we used to sit in armchairs making toast. Dad would have liked a picture on the wall, but the walls were curved.

Then the man came from the council. Nothing was right for him: we couldn't have a wooden door on the shelter; a bomb would turn it into a mass of splinters, and drive them through our flesh as we sat there. We could only have an old blanket over the door. We couldn't have electric light, as the bomb might cut the cable and fry us alive, if the cable touched the metal walls. Worst of all, the shelter should be three feet deep, not two feet six.

Dad told him about the field-drain. Dad said he wanted a shelter, not a well for watering the roses. But the man kept on waving his little steel ruler, and saying if we didn't put it three feet down, the council would come and take the shelter away, and we could do without.

We put it down three feet; I don't think Dad stopped swearing from start to finish. Slowly, the shelter filled up with water like a swimming-pool. We did water the roses from it. We spent the winter raids sheltering in the cupboard under the stairs.

 Boy, aged nine, Tyneside

'ARE YOUR LITTLE ONES used to seeing you in *your* mask? Make a game of it, calling it "Mummy's funny face" or something of the kind. Then if the time comes when you really have to wear it, you won't be a terrifying apparition to the child.'

Radio broadcast, 1939

Hitler will send
no warning –
so always carry
your gas mask

The nearest we ever got to hysteria was about gas masks, before the war had even started properly.

THE ONE THING WE WERE certain of was that the Germans would use poison gas. Babies had gasmasks; horses had gasmasks; both were the same size, except the whole baby went inside, but only the horse's head. The baby's mother had to pump air into it, through a concertina-thing on the side.

Young children had gay blue-and-red ones that looked like Mickey Mouse. Soldiers had very grand hideous ones, with round eyepieces and a long trunk like an elephant. Wardens'

Silly propaganda. An obviously posed photograph with the girls simply standing. Had they tried exercising, their masks would have steamed up immediately.

were similar, but without the trunk. Ours had a short trunk, and a large window for our eyes. The moment you put it on, the window misted up, blinding you. Our Mums were told to rub soap on the inside of the window to prevent this. It made it harder to see than ever, and you got soap in your eyes.

There was a rubber washer under your chin, that flipped up and hit you, every time you breathed in. You breathed out with a farting noise round your ears. If you blew really hard, you could make a very loud farting noise indeed. (You got caned for doing that during gas practices.) The bottom of the mask soon filled up with spit, and your face got so hot and sweaty you could have *screamed.*

Once we had our masks tested; we were led through an air-raid shelter that the wardens had filled with tear-gas. Most of us noticed nothing, but Charlie Blower's mask didn't work. He just sat in class all morning with tears streaming down his face, then the teacher sent him home.

The cardboard boxes that gasmasks came in fell apart inside a week. Our dads bought us long metal cylinders like the German soldiers carried their gasmasks in. We used to carry them round on dog-leads across our shoulders. We used gas-masks in fights, whirling them round our heads, swinging them like swords; they could cut your head open, if you didn't dodge. The guy with the most dented gasmask was the hero. We used to carry bottles of ink and sweets and secret treasures inside. When you had a sudden gas practice, this could be very embarrassing.

Boy, aged ten, Tyneside

1939 A DEMENTED KITE

I GOT TO KNOW our local barrage balloon team very well. They were sited on the tennis courts just below our back garden and I spent many hours watching. We occasionally lost a balloon by it breaking free, when it would suddenly shoot up to a tremendous

height before drifting away, no doubt to be used as a target for some marauding fighter plane. Alternatively, the ears or vanes would tear, and on these occasions the balloon would go out of control and behave like a demented kite. The crew would try and bring it in but it would tear round on the end of its wire, taking off chimney-pots and roofs. On one such occasion the wire crossed the trolley-bus cables and disabled all electric transport along the Plumstead road for hours.

Boy, London

Like herds of silver elephants, their fins rippling in every breeze . . . They brought down few aircraft, but raised morale.

WE HAD FIVE BARRAGE BALLOONS, including one on a ship that went out into the middle of the river during raids. The Germans shot down one, the Fish Quay Buster. But it was replaced the next day, which made the Germans seem pretty pointless.

Sometimes the balloons flew low, sometimes high; no pattern to it. People used to discuss them, like they'd discuss weather in peacetime. 'I see the balloons are low tonight!' It must mean *something.*

Finally the mums decided they were a kind of barometer for air raids. If the balloons were low, a raid was expected. If they flew high, it was safe to let the kids out to play. The higher the balloons, the further we were allowed to roam.

One sunny night, we went off to the Coast Road bridge, about a mile, to watch for army convoys. My mate went fishing for newts. I lay on my back in the dry summer grass, and suddenly noticed the balloons. *Incredibly* high, the sunlight catching their silver sides, making them glint like stars. So many . . . I felt incredibly safe; so many balloons, so high. I hadn't felt so safe since war started. Hitler couldn't possibly win.

I lay on, in a kind of dream, my mate splashing some yards off. The sun set, and still the sides of the myriad balloons glinted.

I called out 'Aren't the balloons like stars?'

'They aren't balloons, they *are* the stars!'

Suddenly, it was dark, and we were far too far from home.

We ran all the way.

Boy, aged ten, Tyneside

CHAPTER 7
DAYLIGHT RAIDS

18 AUGUST 1940 ATTACK ON KENLEY AIRFIELD

EIGHT-YEAR-OLD BRIAN CRANE had been playing football with some young friends when the sight of the large formation caught their attention. The children gazed up in awe at the armada passing overhead. Then, too late, the siren began to sound and bombs began to fall. Instant confusion; the horror-struck boys stood paralysed, not knowing what to do. Then a lady shouted 'Run home to your mummies, quick! They'll be worried!' And run the children did, as fast as their legs could carry them. 'The owner of the ball kept calling "You've left my bloody ball." We hadn't. I was clutching it firmly to my stomach, probably wishing it was my mother.' Half-crying to themselves, the children ran on, people shouting at them from all directions. 'Get off the street! Mind the shrapnel! Get home quick!' All of this intermingled with the crump of exploding bombs and the menacing drone of aircraft. Finally a concerned lady insisted that the boys take cover in her house. They were ushered into a cupboard under the stairs and plied with milk, biscuits and toffee. 'I sat with my knees under my chin, pressing the football into my chest and remembering every good thing my mother had ever done for me.'

From Alfred Price, The Hardest Day, *Scribner, 1980*

1940 LIFE MUST GO ON

THE MISSION BAZAAR is today and I am dressed up as a Red Indian. It is going to be jolly nice unless the Jerries want to pay a visit to us. The siren is a 'stale story' because it goes every night at a quarter past seven. Is there any chance of you and

HOVIS

Daddy getting a house yet? I suppose all this can be blamed on 'Funny Face Hitler?'

Girl, convent boarding school, Hampshire

1 SEPT 1940 LETTER FROM A RAID

DEAR MUMMY

I go down to the farm nearby all the day . . . The siren has just gone and we are in a shelter, ha, ha! The siren always goes when I am at the farm. We have had two more Raids in fact more I am sure. The 'All Clear' has just gone what a short Raid they passed but they were lots and lots of them. Oh dear! No more news.

LOVE, JILL

DEAR MUMMY AND DADDY,

We had an exciting time on Thursday (us). You see we had an *Air Raid* warning in the night. It was funny, mistresses in dressing-gowns. Nuns half-dressed. (I still had my plate in my mouth ha, ha!) We were down in the shelter about an hour. We played games and went nearly to sleep. We said the Rosary too. The next day we were very tired so we had to rest. Most of the school went to sleep.

JILL

Girl, convent boarding school, Hampshire

1940 DAYLIGHT RAID

IT STARTED WITH the sound of aeroplanes. It was a warm, muggy overcast day and raining. We looked out of the classroom window, and couldn't see a thing. We didn't recognize the *zhooooorzh, zhooooorzh, zhooooorzh* of unsynchronized German engines in those days.

Then the sound of a boy running a stick along a set of iron railings, far away. More boys running iron railings. Then the sound of the aeroplanes went really wild, like they were going to crash above the clouds.

Then the sirens went. We had to run to the surface brick shelter down the street. A sloping wet slippery street, and all the time the sound of invisible planes going mad just above us.

Then a Spitfire came diving down through the clouds, vertically, just above us. We thought it was going to crash on us, but it pulled out just above the rooftops, and flew round and round in circles, as if it was frightened a German had followed it. Then it put its nose up, and disappeared back into the clouds as vertically as it had come down.

We were sent home when the 'all clear' sounded. The streets

In our eyes the Stuka dive-bomber was the ultimate magic evil Nazi bird. Only J. R. R. Tolkien, with his Nazgul in *Lord of the Rings,* gets anywhere near the horror today. They were Hitler's personal demons. Like the Nazgul, they cast a shadow of terror, men's hearts failed when they appeared. On the newsreels, we had watched them destroy the terrified streams of refugees, and helpless soldiers of Spain, Poland, Holland, France. They flew in geometrically straight formations, and dived on their prey near-vertically, paralysing them with the built-in whistles on their wings, that wailed like banshees. With their queer cranked wings and fitted spatted undercarriage, we boys found them miracles of evil shapes, impossible to draw. But we impersonated them more often than Hitler or Churchill, cranking our arms wildly and screeching down steep hills to the consternation of old ladies.

At the beginning of the Battle of Britain, Stukas were sent to attack south-coast shipping and radar masts. They flew into a cloud of Spitfires and Hurricanes off Portland Bill, and were slaughtered. There was a radio commentator watching: I'll never forget his hysterical shouts of delight and relief as they started going down. In that moment, I knew that Hitler was going to lose the war. Now, when I read of the Nazgul falling in fiery ruin, at the end of *Lord of the Rings,* it's the Stukas I see.

were covered with little heavy silver mushrooms – bullets that had flattened themselves as they hit the ground. You could still find them months afterwards, hidden under privet hedges.

The news said that seventeen German raiders had been shot down – but they said the battle had taken place over the Farne Islands, about forty miles north of us.

Boy, aged ten, Tyneside

IN 1939 MY SCHOOL was evacuated to Scarborough, but I didn't go, as my parents wished me to stay at home and assist them with our family's holiday camp, as far as a schoolboy could.

One afternoon I was at home, the siren having sounded, and I saw a German bomber circle the lighthouse half a mile away and drop a bomb on Larder's caravan camp. A Mrs Read suf-

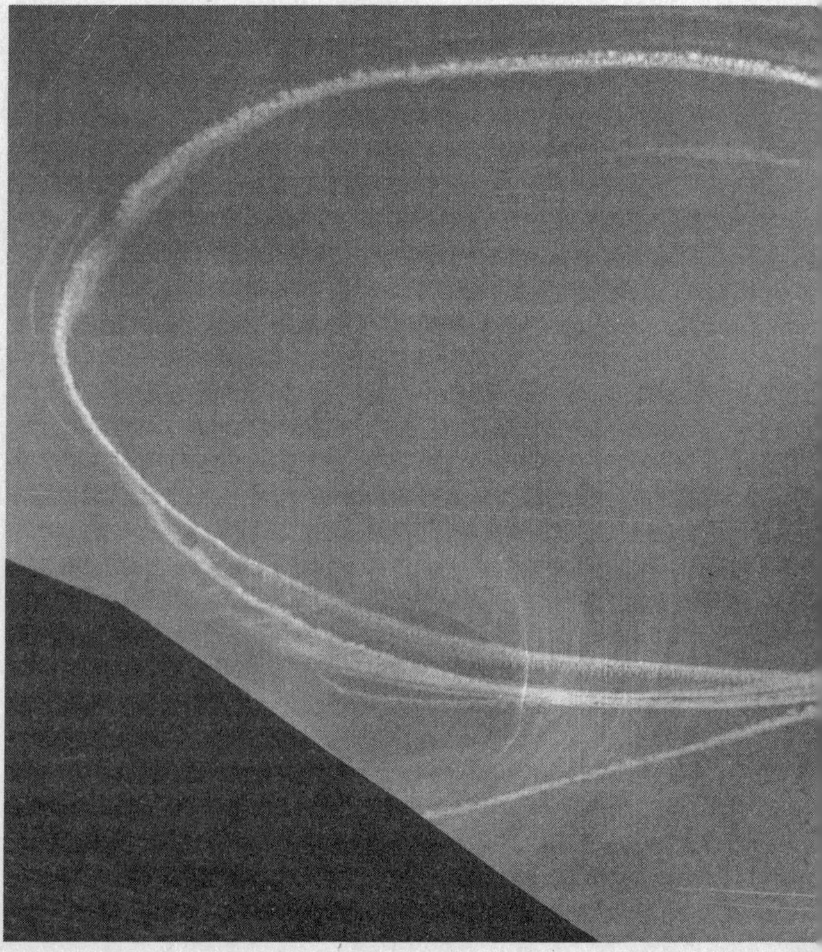

fered a fractured arm and leg when the caravan she and her husband shared was flattened by the explosion. Mrs Read moved subsequently to the Kenwood Camp right behind my parents' home, as this was a chalet-camp used for billeting soldiers and bombed-out people, as was our camp. Mrs Read suffered a great shortening of her leg, and had to wear a high-soled boot on recovery.

One evening at six o'clock I had gone to the Little Kinema with my mother, to see a comedy film. We were inside only a few minutes when the siren went. Shortly afterwards I heard a rushing sound, commenting to my mother that the steam train must have arrived, the cinema being opposite the station. For some reason I was uneasy, and had a strange feeling as I said it, that it was untrue. The next minute we were choking from the dust of two 350lb. bombs. The blast broke the exit-doors and many people were prevented from leaving by Mr Bob Neil, the local sugar-boiler and rock-maker, who suggested we'd be safer inside than in the streets. This was good judgement as only minutes later the streets were raked with machine-gun fire from the planes, a popular local bus inspector

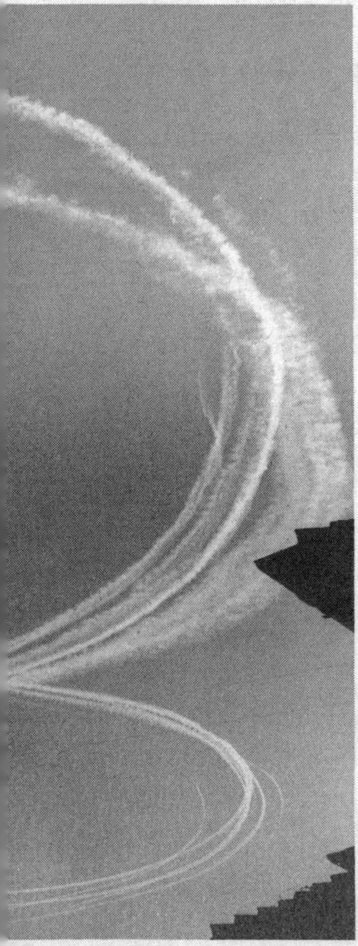

Vapour trails: the calligraphy of fighter combat. Spitfires could turn in a tighter circle than Messerschmitts . . .

being killed in a hail of fire. Fortunately the main street was deserted due to being tea-time, saving many lives.

Later, a lad found an item on the beach and took it to his mother's caravan in Moser's caravan camp. It exploded, sending shrapnel through weather-boards an inch thick. It was a timber caravan, and his mother lost her foot and part of her lower leg as a result of the explosion. The unfortunate lady could be seen being pushed round the town in a wheelchair for many years afterwards. The lad had put it on the table when he came in, not realizing the danger.

Many a night my family would be unable to sleep as we watched the glow of Hull burning and heard the anti-aircraft guns banging away, about fifteen miles as the crow flies. We had an oak dining-table with a top one inch thick with cabriole legs, and we sat under this when we became worried, as the bombers had to pass over our brick bungalow, going to Hull and coming back. Regularly, fresh people would arrive to dwell in our requisitioned timber holiday chalets, having been bombed-out of Hull, many still living there till 1960, when they were found council accommodation.

I played the cornet in the local Gospel Mission Band, being the youngest player at nine. Shortly afterwards, Mr Back the ex-Salvation Army Officer who led the Mission was sent to gaol for allegedly spreading rumours, and the Gospel Mission was closed. I believe he was innocent, but the authorities were very jumpy early in the war.

Another gentleman, Mr Benjamin Smith, was also sent to the local cells for one night, as he had been seen on the promenade, using a pair of binoculars, looking out to sea. He was our local radio repair man, usually short of cash, very kind and helpful, possessing a bicycle that was rusty, decrepit and unique. It only had one handlebar, as he found the other handlebar got in the way. So he took a hacksaw and lopped it off, being able to carry a radio under his arm much more easily while on his cycle. There was only one brake left and he used one foot sliding on the road to supplement the existing brake. This caused much hilarity among us schoolboys.

Our local cinema was run by Mr Vincent Lockey, and owing to the petrol shortage he used an electric battery-driven van. It did about ten miles an hour on the level road and made a whining noise that was rather weird in the blackout. I think it was an ex-laundry van.

I went into Hull one day and forgot my gasmask. Unfortunately I was caught in a test with gas, and although I went into a shop to shelter I had to be treated by Civil Defence for severe eye irritation. I never forgot my gasmask again; it taught me a lesson. It was tear-gas.

There was a young mother by the name of Anne Marie who lived in our camp. I did not know her surname or her husband, as he was possibly away in the services. Having been bombed-out in Hull she was allocated to our number 10, and she had a child with her, about five years of age and went to the local infants' school.

About this time the South Promenade, which had received scant maintenance during the war, collapsed one night when the sea was rough, leaving a gap about ninety feet wide, which about doubled in the next fortnight. Two nice bungalows, known as 'La Plaza' and 'Kingdom's Café', ended up on the beach as the sea ate into the land to a depth of fifty feet.

One day Anne Marie's child was seen playing near the gap in the sea-wall. The next thing the mother knew was the child had disappeared. What happened may never be known – in spite of police enquiries, searches by local people, etc., the child was never seen again. It is almost certain the child was drowned or maybe buried by a fresh fall of earth from under the promenade paving-stone decking but no trace was ever found.

It was the custom to gather money for a wreath in the camp if anyone was bereaved, but what can you do if there is no funeral? Everyone in the camp was very upset, as was the whole town at the time. May the little one rest in peace, may perpetual light shine on the little one!

Boy, aged nine, Withernsea, Humberside

CHAPTER

8

THE LONDON BLITZ

SEPT 1940
THE BEGINNING OF THE BLITZ

A SQUADRON OF HEINKEL 111K bombers were approaching with Me 109 escorts. Six Spitfires thundered over to intercept. In the ensuing battle the bombers were dispersed, the remains of six German and two English planes were scattered over our town. A stick of three 250lb. bombs had fallen close by and we walked around to see the damage. Only one had fallen near a house. The owner showed us the ruined furniture, the broken window and door frames, and the large hole in his garden.

It was our first experience of air attack and I think it gave us a false sense of security. We felt if this was the worst German bombs can do we needn't worry.

On that day we mourned the two pilots who had died in the battle over our heads (they were Polish).

The following Saturday, 7 Sept., the siren sounded again.

It was obviously no repeat of the previous week. The sky was full of approaching bombers. As we watched we could see their bomb-racks opening and bombs beginning to fall. We took to the Anderson shelter in our garden, taking turns to peer out of the door to see what was happening. It was obvious from the noise that bombs were not being aimed at specific targets, but were being dropped in an indiscriminate carpet over the civilians of London.

My brother was at work in the Siemens factory at Charlton and my mother was very concerned for his safety. She kept saying 'If we are to be killed, at least we should all be killed together.'

The raid ended about 18.30 hours. We emerged from the shelter to take stock. Our house wasn't damaged, but an unexploded shell had gone through the house opposite and the road had to be closed until the bomb-disposal men could shift it. Over the river great fires had been started and as darkness fell a red glow lit the area.

About 19.30 hours the sirens went again and we were to hear the start of a winter of endless bombardment. The attacking bombers concentrated on the areas where fires still raged, and further fires were started. We felt sorry for the East Enders who were really 'copping a packet'.

Schools were reopened for children still remaining in London; much of our time was spent in the air-raid shelter, which paradoxically was a cloakroom, with bricked-up windows, three storeys up in the building!

The nightly raids meant that even though we had beds in the shelter we didn't get much sleep. The early bombers would drop incendiaries. If these were not put out the following bombers would drop high explosives. It became necessary to organize firewatchers to quickly extinguish any that fell. My brother organized street-watches. I typed the rotas, which were displayed on hand-made notice-boards around the district.

Once we were showered with individual bombs – there were three on our house alone – one under the car. We quickly put out all visible light. It was only then that one was discovered lodged in the roof of the house next door, owned by an old couple. It had no access to the roof area. The old people were in the shelter and had not been disturbed. We gained entry and located the bomb. We could see the glow through the ceiling in their bedroom. A metal bucket was placed underneath and the ceiling around the fire cut through with a water-jet from the stirrup-pump until the bomb eventually fell through.

When it was all over my brother found that he was wearing his slippers on the wrong feet!

Not all incidents were without humour – a string of incendiaries fell in the cemetery and our firewatchers climbed over the walls to put them out. They were using flower-pots and whatever was to hand. However, on achieving this they

We shared a shelter with a fireman's wife. Every time she heard the fire-engine bells, she said: 'The Jerries aim their bombs at the fires.'

successfully eliminated all light and were unable to find their way out again!

No doubt the relatives of those occupying the graves would have blamed vandals for the emptying of the flower-pots, had it not been for the little piles of grey ash and metal fins left from the bombs.

We knew that parachute flares overhead could mean we had been selected for punishment that night; therefore lights in the sky were viewed with alarm. One night, whilst bedded down in our shelter, a light appeared to hang in the sky. We watched it for a considerable time before we realized it was a glow-worm crawling over the curtain which we had fitted to the opening – quite a relief . . .

Every day brought its own tale of war. We became like a village and tended to disregard the troubles of others three or four streets away.

A bomb fell further up the road, taking out two houses and killing the lodger in one. He had just run indoors from the shelter to make a cup of tea.

Remarkably, the houses on either side were undamaged, although further away roofs were broken by descending debris. The front doorstep of one of the houses came through the roof of the house next door, finishing up on the landing, leaving a gaping hole to the sky. Naturally, next day it rained. Our neighbour, after removing the huge lump of concrete, put a tin bath at the top of the stairs to collect the rain. Their teenage son came out of the bathroom, fell over the half-filled bath and accompanied it downstairs, to the consternation of his mother!

A nose-cap of an anti-aircraft shell penetrated our roof and lodged through the ceiling of the bathroom. When removed this left a small round hole through which dust dribbled when an explosion occurred near by.

 The fixed gun installations had been augmented by mobile units who would roar up the road, clamp down, and fire a few salvoes before rushing off elsewhere. I don't think they ever shot any enemy planes down, but it helped morale considerably.

Nightly the raids continued unabated. During the day through intermittent raids I attended school, spending most of the time in the third-floor cloakroom shelter. Once we were violently shaken by a very near miss. As we left school we saw the rescue teams, ambulances etc., at the factory next door. The bomb had fallen down the ventilation shaft into the shelter where the factory girls had been assembled. The dead and injured were being removed; the carnage was horrible. It was a sobering thought that only 10 feet separated us from suffering that fate. I decided that after I had taken the pending exams I would have to learn First Aid.

I did well in the exams and was one of two to obtain a Grammar School pass. I was sent to Colfes Grammar School at Lewisham, which throughout the war was called SELESSFB (South East London Emergency Secondary School for Boys).

Boy, aged twelve, London

1940 UNNAMED HORRORS

The things that are going on now in these public air-raid shelters are very dreadful. For a young girl to go into a public shelter now without her father and mother is simply asking for trouble.

London magistrate reported in Evening Standard, *4 November 1940*

1940 UNDERGROUND PEOPLE

On 7 September, the bombers came early. That day stands out as a great flaming wound in my memory. Imagine a ground-floor flat, crowded with hysterical women, crying babies, great crashes in the sky and the whole earth shaking. Someone rushed in.

'The docks are alight. All the docks are alight.' I could smell the burning.

'Trust the poor to get it in the neck, why don't they sort out the rich?'

The men started to play cards and the women tried a little sing-song – 'I saw the old homestead and faces I loved' or 'Yiddle mit his fiddle'. But every so often, twenty women's fists shook at the ceiling, cursing the explosions, Germany, Hitler.

'May he die from a lingering tumour,' my mother wailed.

'That's too good for him,' Aunt Sarah said. Yes, cursing got my mother and aunts through those early days. I sat under the table where the men were playing cards, screwing up my eyes and covering my ears, counting the explosions.

'We're all gonna be killed, we're finished.' One of my aunts became hysterical.

'Churchill will get us through, he's a friend of the Yiddisher people.' With these words she was soothed.

This time all my uncles nodded agreement, even the Marxist playing Solo.

The all-clear sounded a beautiful symphony in my ears.

After the terror of that night, people started to flock towards the tube. They wanted to get underground. Thousands upon thousands the next evening pushed their way into Liverpool Street Station, demanding to be let down to shelter. At first the authorities wouldn't agree, and called out the soldiers to bar the way. I stood there in the thick of the crowd, thinking there would be a panic and we would all be crushed to death.

It was the worst experience I had up till then and I wanted to rush out of that crowd, but I was jammed tight. I would have preferred to take my chances in the street with the bombs. Anything was preferable to that crush. I shouted my head off, went limp and was carried along by the surging masses, trying to hold on to my separate identity. The people would not give up and would not disperse, would not take no for an answer. A great yell went up and the gates were opened and my mother threw her hands together and clutched them towards the sky. 'Thank God, he heard me.' As if she had a special line to Him and He had intervened with the Government on behalf of the Kops family.

This underground station was unfinished: people could sleep on the rails as well.

'It's a great victory for the working class,' a man said.

So I dashed with the crowd into the underground and saw the solidarity of the surface disappear as an endless stream of people crushed in after us. We were underground people with the smell of disinfectant in our nostrils and blankets under our arms, standing jammed, shoving and pushing each other. No laughter, no humour. What sort of victory had we achieved? Every family for itself now, and my mother trying to encompass all her family with her bulk, a family that had emigrated into the bowels of the earth. Dignity and joy left the world. Shuffling down, I felt as if I were fulfilling some awful prophecy. Something that everybody knew, but didn't want to talk about.

The soldiers downstairs forced us on to trains, to go further up the line. Liverpool Street, being the closest, was the most popular. So we were forced to move on and we tried the next station along the Central Line, then the next and the next.

I heard sirens. And sirens and sirens. Early in the morning, in the afternoon and in the evening. And we went underground to get away from the sirens and the bombs. Yet they followed me and I heard sirens until the world became a siren. One endless cry of torture. It penetrated right into the core of my being, night and day was one long night, one long nightmare, one long siren, one long wail of despair.

I would scoot out of the train ahead of the family and under the legs of people, unravelling the three or four scarves tied round me. And I bagged any space I could along the platform. The family followed, and we pitched our 'tent' and unwound and relaxed. Out came the sandwiches and the forced good humour. Here we were, involved in a new exodus – the Jews of the East End, gone into exile in the underground. Our spirits would rise for a while, we were alive for another night, we would see another dawn.

No room left on the platform: safety at the price of torment.
Piccadilly Station, 1940.

Now I see that the miracle of Moses wasn't getting the message from God but in getting all the Jews to go in the same direction, one big happy family. For despite the friendliness and sharing of sandwiches, families were going in all directions, each trying to feather its own three feet of concrete. And something had been lost without trace. This is what Hitler had brought to London. The Jewish people of London with their terrific communal feeling were being torn apart, irrevocably for all time. But then, so was the whole world.

'This is what they brought to the world,' my mother said. And an old man with a sharp beard sitting down next to me, shook his head knowingly. 'When they start on the Jews a terrible retribution comes to the world. Look at Haman! Look at Pharoah!'

But I wasn't only miserable; for seizing advantage of my mother's preoccupations, I managed to get some money out of her. And I got bars and bars of chocolate out of the chocolate machines, and weighed myself incessantly.

Here was a new life, a whole network, a whole city under the world. We rode up and down the escalators. The children of London were adapting themselves to the times, inventing new games, playing hopscotch while their mothers shyly suckled babies on the concrete. And I used to ride backwards and forwards in the trains, to see the other stations of underground people.

One night, though, we were very lucky. We were pitched down at Liverpool Street and Phyllis and I decided to venture as far as Marble Arch. As the train moved out of Bank station and entered the tunnel, it stopped and all the lights went out. There was a great thud and we held our ears. When we returned we realized a bomb had fallen down the lift shaft of that station and, apart from those killed by the blast, there were also those who had been thrown on the line and electrocuted, just as our train pulled out.

From Bernard Kops, The World is a Wedding,
McGibbon and Kee, 1963

LATE AUTUMN; we had yellow chrysanthemums on our sitting-room windowsill. That night the grown-ups in our shelter kept saying the raid was specially heavy. 'One night they *will* get the railway line,' said Mother. It was common knowledge that the railway line a quarter of a mile away carried ammunition trains from the factory at Park Royal.

There was a tremendous bang, and the shelter lights went out. I expected the shelter to collapse, but nothing hit me. We heard bricks falling, people shouting.

'My God, we're hit,' screamed Mother, and immediately got out of the shelter. Then she leant back in, outlined by searchlights.

'Come out,' she said. 'I don't believe it.'

We climbed up the ladder. All the hens were cackling wildly and flapping. Fires in the distance, but everything looked the same as usual. We ran up the back-garden path and through the house. Just then my uncle came in the front door.

'Keep those children in,' he shouted. But we all ran past him.

There was a huge hole opposite – two houses down, looking like teeth that needed filling in the semi-dark. Bricks were still falling and a ring of wardens shouting 'Keep back, keep back!' to the people who were pouring in, from up and down the street.

Then Mr Leggatt was helped out of the ruins of his house, bleeding round the head. Then his son, with only a scratch on his hand.

After a long time, bombs falling all round, whistles blowing, planes roaring, searchlights picking out planes and barrage balloons overhead, the ambulance came. A stretcher was carried out, the body covered over completely. Then another, but the face showing, covered with blood.

'It's Margaret,' everyone whispered. 'Then Mrs Leggatt is dead.'

'Here – what about the Joneses, next door?'

'They're all away.'

'It's a miracle.'

A warden yelled at my mother 'Get those kids indoors – there's a bloody raid going on!'

Margaret and Mr Leggatt had been folding a tablecloth by the larder door. Dozens of jars and bottles had been blown into fragments, and Margaret was still having operations five years after the war to remove the glass. She was eighteen.

All our downstairs windows were broken, but for some reason, the upstairs ones weren't. The broken glass had got into the yellow chrysanthemums. My mother immediately picked it all out, and they lived for three more weeks. The house was thick with fallen soot. Precious, my doll, had a white Victorian frilled nightie that had to be destroyed, it was so filthy. I *hated* Hitler.

After the bomb site had been tidied up, our gang used to play there and have secret fires. Until one day a woman saw us and

Wherever the disasters were worst, they were there, listening. When Buckingham Palace was bombed, the Queen said she was glad. 'Now we can look the East End in the face.' This photograph was taken in South London, October 1940.

said 'That's where Mrs Leggatt died. You kids ought to be ashamed.' We never went there again to play, but set up a little stone and put flowers on it in summer, and leaves in winter, and holly at Christmas.

Fatty Waller said we ought to send Margaret Christmas cards, so we all told our mums we were being kept in at school, and went up to Willesden Hospital with them. They took the cards, but they wouldn't let us see her.

On Christmas Eve we all went to the bomb site and sang 'Away in a Manger', then

Whistle while you work
Hitler is a twerp
Goering's barmy
So's his army
Whistle while you work.

Then we didn't know what to do, so we all went home, and got into trouble for being so dirty.

Girl, aged six, London

1940 IN THE SHELTER

WE HAD AN ANDERSON shelter at the bottom of the garden. The three of us shared it with Maude and Laura Rowlands (two maiden ladies who lived next door) and their fat old brown-and-white mongrel, Patch. It was very damp. My mother caught lumbago from the damp and eczema from spring-cleaning with washing-soda, as there was no soap to be had. Every morning she had to drag herself backwards up the shelter steps, in time to make our breakfast before we went to school. If you were late, and there hadn't been a raid the night before, you got caned. Fortunately we lived by the railway. There were raids every night.

Girl, aged six, London

1940 LANDMINE

WE WERE ALL IN OUR SHELTERS, and in spite of an air raid some miles away, most of us were asleep. Suddenly there was a lot of whistling, men shouting 'Everyone to the front of their houses'. Then a loud-hailer. 'This is the police – everyone to the front of their houses, PLEASE.'

My mother said 'They must be mad, with an air raid going on.'

'Perhaps the Germans have invaded?'

When we got to the front, wardens and police were telling everyone they had ten minutes to get out of their houses and go to friends at least half a mile away. If they didn't know anyone, they were to go to Harvist Road School – *my* school. There was an unexploded landmine in Doyle Gardens and as soon as all the neighbouring roads had been evacuated, they would be closed, so the Army could move in.

'Be as quick as you can – DO NOT WAIT TO DRESS. Turn off your gas, electricity and water. If you can find your pets take them. Do not waste time looking for them. Take your ration-books, if you can find them quickly. Take what blankets you can carry.'

'Granny's,' said Mother. The warden marched alongside us; we were all still in our nightclothes. The raid was now overhead. Ack-ack guns fired from Roundwood Park. We heard a plane crashing. Searchlights all over the sky.

'I'm frightened, Mr Leggatt,' I said to the warden.

'Here's my tin hat,' he said, putting it on me.

'I want one,' said my brother. He was only four, and my mother kept carrying him, then putting him down. Mr Leggatt left us, to hurry other people on. One woman was carrying a budgie . . .

It didn't feel like half a mile – more like ten. Grandmother lived near Harvist Road. She was very frightened, being knocked up at two in the morning, as my uncle was a warden and she thought he'd been killed.

My mother gave her the big blanket, and she settled Mother on the couch in the living-room, and my brother on cushions on the floor by her side. Then she wrapped me up in the big blanket, found a pillow and put me to bed in the bath. I went to sleep at once, the helmet beside me.

I dreamt I was drowning, slowly. Then I awoke to find the cold tap dripping in my face. 'I can't go to school in my nightie!' I told my mother.

'Don't be silly,' said mother. 'They're using the school as an Emergency Shelter.' She borrowed clothes for herself from Granny and went out. Granny made me and my brother a huge breakfast.

My uncle came home. 'They've not moved the damn thing,' he said. Mother returned carrying clothes for my brother and me – some borrowed from friends, some bought without coupons, with a promise to take coupons as soon as she could.

'I had to pay Mr Spillman double for this dress,' she said.

'I don't like it,' I whined.

Crack! 'Don't be so ungrateful,' she said. I knew better than to argue – it would only mean another smack.

That afternoon we wandered down to the school to see our friends. Many were still in their nightclothes. Mrs Murphy, who had *six* children, had them all in day-clothes, and herself. People said afterwards they never wore nightclothes, just in case . . .

Two days later, three army cars came to Harvist Road School to say the Army had taken the landmine away. We could go home. Only then we found the ack-ack gun in Roundwood Park had received a direct hit. So that was what the Germans had been aiming for.

'Would we all have been killed,' asked my brother, 'if it had gone bang?'

'Depends,' said my mother, and got on with peeling the potatoes.

Girl, aged six, London

A NASTY NERVOUS FEELING in the kitchen. Every thud, Mrs R would say 'Is that a bomb?', and Mr R would say 'No, it's a gun, dear.' As time went on, they'd said it so often Mr R would answer 'No s'a gun', then just 'S'a gun', then finally a noise that sounded like 'S'gun'. She could see he was getting irritated and tried not to do it; muttering the question under her breath instead; which of course made it more irritating still. I felt all swollen up with irritation, bloated, but actually it was fear.

E says to me 'Let's get some air.' Out we go . . . a beautiful summer night, so warm it was incredible and made more beautiful than ever by the red glow from the east, where the docks were burning. I tried to fix the scene in my mind, because one day this will be history.

I wasn't frightened any more, amazing. Being out in the open, you feel more in control when you can see what's happening. The searchlights were beautiful, it's like watching the end of the world as they swoop from one end of the sky to the other. We didn't see any planes, though we could hear them bumbling about somewhere.

We sat on the grass. Very long and unkempt – Mr R is normally a besotted gardener, but he has let the garden go to rack and ruin this summer . . . the uncertainty.

Two bombs fell in the distance. I felt no fear. E said he could smell burning from the docks.

Another bomb, nearer. Then, suddenly, the weirdest scratching sound just above the roofs – as if someone was scratching the sky with a broken fingernail. Then the most God-awful crash – it seemed only a couple of gardens away, I felt the earth juddering under me as I sat.

'Hey, it's not too healthy out here!' E dragged me up from the grass. I didn't seem to be doing *anything* – just cowering. I don't know what I meant to do, or what I was feeling . . . a funny blank.

I remember racing towards the house, E pulling me and

yelling. The oddest feeling in the air all around, as if the whole air was falling apart, quite silently. And then suddenly I was on my face, just inside the kitchen door. There seemed to be waves buffeting me, one after another, like bathing in a rough sea. I remember clutching at the floor, the carpet, to prevent myself being swept away. This smell of carpet in my nose and trying not to be swept away, and I could hear Mrs R screaming. E was nowhere, the lights were gone, it was all dust. I didn't even wonder if he was all right . . . didn't give him a thought. Seemed to be nothing in the universe but this dusty carpet I was breathing and having to hang on like grim death. I clutched the floor as if it was a cliff-face; why I had this feeling of saving myself from falling, I don't know. Mrs R seemed to have been crying

This terrace had fallen like a pack of cards.

for ages, and calling out something or other, but I couldn't think of answering her. I discovered later my mouth was full of plaster and dust, but I had no feeling of that at the time. I just didn't *think* of answering or doing anything about anything. Almost a tranquil feeling. I could hear Mr R yelling: 'Down, everybody, get *down*. Do what I tell you, get your heads down!' Over and over – no sense in it, because we'd had the bomb now and everybody was down, heads and all.

E had a torch, he flashed it round a bit. Plaster and glass everywhere, mountains. The whole ceiling had come down, it looked like a builder's yard. You couldn't see the furniture, only

They rescued people . . .

the clock and a cushion sticking out. Mr R was still shouting, giving orders, very contradictory. 'Don't move, stay where you are! Someone tell the H's next door. Don't move till I tell you!' and so on, and so on.

We got to the front door, quite a job as the ceilings were down right along the passage, and pitch dark. I could hear Mrs R stumbling along behind, Mr R scolding her, 'Watch out – can't you look where you're going?', every time she stumbled. Actually, he was stumbling just as much, and he's normally a very amiable, detached, good-natured sort of man who rarely raises his voice.

. . . and pets.

The front door was wedged tight, wouldn't budge. There were men outside and someone saying in a high-pitched voice 'Naomi, ask Naomi, Naomi will know. Has anyone seen Naomi?'

We went back through the front room, it wasn't so bad there, the ceiling had held and we crawled out through a broken window. It looked so bright outside I couldn't believe it, a sort of white haze, a halo over everything, though there was no moon. Two of the women cried when they saw us; how terrible we must have looked, smothered in white plaster all over, and streaks of blood from the glass. 'Are you hurt . . . are you all right?' people kept asking. It was only then that it occurred to me I *might* have been hurt – I had been in *actual danger*. Up to that minute I had taken everything for granted, in a queer brainless way, as if it were all perfectly ordinary.

We spent the night at the F's, Mrs F insisting on piling about seven blankets on top of me, and a hot-water bottle as well. 'For the shock,' she said. When I pointed out that I was feeling perfectly all right, she referred darkly to '*delayed*' shock, implying this dread phenomenon would hit me before the night was out.

It didn't. I lay there feeling indescribably happy and triumphant.

'I've been *bombed*,' I kept saying to myself, over and over – trying the phrase on like a new dress, to see how it fitted. 'I've been bombed – me.'

It seems a terrible thing to say, when so many must have been killed, but never in my life have I experienced such *pure and flawless happiness*.

Young girl, London. Taken from Tom Harrison (Mass Observation), Living through the Blitz, *Collins, 1976*

1943 ARP MESSENGER

I JOINED THE ST JOHN'S CADETS, but found I was mostly being chosen as a casualty; finding myself bound head to foot whilst others broke for tea. So I decided I would be more useful in the Civil Defence as a messenger. The District Warden, a Mr W. H. Munday, suggested that though I was well under age, they could use me at my local wardens' post. I joined Post KK6 in early 1942 and accompanied the Post Warden on his patrols.

My job was to ensure communication between the incident and the wardens' post, should a bomb fall in our area.

Early in 1943 there was one of the strike raids and our home area was saturated with incendiary bombs by the first plane in.

We worked tirelessly to extinguish the light from the fires before the next planes came over. We achieved this, although a couple of wardens were hurt by the anti-personnel devices, the worst being the German flower-pot bomb, which consisted of an assortment of prisms and flower-pot shaped incendiaries, surrounding a small but lethal explosive device, timed to explode and kill the firefighters.

I was patrolling with the Post Warden, when we came upon a man running hysterically along the road. We eventually ascertained that as he was sitting in his front room a vivid green flash occurred in his hall, together with a loud crashing. He had been so startled that he jumped clean through the glass of his front window.

Surely enough the front window was broken. On entering the hall we found the wallpaper and woodwork had been burnt. A hole through the roof marked the passage of the bomb, and a further hole running under the house showed its direction of travel. We knew that we had here a phosphorus bomb; a canister filled with a chemical which burns when exposed to air, but can be extinguished in water, only to burn again once it is dry. The bomb was buried under the house in soft earth and was leaking slightly. We notified bomb-disposal, but they were completely occupied and couldn't come for at least a week.

To save this house from burning, and perhaps the whole district from further attack, we had to ensure this bomb did not ignite. At fourteen I was by far the smallest member of Civil Defence, and therefore most able to crawl through the tunnel made by the bomb.

I was given a bucket of water, which I pushed ahead of me, until I came to the tail of the bomb. I then tipped the water over the bomb and retreated. Twice a day, until it could be rendered safe.

We also had unexploded HE. Two of these were in the centre of Flaxton Road. It was customary to see groups of young mothers with their babies in prams, gathering round the two holes to watch the disposal men as they worked. They had lost all sense of fear – unfortunately.

There was a third, which wasn't found until the Saturday, long after the other two had been made harmless. This was in the front garden of a house in our road – the occupants were away – on the Saturday my mother had carried out a long conversation, not two feet from the weapon. That evening it was discovered to be in a dangerous condition.

In the clearing up, we discovered a nearly complete canister of incendiaries in a playing field close to the wardens' post. I held my arms out as the wardens loaded up the unexploded incendiaries. With about twenty-five of these little monsters I started to walk back to the post, being careful to see that the pins which activated them didn't fall out in the process.

I kept one of them as a souvenir. One day I took it to school in the saddlebag of my bike and showed it to my friends there. It passed from hand to hand and during assembly one of the 'wags' saw fit to test it by dropping it on the floor. The bomb detonated and in the chaos that resulted the hall filled with smoke and the boys evacuated it in record time to reassemble in the courtyard.

The porter, in his zeal, up-ended a chemical fire extinguisher and played it on the fire. This caused the bomb to explode and shower burning particles over the end of the hall. It was eventually put out, but left a crater in the parquet flooring and damaged the Honours List.

We reassembled, and prayers continued as if there had been no interruption – no mention was made of the incident. After assembly I grabbed the fellow who had dropped the bomb and we reported to the Head – he to say he'd dropped it and me to say I'd brought it. We were sent to his study, where my accomplice chickened out and said it was an accident; he was excused. I, naturally, felt I was really in for it. Dr Reece suspended me and sent me home. When I told my father he took it very well and immediately phoned Dr Reece. His eloquence enabled me to return to school, where I was viewed with caution by the staff and admiration by the boys.

Being a district group, we also assisted in training exercises, usually acting as 'casualties' in staged incidents. One of my messengers was dropped from a building and broke an arm while being 'rescued' by the trainee team. For my pains I was put under a derelict house which was collapsed above me. There was a label attached to my coat which stated 'coal-gas poisoning, not breathing'. I lay there for what seemed an age, covered in dust under the stairs, completely entombed, whilst the 'rescuers' dug for me. Not a very nice experience. When light started to filter through I noticed a newspaper dated 1927 lying beside me. I could not help but moralize, that being the year of my birth.

I was eventually dragged from the ruins and laid on the brick-strewn path whilst being given artificial respiration. My ribs were bruised both front and back. I did not volunteer again!

Another task we had was to umpire the war-games between the Army and the Home Guard, the former being attackers and the latter defenders of London. The former always won, as there was a hot cup of tea for prisoners!

Once, we set up our observation post in a bush alongside the cemetery, at a junction of two footpaths, and settled for a long night. My colleague was a local barber, a Jew with a very fierce manner.

He fell asleep, and started to snore. I kept watch. About 2.30 a.m. I heard the cautious approach of a number of men. As they drew near I woke Jack in case his snores betrayed our position. He had been dreaming about German paratroops. He came to with a roar and leapt from the bush.

The six-man patrol, confronted with a black figure (Civil Defence uniform was dark blue) leaping from out of the cemetery in the middle of the night, dropped their rifles and fled. I understand they gave themselves up to the first opposing patrol. Jack and I were in hysterics when we realized the implication – that cemetery was a very frightening place.

Boy, aged sixteen, London

CHAPTER 9

THE PROVINCIAL BLITZ

1941 A NASTY ONE

MY FATHER CAME OFF DUTY looking pale and sick, and said the Germans had scored a direct hit on Wilkinson's Lemonade Factory, and hundreds had been killed, and some were still trapped down there in the cellars. He said there should never have been a shelter down there. There'd been heavy bottling machinery on the ground floor, just standing on wooden boards, and when the bomb hit, it all just collapsed on the people below.

Terrible rumours started going round. People so crushed they couldn't be recognized; people sitting down there without a mark on them, just dead. Mothers with babies still in their arms. A man still holding his accordion . . .

Everybody was just stunned; couldn't cope. Why had God let it happen?

Then the stories changed. Wicked things had gone on in that shelter. People had taken drink down there; held parties. Music and dancing every night. Immorality, and they didn't care who saw it . . . People went there even when there wasn't a raid going on. Gambling . . .

People said it was a Judgement. God is not mocked! It was like Sodom and Gomorrah.

Everybody felt much better after that.

Boy, aged twelve, Tyneside

1941–1944 WINDFALLS

MY EARLIEST RECOLLECTION was a bright red glow in the sky from my bedroom window. 'Are you frightened?' whispered my brother.

No, I just couldn't understand the sun rising so late at night. Next morning we discovered it was an RAF plane that had crashed on to the cricket pitch at the back of the 'Bull's Head'. Just a mass of twisted metal burnt beyond recognition with one wheel sticking up like a toffee-apple. Did he crash on to the cricket pitch to avoid the houses? It was a dark night, how could he have seen it?

The next plane I saw crash was also RAF. Brought down by a barrage balloon operated by WAAFs on the common at the top of our road. I watched it fall, twisting round like a sycamore pod, till it finally disappeared behind the houses. The local fire-engine was on the scene within minutes; I followed behind on my bike and arrived in time to watch them carry away the pilot's body covered by a blanket. The plane crashed on allotments surrounded by houses; another miracle.

Underground shelters were built in Primrose Hill Park. I spent many a long night in those shelters, listening to bombs dropping and an old man playing the accordion.

My mother took my younger brother and I to Evesham, to escape the bombing. Dad stayed behind working in the Daimler factory. We stayed with friends living over a cobbler's shop. My mother's friend, who I called Aunty, had a son my age called Donald. Next door lived a witch. Don and I discovered a way into the Witch's House; up into the attic, across the sloping slate roof and into the witch's attic window. Lo and behold, treasures beyond our wildest dreams! Cardboard boxes, dozens. We opened one – candles. In the next, tins of peaches. In the next, pears, pineapples, plums. On a rainy day we spent many a happy hour in the witch's attic, eating tinned fruit by the light of a candle.

One night, Aunty's husband came home drunk and locked Mum and us out of the house. We went to the Police Station and a very large sergeant took us back.

'Open in the name of the law!' said the bobby to the door, and we were let in. Next day, Dad came to visit us. Later I noticed Aunty's husband had a black eye; good old Dad!

Mum and my brother returned to Coventry, leaving me with Aunty. I have unpleasant memories: standing outside the cake-shop window with my nose pressed against the glass; sitting in the park watching a father and son having a picnic, and me eating the pork pie they left behind. My mother found another house in Coventry. I was sent for and the raids started again.

I found an old rusty bike in the shed of the new house and painted it silver; to me it was the best bike in the world. Riding through Brinklow Woods we found an unexploded bomb. Small enough to fit on the crossbar of my bike. We tied it on with string and covered it with my coat, and set off for home. We had to cycle through the city centre with the bomb between my legs. The string snapped, and the nose of the bomb fell on to the lug that holds the bike pump on to the frame and bent it.

'I can tell people a bomb did that, can't I?'

We tied it on again, and arrived at Derek's house. We dug a hole in the back garden and stood the bomb upright in it, covering it with soil. I told Derek to go and tell his father, who happened to be an ARP warden, that there was a hole in the garden. He came out a few seconds later, followed by his father.

'Look, there it is,' said Derek', pointing a very soily finger at the hole. His father bent down and scooped away a little soil, exposing the fin. He stood up with his mouth wide open; no sound came from him. I looked at Derek; Derek looked at me. Still not a word from his father; his mouth was still wide open.

'Sta . . . stand still,' he finally spluttered, and ran into the house. Derek put his hand over his mouth, stifling a laugh. His father reappeared with his ARP helmet on. 'Out of the garden, quick, it's an unexploded bomb.' We ran out and stood across the road. The Bomb Disposal Squad came and took it away. We never told him it was our bomb.

Schooldays were awful, but I could escape by volunteering for potato-picking. I'd turn up for school in old ragged clothes, get my name ticked off, and then grab the back seat of the coach. Lucy sat next to me; I fancied her in my youthful way. Not like they do nowadays (I never thought about it then). The coach took us to Kenilworth. The tractor dug the spuds up, and we filled the sacks. Hard work but better than school. At lunchtime a large bucket of cocoa was brought round; it was foul, no sugar, no milk – but we drank it.

There was an Italian POW camp near by. We took potatoes to the POWs and they fried chips in butter for us. I haven't had chips as good as that since. Happy days! Sugar was rationed; I had treacle in my tea. I still have all my own teeth. I remember a boy at school had a banana. Where he got it I never found out. A lot of kids had never seen one, never mind tasting one. Anyway, after he'd polished it off and thrown the skin away, I picked it up and kept that skin till it turned black and snapped in half.

And of course we had the cinema. The 'Rex' was in the centre of town, one of the largest. *Gone with the Wind* was the latest film showing . . .

The enemy obliged; it was destroyed that night by a stick of bombs.

American soldiers appeared in the streets, the place was full of them. They had smart uniforms and big cigars; I thought they were all officers. They all chewed gum; us kids would say 'Any gum, chum?' they always obliged. They played baseball in the park. We called it rounders, a girls' game. I collected cigarette packets they threw away, Camel, Lucky Strike and many others. Then aeroplanes towing gliders with white strips on the wings flew across Coventry and there wasn't an American in sight. It was D-Day, the sixth of June.

Boy, Coventry

1941 THE NEW SHELTER

THE WAIL OF THE SIREN brought my mother upstairs, to shepherd us down. This was great fun! We tipped our old settee on its ends; this was to protect our heads, the three of us! The big old kitchen table was pushed up to it. Hey presto, a home-made air-raid shelter! We cuddled down into makeshift sleeping-bags. The living-room fire was kept on. We were cosy, warm and safe.

Girl, aged nine, Cheshire

1940 THE WAR IN EDINBURGH

THE MORNING AFTER DUNKIRK, there was a bren-gun carrier in our school bike-shed, under a tarpaulin. Nobody knew who'd left it there. We got under the tarpaulin, but it didn't have any guns. The Head told us to keep away, but we played in it regularly. It was used by the Home Guard at nights.

My father was in the Home Guard. They guarded the main road south, at Kainies Crossing. There was a smithy with a gun-slit in the wall, under the blacksmith's furnace. They had to put

Very early days. Rifles have replaced the pitchforks and shotguns, but there are no uniforms, few tin hats, and the 'armoured car' is an amateur job: workers at a jam factory have covered a Morris saloon with boiler-plate to make their own armoured car.

the furnace out, before they could put the gun in. The gun was a smooth-bored thing called a Blacker Bombard – a mortar, only aimed horizontally. It was supposed to throw bombs at tanks.

In front, the first line of defence was a pillbox full of riflemen, and a row of round blocks of concrete, that could be rolled into the road, then up-ended to block it. Then someone had the bright idea of stopping the Germans by pouring petrol on the road and setting it alight. They got hold of a twenty-five gallon drum of petrol, and thought they'd try it. They poured the lot on the road and put a match to it. Unfortunately the flaming petrol ran down the drains, and out into the Burdiehouse Burn, and down it, floating on the water, still alight. I remember the line of fire, spreading, spreading, as fast as the burn ran, setting fire to the fields and trees. They had to call the fire brigade out.

It was very dark walking home from school in the blackout – in Scotland it got dark at three o'clock. One night I saw an enormous soldier walking along in green-grey overcoat and funny pointed cap. I followed him a long way. Then he heard my footsteps behind him. He whirled round and drew a Luger pistol from a big leather holster and pointed it straight at me. When he saw it was only a child, he burst out laughing uproariously. I was terrified. He was a Pole.

Just behind our house were the Braid Hills. There were two sledge-runs up there, we called the Cresta and the Livershaker. That winter, going up past the golf course, we noticed it had been wired-off, but not very well, not enough to stop us. On the golf course were two Spitfires and a hangar.. But when we got up to them, the Spitfires weren't real, just full-size models made of plywood, just the tops of the wings and a body hollow underneath. The hanger was also a fake, just an empty Nissen hut. It was a fake airfield, built to deceive the German bombers from the air. We used to swing about inside the Spitfires, and camp inside them in summer. We didn't think they were good enough to fool anybody.

We didn't have many raids – only spent one night in the Anderson shelter. The Germans tried to hit the Forth Bridge, but all they got was Willy Younger's whisky distilleries at the bottom of Canongate. I remember the flashes from the Bofors guns, banging away on the bridge. Also the incredible blaze of the burning whisky, like an oil-refinery going up. People were lying in the gutters, drinking the whisky – the fire brigade couldn't get past for the bodies. Next day in Edinburgh there were thousands of drunks.

I saw one dogfight between a Hurricane and an Me 109 – over the Pentland Hills. We heard the guns firing, far away. Then smoke came out of the Messerschmitt, and it vanished over the hills and we heard the bang.

As we got older, we explored further and further. The firing-range on Alnwick Hall Road, from the 1914–18 war, still being used. We spent a lot of time collecting empty cartridge cases and stray bullets. Kids would pay you 1*d.* for the bullets, but the cartridge clips from the magazine fetched 3*d.* Better still were the ranges behind Dreghorn Castle. They used 2" and 3" mortars there. We used to search for bomb fins and the odd unexploded mortar bomb. When we found one we used to lug bricks at it, and occasionally we got one to explode. A bit dicey – they had a killing-range of 24 yards. One kid got killed picking up bombs and taking them home. Once they'd been fired they were fused, and if you turned them upside-down, the ball-bearing dropped down the tube and . . . wham!

Best of all were the mobile ranges at Glencarse. A circular railway track, with little bogies pulled on a chain by an engine. The soldiers arranged themselves so they could fire through the bogies into the bankside. The bogies carried plywood cut-outs of German soldiers, with helmets and grey uniforms, larger than life. As the bogies went round and round, the targets went up and down. There were target-tanks too, but the soldiers only used rifles, pistols and sten-guns.

The best place was the POW camp for German prisoners. But they weren't Germans, they were Ukrainians, who'd fought for the German army against Russia, then run away from the Russians to the West. They wore light-brown denims with big green or orange circles on the back, and German peaked forage-caps or little circular caps. They worked on the farms during the day, short thick-set Slavs with broad cheekbones.

There were a hundred huts, surrounded by a big barbed-wire fence and watchtowers. Outside, there were trip-wires in the long grass, and barrel hoops honed razor sharp, that shot upright as you stepped on them. We used to get through the wire at night, to take the POWs fags and fish and chips. The guards were watching for POWs trying to get out, not kids trying to get in.

They were so glad to see children – used to take us into their huts. It could have been very dangerous, I suppose. But they made toys for us, model boats and tanks, really beautiful. And Russian-style tommy-guns with round magazines, not like ours. They used to stain them brown with tea or coffee – the stain came off on your hands when they got wet in the rain.

(After the war they were all shipped back to Russia against their wishes, and the Russians shot them.)

In January 1942, my father got his call-up papers – a buff envelope dropped on the doormat. Father was locked in the bathroom at the time, shaving. Mother told me to take it up and slip it under the bathroom door. That was the first time I ever heard my father swear. He swore continuously for a *very* long time.

We could always tell when we wakened up in the morning that my father had come home on leave – that lovely smell of khaki and boot-polish and gun-oil. He used to bring us home Service-issue boiled sweets from his compo-rations. All the soldiers did. Then they used to tell the Quartermaster that they'd lost them, and indent for more. They were the only sweets we saw in the war.

My mother took us down to London for the wedding of my uncle, who was a parts-pusher – a man who went up and down the country finding out why deliveries of small parts for Spitfires were late, and holding up production. He would get them moving again. We went down to London by train. We had to stand all the way – twelve hours. A soldier gave my mother his seat, then tried to pick her up. After the wedding, my uncle took us round London. Cannon Street station was flat. High Holborn church was just a hole in the ground, with a single bell lying where the tower had been. But all the ruins were covered with the plant that Londoners called 'Bombsite' – rose bay willow-herb. My grandparents' house had had its back blown in twice – the back was just plywood, with no windows in the bedrooms – you had to have the light on all the time. All the streets were blocked with huge brick air-raid shelters, half-buried underground.

Boy, aged six to eight

CHRISTMAS 1941

I WOKE EARLY, my brother was asleep, so I made sure the black-out curtains were over the windows, and with my torch I had a little peep at my presents. I had a pair of slacks (Mummy made them out of a blanket), a paint-book, a pencil-box, and a very nice handkerchief, a book of poetry from Mummy, a bar of chocolate, a whole orange.

I have a very nice present for Mummy, I made it myself, a kettle-holder. And a present for Daddy, I made it, it is a case with needles and cottons and buttons in, so when he goes away he can sew his buttons on. I also made him a shoe-polisher. We had a lovely breakfast, fried bread and a nice egg. We're both very lucky, Richard and me, because Mummy and Daddy don't care much for eggs, or sweets.

Girl, aged 10. From Norman Longmate,
How We Lived Then, *Hutchinson, 1971*

My daughter had asked Father Christmas for a doll's house. We looked at each other in dismay. Then my brother found an old bird-cage. During the raids he worked on it; found bits of card-board for the walls. The office waste-paper basket provided an old file which made the roof. He painted the floors. We hunted for all kinds of bits and pieces and a miracle was achieved . . . a piece of hessian, dyed red, fringed, made an elegant carpet. Never will I forget her face that dark Christmas morning and her childish voice piping 'There'll be bluebirds over the white cliffs of Dover' as she saw those tables and chairs, tiny pictures made from cigarette cards, her cries of joy as she discovered each new thing.

From Norman Longmate,
How We Lived Then, *Hutchinson, 1971*

WINTER 1942–43 NUISANCE RAIDS

THE NUISANCE RAIDS were the worst. Single bombers, only dropping a few bombs, but the siren would get you out of a warm bed into an ice-cold shelter two or three times a night.

The first time we'd be well organized, folded blankets and thermos flasks; but by the third time people would be tripping over armfuls of bedding trailing along the wet ground, little kids bawling, getting slapped, couples screaming at each other, not from fear but because they were totally disorganized. You got punch-drunk, half-asleep, half-awake, day and night. All except our Norwegian neighbour, John Asmussen, a trawlerman. He used to come to our shelter, to see if we were all right; always gentle, cheerful, singing songs. Except he'd be sitting there and you'd suddenly realize he'd gone to sleep sitting up, still wearing his tin hat. He could sleep for five minutes whenever he wanted to, like a cat, and wake up better for it. Mam said it was him being in the trawlers; he'd learnt to snatch sleep between hauling in the nets, night-fishing.

One night, after he'd gone, I fell asleep in the bottom bunk of our shelter. I wakened in pitch darkness. The tiny oil-lamp above my head seemed to have gone out. I peered round, and couldn't see any red glow on the curved metal ceiling, from the candle in a flowerpot which was our only means of heating. I listened for the reassuring sound of my mother's breathing in the bunk above. Total silence. No sound from Brian Spedding, who slept opposite, only two feet away, or his Mam above. Just silence and pitch darkness.

I called: no answer. A bomb had killed them all, while I was asleep. There was no trickle of dim blue light round the shelter door curtain . . .

I was buried alive! In blind panic I rolled out of my bunk on to the floor – that was the way I always did it – the bunk was only six inches off the shelter floor. I was screaming my head off.

Instead of falling six inches, I fell two feet, with a hell of a thump. On to carpet, not bare earth. The world was *insane*.

Then the light banged on, and Mam was standing there in her dressing-gown. I was in my own blacked-out bedroom. She told me the all-clear had gone hours ago, and I'd walked back from the shelter when she told me to, and got into bed.

I had walked in my sleep.

Boy, aged thirteen, Tyneside

1943 THE BIG BANG

EVERYBODY AROUND NORTHWICH believed that if a German bomb hit ICI the whole of the town of Northwich would explode, and vanish. One day in 1943, the roof blew off the ICI prototype polythene plant. We got quite used to that in later years, but then everyone went rushing in to see how Northwich had vanished. We were quite disappointed to see everything was quite normal.

Girl, aged fifteen, Cheshire

ENCOUNTER IN THE DARK

OUTSIDE THE HOUSES they had things called pig-swills, that was every ten yards or so on the pavement, where people put all their orange peel if they got any, potato peel, etc.

My sisters, brothers and I were all going out to a dance, but they had gone on a little bit, so I had to follow on my own and you had to go up a dark street.

So my mum and dad gave me a torch and said 'If anyone creeps up behind you, shine the torch in their eyes, kick them your hardest and run.'

So I took the torch and was walking down the dark lane when I heard footsteps behind me. So I turned on the torch and shone it in the person's eyes . . .

It blinded him for a few seconds and he fell in one of the pig-swills. He staggered up and had orange peel and all sorts of rubbish on his hat and over his coat. So I took to my heels and ran all the way to the dance.

When I got home my mother said 'Eeh, don't let your father know it was you shone the torch in his eyes, because he has got his new hat spoiled and his temper's foul.'

I didn't recognize my dad because it was a cold night and he had his hat down over his eyes and his coat pulled up round his ears.

Girl, aged sixteen

A LIVELY GIRL

ONE DAY, DURING THE WAR, I wanted to join the ARP, so I stayed out all night helping with the air raids. When I arrived home my mother battered me for staying out all night.

Another time I wanted to join the WRNS but my Mum wouldn't let me. Then I wanted to join the Army with my friend, and get posted to different countries. But when I saw the uniform, I didn't want to join because I didn't like the colour of the stockings. They were a horrible green colour. But my friend joined and got posted to Canada, and there she met a Canadian and lived there.

Girl, aged seventeen

WAR BABY

My mum lived through the war by herself with my dad at war for five years. Then my mum had a baby in the last two years of the war. Sheilagh was the baby's name. In a newspaper

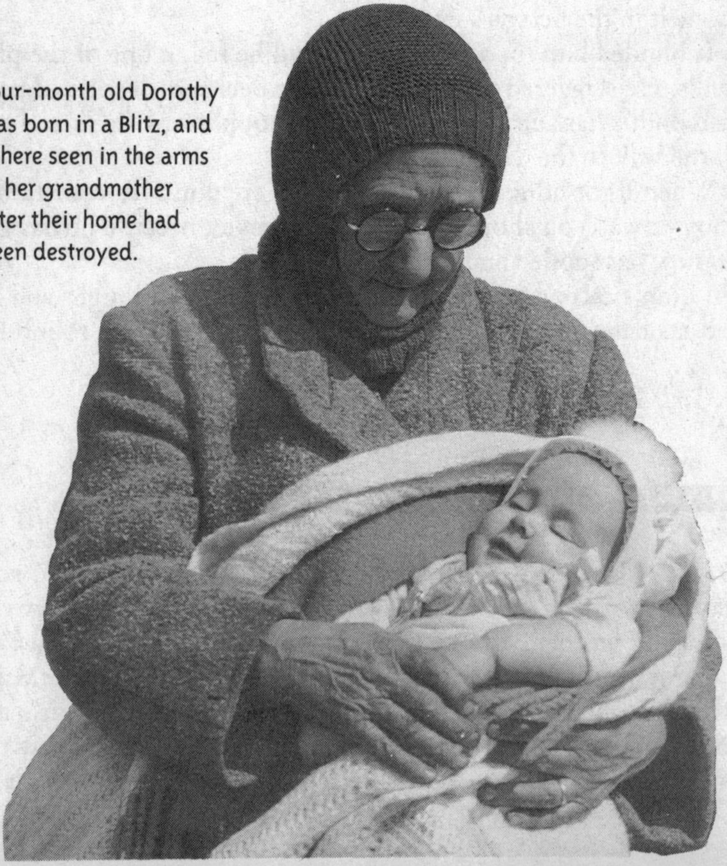

Four-month old Dorothy was born in a Blitz, and is here seen in the arms of her grandmother after their home had been destroyed.

my mum's photograph was taken and underneath it said 'This little girl is waiting for her dad to come home from the War.' And it was published!

Girl, aged seventeen

1941 LANDMINE

THERE WAS A PARACHUTE and a landmine. The parachute was stuck on the school railings and a man pulled the parachute and the school blew up to pieces and so did the man.

Girl, aged six

1941 NEW GAMES

WE USED TO PLAY A GAME where you used the bricks off wrecked houses and you had to build a little base big enough for yourself to get in. They called this game the Shelter Game. This was not the only game they played with bricks; they also played a game where you had to balance as many bricks as you could on top of each other.

Girl, aged fifteen

GRANDA

GRANDA, DURING THE BLITZ, always went around with about twenty felt hats on his head, to keep the bombs off. One night he was walking home with eggs in his pockets. The siren went but he kept on walking until the bombs came whizzing down so he dived for cover and suddenly realized he'd smashed the eggs . . . We lived at 38 Mighall Street. Granda didn't like Mr Scott who lived next door at No. 36. One night an incendiary bomb landed in our yard. It did not explode and Granda went out and the bomb had the number 36 on it. 'There y'are,' said Granda, 'I knew it was meant for him next door,' and he threw the bomb into 36's yard, but it never went off.

Boy , aged ten

'THERE WAS NO HOME'

WHEN MORNING CAME we left the shelter and made our way home. There was no home. All that was left was a pile of bricks. We had nowhere to live except the shelter, and that was to be our home for six months. We had our meals at different relations'.

NOT MUCH USE

ON OUR WAY HOME from a dance with my brothers and sisters, the siren went. We were quite a way from home, so we ran into this square, where Tommy, the eldest, saw an air-raid shelter. So we all ran into it. Bombs and machine-guns filled the air. Everybody was scared stiff, so we huddled together with our eyes shut, to seek comfort from each other. Then Peggy looked up and said, 'D'you want to know something? But . . . erm . . . this shelter hasn't got a roof on it.' Everybody looked up, and Tommy said 'Run home, quick.' It was about half a mile and all the girls were crying, but to make matters worse we were running through an air raid.

At home we all dived down the shelter, then after a cup of tea Dad said 'Right, where was that shelter? I'm going down tomorrow to see that council. These shelters are a disgrace. They'd better do something about them, or else.'

Girl, aged sixteen

CHAPTER 10
FOOD

SOME FUNNY THINGS

We never starved, but we ate some funny things. Best was American dried egg. You poured a thin trickle into the frying-pan, then as it cooked it blew up like a balloon, till it was two inches thick, like a big yellow hump-backed whale.

And we had whale meat, that tasted strongly of fish, unless you soaked it for twenty-four hours in vinegar, after which it tasted of vinegar. But there was so much of it – great big steaks as big as your plate – that we didn't care what it tasted like.

Sausage-meat was pale pink – I don't think it had any meat in it at all. Late in the war, my mother got a pound of 'butcher's sausage' – the sausage a butcher made for his own family. It seemed indecent, cos lumps of real meat kept dropping out of it – it nearly made us sick.

I lived a lot on chip-butties – but you had to eat them quick, before the chips turned dark blue.

The government posters made us all hate the 'Black Market' – though no one ever knew what a 'Black Marketeer' looked like. But all through the war, things kept 'appearing' in our house. One Christmas, a whole unopened box of Mars bars. Another time, a seven-pound tin of butter, which for some reason we kept in the bath. I enjoyed carving great caves out of it. When I asked Dad where these things came from, he'd say 'bought it off a feller at work' or 'off the ships', so matter-of-factly that it never occurred to me till after the war that my father must have 'received goods knowing them to have been stolen' – from the Black Market.

Luckily, we had a neighbour on the trawlers. My parents looked after his wife while he was at sea, especially when she was pregnant, so we were never short of fish. And we had a large greenhouse – immediately after every raid my father would go and check how many panes the Germans had blown out – by the end of the war, it wasn't so much a glasshouse as a cardboard-house, but all through we had so many tomatoes, we sold them to other people.

My mother spent our week's holiday in Cumberland collecting eggs from all the surrounding farms, a dozen at a time. At first she was treated with great suspicion, as a Ministry of Ag. and Fish snooper, but by the end of the war, she'd come home with twelve dozen in a carrier bag.

My friend Ally Johnson dropped his mother's carrier, containing twelve dozen eggs, in Newcastle Haymarket Bus Station, right under the nose of a policeman. He said the yellow egg yolk just spread and spread, all over the road; the Johnsons took to their heels.

In 1939, I was a thin child; by 1941, I was an enormous fat elephant. I think my mother saw fattening me up as a patriotic duty. Our dog got very fat as well. Our neighbour in the trawlers used to see it as a good-luck mascot – when he went on a trip, he used to always come and stroke our dog first. When he came back safe, he would give our dog a whole pound block of Cadbury's chocolate. The dog used to bring it home in its mouth, with half the wrapping chewed off; my mother would immediately requisition it. The number of times we handed round tooth-marked chocolate at Christmas . . .

My mother seemed to have no appetite in the war. She'd sit my father and I down to something tasty, then announce 'I'm not really hungry. I'll have my share later. I think I'll just have a little bit of bread and butter . . .'

Boy, Tyneside

WELCOME HOME

WHEN PEOPLE who'd been out at the war for a time returned to their home town, people put up banners saying 'Welcome home, Peter!'

Well, when rationing was on, mums had to queue for hours. One day, my mum was gone all day queuing for potatoes, and when she came home there was a big banner across the street saying 'Welcome home Mum', because she'd been gone all day for a couple of spuds.

Girl, Liverpool

NOT ENOUGH RABBITS

ONE MORNING I went to the market to buy apples and I had to stand in a long queue in the cold morning air. When at last it was my turn to be served he gave me a pound of apples. As he was doing so I noticed he placed two bad apples in the pound I had. So I told him that I didn't want them, and could he replace

them? With that he took the bag of apples off me, gave me my money back and told me to go. I was very angry because the apples were not for me but for my children. I swore at him then I went away. When I arrived home my husband said, 'If I'd been treated like that I'd have knocked his stall over and thrown his rotten fruit at him.'

A week later I went to the market again for some meat. On the meat stall was the same man again, selling rabbits. I stood in the queue hoping he would not recognize me because I knew if he did I would not get my rabbit. He started counting how many rabbits he had, so that them waiting would not be waiting for nothing. When he'd finished counting the rabbits he started to count us. When he came to me he said 'Sorry, love, not enough rabbits'. If he'd been lying I'd have tipped his stall over and thrown the rabbits at him like my husband said.

The queue was seen by some women as a misery, by some as essential war-work to beat Hitler, by some as a free social occasion.

Local papers were not allowed to write about their local war for fear of helping German Intelligence. No doubt smuggled-out pictures of these block-buster marrows, grown in Paignton, Devon, must have made Adolf's heart sink!

FOOD
GROWN BY
EVACUEE
BOYS
AT
TWEENAWAY

CIGARETTES

When me and my sister were about nine and eleven years old, my Dad used to smoke Winston cigarettes. So every morning about five our Dad woke us up. There were two tobacconists. So one of us went in one queue, and the other in the other queue. When we got the cigarettes we swopped queues to get some more. We done this every morning for two years, every morning except Sunday.

Girl, aged nine, Liverpool

PIGS

OUR FAMILY never went short of food. My uncle was a farmer. He used to breed pigs. He was allowed to kill so many pigs for himself, and the rest went to the government. So he used to kill one on the sly and give it to my dad. They used to put the dead pig in the bath, to soak overnight. My aunty went to the toilet in the night and she saw the pig lying in the bloodstained water. She didn't know it was a pig and she let out a scream that woke everyone in the house.

Girl, aged fourteen, Liverpool

KEEP
A PIG
Join
or start
A PIG
CLUB

Nobody kept a pig round our way: the smell was too bad, the neighbours would have complained. But at one time, I had twenty-seven rabbits – a whole village of hutches. Then I lost interest and my mother had to feed them – toast and dandelion and baked potato-peelings. They died or vanished somewhere, one by one. We ate the last one – a buck called Big Lugs, a friend of four years standing – for our Christmas dinner, 1944. I couldn't eat a bite. My father kept Big Lugs' tail for pollinating his tomatoes.

SHORTAGES

AS A YOUNG GIRL I loved to go to the dances. I only had two best dance dresses, which I had to alter every now and then to make them look different. We used to get some material or nice paper and fold it carefully to make belts.

We had an open coal fire, but coal was on ration. I remember my dad going into the woods and chopping down one of the trees so we could have wood for the fire. My dad and brother spent all day chopping it up. I remember my dad with a wheelbarrow going round the neighbours giving out logs.

I can remember the state our whole estate was in when the Co-op got a box of bananas. Everyone queued up for hours. My mam dragged me to the shop with her. Just one banana and we had to wait all day. I was really bored.

You could hardly get wool and so my mum used to undo all my dad's old jumpers to make us hats, gloves, wool socks and scarves; if she had enough wool, all to match. I used to be the envy of the street.

Sometimes the coal ration would run out, so we would put the gas oven on and put our feet inside to keep ourselves warm.

Nobody could afford to make a birthday cake, so instead you had a decorated hatbox as a cake, or a wooden cake with candles on.

Girl, aged sixteen

1941–42 LIVE BULLETS

Once my uncle came home on twenty-four hours leave. He had all his Army things. Once we got our hands on them, we soon had so many each of the bullets. But we started complaining on the amount we should have each, so my mother came in, in a rage. Not knowing what they were, she took them off us and threw them on the fire and said 'No one will have them.'

Then a sudden burst of gunfire broke out in our living-room, so we took cover behind the settee.

Girl, aged six

THE HOME GUARD used our schoolyard to drill in. We regarded this schoolyard as ours – and them as trespassers. We used to peep over the wall at them drilling, and rag them. Some stupid members didn't know their left foot from their right. We used to shout out commands, left turn, right turn, while their sergeant was shouting them. In the end the sergeant would get so mad it became a chase-job . . .

They caused my grandfather great inconvenience, because all they ever seemed to do was set up checkpoints on the outskirts of Carmarthen town – a mass of sandbags that reduced the road to half-width, so they could stop every car and search it for spies and fifth-columnists. My grandfather was neither – he was a farmer, and before the war he used to buy in butter from the other farmers and blend seventeen different kinds of butter. Now all his milk went to the Milk Marketing Board, and he didn't blend butter any more. But he still had plenty of contacts in the butter trade, and none of our family ever went short of butter. . . . He had an old Standard 9, with the boot under the back seat, and into that would go these pounds and pounds of butter, and off we'd go through the Carmarthen checkpoints with me sitting on top of it. A bit hair-raising, if they'd decided to search the car, in spite of the innocent child sitting in the back . . . we could've both gone to prison.

But my father's in the Carmarthen Home Guard as well . . .

Boy, aged eleven, Carmarthenshire

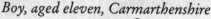

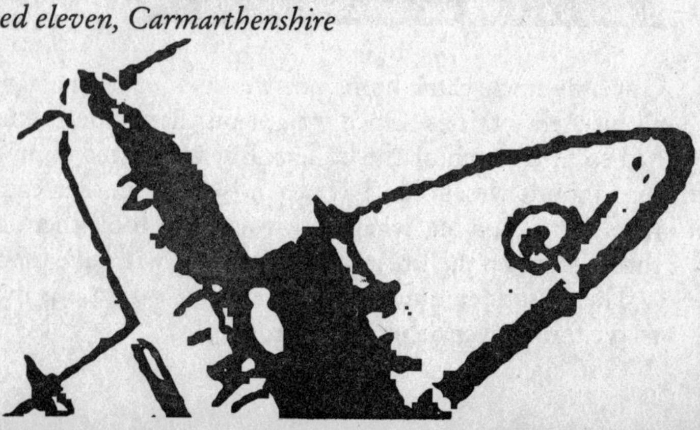

CHAPTER

11 SPIES

1940 SPY!

THE NEWS ON THE WIRELESS was a must. Each word of Alvar Liddell was savoured and recorded, not only for discussion with your peers, but to relate to your dad on his return from the pit.

'The RAF have bombed Tobruk, Dad!'

'The Eyeties have been chased out of Sidi Barrani.'

Atlases were pored over; the disposition of troops, Allied and Axis, faithfully recorded. A broadcast announcing a victory, or even a partial success, was inevitably marked by the raising of a small Union Jack, a relic of the 1937 Coronation, on a tall garden cane affixed to the back-yard gate. Anyone entering the back lane couldn't but be aware of the state of the nation in its historic conflict.

His Majesty's Government, in their wisdom, had told us that 'Walls have ears' and 'Look out – there's a spy about'. Wall-posters – by far the most fascinating to me was the Spy Poster. Depicted was a city gent in bowler, with brolly, striped trousers, black coat and carrying a briefcase. This person, we were confidently informed, could be a spy.

In a community used to its menfolk in coal-grimed work-clothes and blackened faces, the sight of such sartorial elegance was utterly alien. Even the doctor did not aspire to such heights!

We re-enacted the various battles on the piece of waste ground at the end of the colliery row. Small, nondescript, it became in turn the sands of North Africa, the Jungle of Burma, the Beach of Dunkirk. Dunkirk became a historic victory on our 'beach' – two valiant Britishers against the overwhelming odds of four 'Nazis' reluctantly recruited among our companions.

The government followed our lead. Very soon, the ignominy

which led to Dunkirk became, as we had already portrayed, the brilliantly organized evacuation which has been recorded in history.

The aftermath of the real Dunkirk was that the village was invaded by hundreds of troops to be billeted in the church and miners' halls. Trucks were deployed in nearby farmers' fields and – joy – *real* tanks rolled into the bed of the sand quarry. Our war-games took a secondary place as, encouraged by *real* soldiers, we joy-rided in bren-gun carriers and explored the depths and mysteries of the gun-turret of a real tank. The days were all too short; we had much to thank Hitler for.

It was about this time that our portrayal of the Siege of Tobruk (or was it the Ordered Withdrawal From Greece?) took place on the waste ground at the end of our street. Fighting had been heavy all morning, until our respective calls to dinner. Battle recommenced immediately thereafter with numerous casualties, and immediate resurrections, on both sides. Honours were about even, and calls of 'skinch' announced that this sector of the world conflict wanted a breather. Our makeshift rifles were set aside and we sank to the grassless earth.

'Who's he?' asked General (later Field Marshal) Erwin Rommel. The eyes of friend and foe alike were directed towards the bottom of the street. There, setting up a tripod on which was a 'telescope thing', was a man the like of whom had never been seen outside the wall-posters.

'Bowler hat?'

'Yes!'

'Black coat?'

'Yes!'

'Striped trousers?'

'Yes, yes!"

'And he's got spats too!' whispered a ten-year-old who only minutes before had been General Alexander. We watched curiously as the intruder set up his instrument and pointed it at the end of the row of houses. He peered into the eyepiece, made slight adjustments and peered again. Then he straightened up and reached for a leather satchel, nearby.

‘A briefcase!’ we whispered. Conclusive and damning. ‘He’s a spy!’

By this time the spy had taken from his briefcase a notebook and pencil and, after more peering and adjusting, wrote down what were undoubtedly facts of vital importance to the outcome of the war relative to a row of colliery houses. The spy and his equipment now moved nearer our battlefield.

‘Shall we capture him?’

‘He’s a big feller, mind!’

General Rommel, temporarily retired but still with the astuteness of his recent role, suggested ‘Let’s tell PC Wilson!’

Some, mainly those who had recently been ‘Germans’, were in favour of tackling the spy and taking him by force. Already they were brandishing their broomstick rifles. Good sense and generalship prevailed, and we agreed to inform PC Wilson, who lived in a neighbouring street. Our main force would make its way the long way round. To allay suspicion, two of our force would need to make their way past the spy. They could, if opportunity arose, gather more damning evidence as they passed him. Two dirty-faced, sweaty, khaki-shorted, sand-shoed troopers made their tentative way down the lane. Step by step they neared the bowler-hatted man, who continued to devote his attention to the lens of his theodolite. Young Denis was tempted to blurt out ‘Are you a spy?’ as they got abreast of him. Alan, proud of his meagre knowledge of German, thought of astounding the Nazi by shouting ‘Achtung! Achtung!’

That might allow him to escape though, and neither uttered a sound as they passed.

PC Wilson was standing in his shirt-sleeves at his back door, listening to the other boys, his face impassive as he towered above and listened to the motley band of erstwhile warriors.

‘A spy, eh? Well, let’s see then!’ The group stood to one side, as he donned his police jacket and peaked hat, en route to the backyard gate. The strange procession began its trek. Perhaps a little pity developed in all of us for the spy. All of us had experienced the wrath of PC Wilson; his cuff about the ear for minor, and his heavy service boot in the rear for major, misdemeanours were well known and respected.

Then our mothers appeared, as if by evil magic, at back doors.

'Alan, come here this minute!'

'Your tea's been on the table for ages, our Billy!'

'TOMMY!'

'Ah, Mam, just a couple of minutes . . .'

All pleas went unheeded. PC Wilson alone turned the corner to confront the representative of Hilter's Germany.

Teas were hurriedly downed, and chores done with hitherto unknown alacrity. Once free, the group raced down the street, rounded the corner to the scene of the 'capture'.

Deserted. No policeman, no spy, nothing!

'Mr Wilson will have handcuffed him and taken him to prison.'

'Probably has him locked up in his coalhouse.'

'He'll be int . . . introg . . . questioning him.'

'The Army looks after all spies because they have bullets and guns to shoot them.'

So the speculation went until dusk and our maternally imposed curfew. The six o'clock news was listened to with great anticipation . . . When nothing materialized, we gave an enigmatic hint to our parents to be sure to call us should PC Wilson call, or should there be any particular item on the nine o'clock bulletin after we'd gone to bed . . .

When we gathered on subsequent days, we agreed that no news is good news. National Security was the reason our exploit could not be publicized.

'They won't want old Hitler to know he's been captured.'

Our 'Hallo, Mr Wilson,' when we met our fellow spy-catcher in the street met with, disappointingly, only a smile, a pat on the head and a cautionary 'Now don't get into any mischief, boys.'

Jimmy the postman was closely watched and followed, in case he omitted to deliver any official-looking letters to our homes.

'Surely Mr Churchill will write. Or mention us in one of his speeches.' He had mentioned one 'Few', and we had been even fewer.

Boy, Tyneside

1940 A SPY AT ROEDEAN

OUR HEADMISTRESS was the sort you automatically placed in the category 'dragon'. Not the flame-breathing variety – worse. Cold and austere and you knew she would never lose her temper or shout, which at least would have made her human. Tilda was tall, and went straight down back and front without any bulges, so you couldn't even titter about her large bosom/fat wobbly bottom. She had grey cropped hair and a thin-lipped mouth. And taught Maths. That was *it*, as far as I was concerned. At nine, I couldn't do Maths and I was terrified of her.

We had to write down impossible numbers like five million, twenty-five thousand and two . . . I could never get it right. I couldn't remember how many noughts . . . The awful business of being called on to give an answer, mine inevitably being wrong. Our grand totals would be announced to everyone. If you got nought, you were never shouted at, only subjected to a look of withering scorn, so I wished a hole would appear in the floor.

However, life had its redeeming features. We all collected in Tilda's room and sat on the floor and were read to. Whole books from start to finish, in good big chunks and usually our choice, while we sat industriously knitting shapeless grey garments for the Troops. God knows what the Troops must have thought, when the parcels were unpacked in far-off POW camps – my first effort was a scarf that reached record proportions lengthwise, and zig-zagged in and out as I alternately acquired and lost stitches.

Sometimes I was asked to read aloud, when Tilda had a sore throat – Biggles books – I always thought girls' books were soppy, like *Little Women* and *Good Wives* and that ghastly *Anne of Green Gables.* Captain W.E. Johns wrote about *real* things happening *now.* Aeroplane dogfights – invasion by Germans – spies.

One day, in a fit of loathing for Tilda engendered by coming bottom in the Maths test again, I thought 'Perhaps *she* is a German spy?' She seemed quite horrid enough. I mentioned it to my friend Tony. She thought it a definite possibility. But how could we actually *prove* it, before writing to the authorities? Even Biggles had to act on proof. But, how?

Tony and I slept next to Tilda, high up on the third floor of the converted Keswick hotel that was our wartime school. The windows were dormers, with a nice piece of sloping roof below.

'Get into Tilda's room along the roof and search for evidence?' suggested Tony. Tony said she'd go first, while I kept a look out. We chose one long summer's evening just after lights-out, when it was impossible to lie in bed and just go to sleep. I positioned myself at the top of the stairs, and Tony opened the window and crept out on to the roof. After a few minutes she was back, all excitement.

'Just what we wanted,' she said. 'She has newly washed handkerchiefs stuck all over her window in a funny pattern. They are obviously a specially coded message for the ENEMY. The window's visible from the mountains, and another spy's only got to train his binoculars on Tilda's window . . .'

Of course, I had to see the Message. What did it mean? Troop movements? Invasion Imminent? The view from the high roof was marvellous, but I didn't like the feeling in my tummy when I looked down at the ground. It seemed a long way below.

I scrambled back into our bedroom.

Footsteps coming upstairs . . .

Tilda, of course. 'Now, Antonia and Elizabeth, just what are you doing?' The voice was icy with suppressed fury. 'I think you'd better come to my room and explain . . .'

Girl, aged nine

TITTLE TATTLE
LOST THE BATTLE

The Government were nearly as hysterical about spies as about gas. Adolf is listening, but he is also dressed as a humble waiter, and lying on his belly on the floor.

1941 CATCH 'EM YOUNG

A LAD I WAS AT SCHOOL WITH was, as a fourteen-year-old, approached by MI6. He'd returned to England in 1939 because his German mother had just died (his English father was already dead), to live with his uncle. He was quizzed as to his life in Germany and was told they would 'be in touch' and was asked if he would be 'willing to return to Germany' one day. He did, in 1945, as an NCO interpreter with the Intelligence Corps.

Boy, aged fourteen, County Durham

1943 SPIES

I READ IN THE *EXPRESS* that they've shot another German spy. His photograph looked pathetic. Why do they shoot spies? Why do they pretend they're so wicked, like murderers? At least *their* spies are wicked; I suppose *ours* are gallant men doing a wonderful job, giving their lives for their country . . . and I suppose the Germans are telling their people the same thing. Why don't both sides agree to just put captured spies in a POW camp? Who'd be the loser? They couldn't do any more harm.

It's the same with the U-boats. They're cowardly murdering swine, the scum of the sea, because they attack unarmed merchant ships without warning. I heard a destroyer captain talking on the radio; he said when they'd sunk a U-boat, they collected bits of the dead German sailors in buckets out of the water, and everybody cheered. If U-boats are the 'jackals of the sea' what does that make the crews of our own submarines, who, it is announced, have just sunk another German merchant ship off Norway? If that destroyer captain was introduced to a British submarine captain, would he call him a murdering scum too?

Boy, aged thirteen, Tyneside

CHAPTER 12

THE HOME FRONT

THE OILY WIZARD

I WAS OFTEN BOMBED in the war, but never afraid. Tense, when a screaming-bomb was coming down, and I was counting to ten to see if I was going to go on living or not. But only *afraid* once; when my mate caught diphtheria and I thought he'd given it to me.

I wasn't afraid because of my father, who I regarded as some kind of wizard. A very oily wizard; the foreman – fitter at the gasworks. Even before the war, I regarded him as a wizard; sometimes he'd forget his 'bait' and Mam would send me down with his bait-tin, wrapped in a red spotted handkerchief. I would creep into the great smoking, steaming gasworks, beneath the window of the time-office man (who for some reason I always regarded as a mortal enemy), then I would wander about till a 'real' workman, with blackened face, asked me what I wanted. Then a group would gather.

'It's Bobbie's lad. Go an' fetch Bobbie. Where's he working?'

In an instant my father would emerge, black as the rest with shining white teeth, so I could hardly recognize him. Always two or three men walking with him, asking what to do. He was always in a hurry; not flustered, but driving on through an endless sea of problems like a black tramp-steamer. I always regarded the works as my father's kingdom, gorgeously evil-smelling, mysterious. There *was* a manager; but he only saw to the paperwork for my father . . . My father loathed paper; he would defile it with his black thumbprints, then toss it aside with total contempt. His biggest condemnation was: 'It's all right on paper, but it'll never work in practice.'

My father's body was part of his wizardry. His thumbnail grew in five parallel segments, where he'd 'hit it with a hammer at the old North-eastern' as an apprentice. I used to press it, to see if it hurt him. It didn't. He would scrub himself when he came home, but could never quite get rid of the black grease, so that he had the shadowed eyes and swarthy good-looks of the silent-film star, Rudolph Valentino. He always polished his shoes but never his work boots, which lay by the gas stove, black, caked and dreadful. His work overcoat reeked of benzene, ammonia and gas. He never had colds; because, he said, the germs couldn't live in the gasworks air. The primary school beneath the high gasworks wall didn't have colds, either. And somehow his heavy smoking was part of the strong-smelling mystery; the split thumbnail was an awesome brown; when he cut me a piece of bread, it would taste faintly of nicotine. He smoked in the outside toilet (my mother was terrified that for some reason this would lead to him setting himself on fire) and there too, during air raids, the lingering smell of him was a comfort.

He did miraculous things; one day he brought home a full-sized model of a Vickers machine-gun he'd made for me at work. Another time a three-foot model of HMS *Exeter*, victor of the River Plate. He could mend *anything*. Cabinets and model galleons flowed from his non-stop fingers. The cupboards were full of broken brass lumps of model machinery he'd made as an apprentice. And there were his five huge green books, full of drawings of reciprocating triple-extension engines that I stared at for hours in awed incomprehension.

When war broke out, he became a section-leader in the wardens; it was just an extension of his wizardry. As foreman, he wore a filthy boilersuit; as a warden, a clean one. Wardens clustered round him as he walked, just like the workmen. He knew more about the raids than anybody else. He'd come home from work and say 'There's still a yellow alert on. The beggers is hanging around somewhere.' (Red alert meant the siren had gone.) He knew where raids had taken place; where they'd been bad; where an enemy bomber had been shot down. He always gave the impression of being in good control of the situation.
 He never used dramatic words like 'Hun' or 'Nazi'; always

'them beggers' said in the same tone of voice he might use about a stroppy Irish boilermaker, or the Nigerian labourer who always went for a snooze in the heat of the retort-house.

They came for him at any hour of the day or night. When he was home, my mother dreaded the knock on the door, the anxious black-capped figure with the inevitable question 'Is Bobbie in?' Sometimes, when he had dropped to sleep in a chair, exhausted, she used to tell them he'd gone out. But he always slept with one ear cocked; she was always pulled up in the middle of her lies by his call of 'Who's there, Maggie?'

During raids, he toured his district, talking to the people in the shelters. He always believed in telling people what was going on. Anything was better than the chaotic series of thuds,

Wardens in their post, in company with a special constable. Only a garden hut, but the nerve centre of a whole suburb.

bangs, crumps, whistlings and hisses that was an air raid. Women used to stop my mother in the street and thank her for my father 'keeping an eye on them'.

He seemed to go through air raids with the wonder and gusto of a small boy. He would talk of the weird beauty of the 'Chandeliers' – the marvellous cages of blue lights that dropped slowly by parachute, lighting the target for the German bombers; he liked it even better when the ack-ack gunners blew them to bits. One night he heard the soft whispering of a cluster of incendiaries coming down, straight above his head. Just managed to get under a costermonger's barrow before they hit. Then there was a ring of them burning around him, and several burning through the barrow on top of him, and he thought 'his last moment had come'. He escaped by taking a flying kick at one of them, to make a gap to run through.

'Scored a goal, an' all!'

All night through we listened for his footsteps; the clink of hobnailed warden's boots. Mostly they'd walk steadily, even when German bombers were overhead. But sometimes they'd start to run, and then we'd hear the whistle of the bombs. He'd come through the shelter door-curtain in a flying leap, and land on his knees between the bunks with a shelter-shaking thud. Then sit up and say, 'By, I could do wi' a drop o' coffee, hinny.'

My mother only worried when he was on night shift at the gasworks. Climbing the ladders of the great gasholder, to kick burning incendiaries off the thin top plates. Chipping ice off a conveyor a hundred feet up, with a raid in progress. All he would say is 'I'm all right. I know those old works better than bleddy Hitler.'

He seemed to love it all. In 1939, he had incipient stomach ulcers; they seemed to vanish on 3 September. He always said it was the meat-shortage cured his stomach; I think it was the danger. My dearest ambition was to reach the age of fifteen, and be his official ARP messenger. Sadly, the end of the war beat me to it.

Boy, Tyneside

MY MOTHER WAS ALWAYS very calm; I only saw her go to pieces once. To listen to her, the only important thing about the war was getting enough cigarettes for my father. Father never sat still between 1939 and 1945. All that kept him going was twenty full-strength Capstan a day. Without nicotine, he was like a Spitfire without petrol. Some of his mates would call at the shop on their way to work. If the shop had fags, they'd go on to work; if not, they'd go back to bed.

So crisis-point for Mam was Friday afternoons, when she walked round the whole town, looking for cigarettes. She was pretty, in a ladylike way, and had a lot of charm, all of which was used on the tobacconists. It used to outrage me; we'd be walking round the town in the rain, and she'd be giving me stick cos she was fed-up, then at the tobacconist's door she'd turn on the charm like a searchlight. I once called her a hypocrite, and nearly got a clout.

Worst were the shops that only had Turkish cigarettes – you'd see a horrible little hand-lettered sign in the shop window – PASHAS ONLY. My father said Pashas were made from camel dung. But they were better than nothing. Only, if she was offered them early-on, she didn't know what to do. If she bought Pashas, she wouldn't be able to afford better cigarettes further on round the town . . .

When we got to Gran's for tea, Dad would have got there from work. He'd be smoking half-inch dog-ends, burning his nose with the match as he lit them. Or just sitting there panting. Mam would always play a trick on him – get any Pashas out of her shopping-bag first and watch his face fall. Then she'd bury the Pashas with Gold Flake and Players, and every packet she pulled out, his face would light up more. And her face used to look so proud, like she'd presented him with a bouncing baby boy.

In 1941, any woman's most prized possession was a pair of 'Russian' fur-lined boots. Unobtainable in the shops, with or without clothing coupons. But Dad met a 'chap at work' who had two pairs for sale, Mam's size. Mam asked what colour they were – Dad hadn't bothered to ask. Mam had a very subtle taste in colour – Dad's taste could only be described as 'garish'.

That night, he brought home a superb pair of boots, which were quite the foulest shade of acid-green I have ever seen before or since. Mam stared at them in agony.

'I thought they looked bonny,' said Dad.

Silence.

'They'll mucky-down, given time . . .'

Silence.

'Well, they'll keep your feet warm, anyway . . .'

Silence.

'I'd have got the other pair, only they were only a dull brown . . .'

Mam weighed the boots in her hand, and contemplated Dad's head. Then 'They're lovely', she said, with a smile of pure agony.

Boy, Tyneside

1941 SALVAGE

ON ONE OCCASION, following a government scrap-metal collection (aluminium teapots, pans etc.) a story spread around amongst the children that if you collected a bag of shrapnel and took it to the local army barracks, you would receive a toy. Using a spare kitbag of my father's I spent many weeks gathering shrapnel from people's gardens and backyards. When I finally gathered what I thought was a lot (about 30 lb.), I took it to the barracks which was about three miles away. Upon arriving, I was thrilled to see many boxes, sacks and bags of shrapnel

Each newspaper left neatly bundled by the dustbin was regarded as a direct poke in the eye for Hitler. This lady in her 'turban' was the height of chic, and was trying to make bomb-cases seductive. The 'turban' became popular in the factories, where it stopped most women with long hair from being scalped or killed by having their hair caught in moving machinery.

FROM WASTE PAPER TO MUNITIONS OF WAR

outside the gates. Two soldiers with rifles and fixed bayonets were marching up and down on guard duty. I approached them, dragging my bag and asked them where did I go for the toy? One soldier began to swear at me and the other turned round and pointed his rifle and bayonet at me, shouting he would 'stick it in my behind if I did not clear off'. I ran a short distance, leaving the bag, and tried to impress the soldiers by telling them my father was in their regiment (which he was) but they were not impressed and still chased me.

Boy, Liverpool

1941 METAL

METAL WAS IN SHORT SUPPLY. Park railings were cut down with

Aluminium to make Spitfires – anything from silver paper to colanders and circular hot-water bottles. This 'plane' is being built in Sidcup, Kent.

acetylene torches, and taken away to be melted down. Yet there were some first-rate metal toys to be had – Spitfires, Hurricanes, Wellingtons, and ships of the Royal Navy. I was particularly proud of my little fleet, which consisted of the battleships HMS *Hood* and *Nelson*, the cruiser *Exeter* and two or three nameless submarines which stood less than a centimetre high at the conning tower. I had some grand naval battles on the lounge carpet, with my submarines carefully submerged under the long Indian pile, a trap for any unwary person who crossed the room in stockinged feet. When we heard the news that the *Hood* was sunk, I could hardly believe it. How could anything defeat a ship with such a formidable array of guns? After that, I could take no more pleasure in my games.

I still had the ships but their magic was gone, and although I still played with the others occasionally, it seemed kind of cheating to use my favourite ship.

Boy, aged twelve, Manchester

AWFUL WARNING

MY MOTHER OFTEN SAID TO ME 'The Germans will come for you if you are a naughty girl.'

This led to vivid pictures in my mind of a German soldier climbing through my bedroom window, to literally take me from my bed whilst I was asleep. I went to bed night after night, almost afraid to go to sleep, wondering if the Germans would come for me during that night. (I do not remember being particularly naughty either.)

If we went for a Sunday walk I would close *all* the windows prior to going, to prevent the Germans getting in.

This gave me an extreme fear of the dark, because I feared being taken away by night. This fear of the dark has dominated me for years.

Girl, aged five, Warwickshire

Another piece of misplaced Government zeal – handkerchiefs, constantly flapped about, spread more germs than sneezing. Still – the words stuck. They were a 'pre-TV jingle', quoted at you by friends every time you sneezed until the 1950s.

We loved the squander bug, because he made a fool out of grown-ups. The swastikas on him were only part of the joke – really he was a British, and purely malicious, child. We enjoyed his antics, and cheerfully spent every penny we could lay our hands on. He had as much effect on our finances as 'Desperate Dan' or 'Lord Snooty'.

HAPPY YEARS

FOR ME, THE WAR YEARS were happy. We had more freedom than we would have done had the men been at home. We were allowed to roam in the woodlands and on the golf course without supervision. Parents didn't fear lurking prowlers in lonely places, as they assumed all the men who might do us harm were busily occupied.

Girl, Sheffield, From Norman Longmate,
How We Lived Then, *Hutchinson, 1971*

MAY 1942 A CHANGE OF HEART

I'M SITTING in the warm sunshine writing this. The weather is so gorgeous that it's a great temptation to spend much of the time punting on the river, instead of working.

Yesterday I marched in a May Day procession, to demonstrate Anglo-Soviet Unity, through the streets and parks. The Home Guard band marched in front, but were sometimes not sure of what they were supposed to be playing, which caused some amusement. They finally broke into a very slow and sentimental rendering of the 'Volga Boat Song' which proved most difficult to march to.

In the Easter vacation I went to Birmingham to a student congress. I hitch-hiked with another girl, there and back. We travelled mostly on lorries which is much pleasanter than going by train or car, as lorry-drivers are very interesting to talk to; they told us about their families, about the loads they were carrying and the journeys they made every day and about the country we passed through. We felt we had learnt a lot about lorries and lorry-drivers by the time we got home.

 Girl, aged nineteen, Cambridge

We heard at school that a German bomber had been brought down south of Holmpton. Following our usual practice, we rode our bicycles five miles to the crash. We were some little distance away when a large explosion occurred, shrapnel flew over our heads and a large cloud of smoke appeared. We turned tail. (Unknown to us, the aircraft carried two landmines and one had exploded, killing some of the bomb-disposal team.)

Next day we went again, to find that the guards, fearful of a second explosion, had withdrawn to the farmhouse and left the wreck unguarded. The tail had broken off and was some 150 yards away. The aircraft had not burned.

The farmhouse containing the guards was out of sight over the hill, so we had free access. I remember I stood on a large cylinder painted dark grey-green (that turned out later to have been the remaining landmine). Various people took objects they fancied as souvenirs. Alec Allen took the radio set, Ian Wilkinson the top of the control-column, and myself the altimeter.

Then we found the guns; a machine-gun and an aircraft-cannon with belt-ammunition. We carried the cannon and machine-gun, plus three hundred rounds for the machine-gun and about 200 rounds in belt for the cannon, and laid them under bushes well away from the crash. We returned home and went back after dark to collect them, transporting our loot home on Tony Cockerill's mother's bicycle.

Not all of us were in the choir, but as I had a tower-key and in those days the church was never locked, we hid the guns in the 'pulley room' of the church tower. It was a three-foot space, above the ringer's chamber and below the belfry.

As most of us were in the Air Training Corps, we reckoned we knew about guns, and we did know enough to strip and clean both weapons. We also knew the dangers of firing a round up a crash-distorted barrel, so after cleaning the guns, we smuggled them out of the church and on to the beach. We put a round in each, laid the guns on a sack, and tied long strings to the triggers. We then retreated behind an outcrop of cliff, and pulled on the strings. The first was the machine-gun, and all went well. But the cannon not only jumped off the sack, but sent a large ball of fire out to sea . . . We did not know the colour-codings for German ammunition and had chosen a tracer-round for the cannon.

As thumps and bangs were commonplace in those days we had no fear of being caught from the noise, and we smuggled the guns back to the tower.

In those days the German bombers were in the habit of flying in very low over the coast, and often passed between St Nicholas church and the 120-foot Withernsea lighthouse. Our idea was to set up the machine-gun on the north-east corner of the tower roof, and the cannon on the north-west corner. The weapons were to be tied down to the parapet with old bell-ropes, and we intended to shoot at the next aircraft, first with the machine-gun and follow with the cannon. That way we intended the aircraft to crash in the fields beyond the town and thus not do any damage.

For the next two weeks there was not one raid, even though there was a full-moon period.

By this time, of course, the RAF had discovered the loss of various parts of the aircraft. No wonder, since Cecil Bickley had taken a hacksaw and sawn the swastika out of the tail. The RAF were hunting the guns, aided by the local police. The local inspector of special constabulary, Inspector Stathers, was surprised to find a perfect specimen of a German bomb-sight in his son Harold's wardrobe. Questions followed . . .

Several hasty conferences were held, near the lighthouse, by the choir and others who had stolen gear, as to how to dispose of it before being caught in possession. There were many lads up early next morning to dispose of gear in the dike bottoms (irrigation ditches).

Before long, the whole story was out. The guns and ammunition were collected from the church and taken to the local juvenile court on a builder's handcart. Sixteen of us were hauled before the court. There was a large table piled high with our loot.

The RAF sent down a young officer to prosecute. The vicar, the Rev. Willie Passmore, appeared to speak on our behalf. Some parents attended, including a certain Mr Todd, something of a political speaker locally and a strong supporter of the Workers' Education Association. He spoke with passion in defence of all the boys, and particularly his son Alfred, a pal of mine who confided in me afterwards his embarrassment, and said he wished his old man had shut up and paid the fine like everybody else.

At the time I thought the police and magistrates took a serious view of our escapade. But later, my father told me all the adults concerned were amused and sympathetic, and somewhat annoyed by the attitude of the RAF. It appeared the RAF were covering up a blunder and trying to save face. Later I realized our escapade must have resulted in some poor RAF person facing a charge.

We were all given a conditional discharge, and made to pay four shillings costs. There was severe criticism of the authorities for their failure to mount guards on the plane. The vicar wrote to the Archbishop of York, apologizing on behalf of his choirboys. The Archbishop's reply consisted of one line, and indicated his sympathies were with us boys.

The machine-gun had turned out to be an MG 41, of the latest type, and the RAF hadn't had a chance to inspect one before.

Boys, aged fourteen to fifteen, Withernsea, Humberside

1942–45 WEAPONS

I WAS SENT AWAY to a boarding-school, run by Dominican monks at Blackfriars in the Northampton countryside. I became interested in chemistry for its potential in making explosives, stick-bombs and smokescreens.

Not far away was a Polish camp. The Poles were reputed to

fly their aircraft into the German planes when they ran out of ammunition, but security was not their strong point. After discreet investigation I chose a rainy day so I could ride through the park in my bicycle cape. The Poles were nowhere to be seen, and I opened the unlocked door of their armoury. Inside, I swathed myself with bandoliers of ammunition, resumed my cape and rode off. Back at the school, I emptied each cartridge into an Ovaltine tin, and built up my store of cordite.

It seemed to me that I would get a bigger haul if I paid a visit at night so that I could load a pack. So I broke out of school at midnight and crawled across a field. There was no need for this precaution, there were no sentries. As I entered the armoury I felt something under my feet; when I shone my torch I discovered I was standing on detonators which were scattered loose about the floor. This time I loaded up with Mills grenades and 2" mortar bombs, and the following day in the boot-room I had an interesting time finding out how the safety mechanism of the mortar bomb worked with the help of a tin-opener.

I repaired to a gravel pit and threw the bomb over the edge. Unfortunately nothing happened, so I had to scramble down the side of the pit, stones bouncing around the bomb, in order to retrieve it and have another go. Finally I was obliged to lay a Mills grenade beside it; I withdrew the steel pin and inserted some sticks of cordite in its place, laying a fuse with further sticks of cordite which I ignited. This did the trick and produced a satisfying explosion.

One day a Flying Fortress crashed in the woods and we hared off to see what we could find. Several of us tried to haul a machine-gun out of it, but without success. However, one boy of unusual strength got it out on his own and was subsequently seen in the showers banging the butt on the floor, trying to fire the bullet that was in the breech.

Another boy recovered part of the jawbone of one of the aircrew, complete with teeth. This he passed round the refectory, which had the desired effect of putting a number of people off their meal, so that there was more for the others to eat.

Somehow or other our headmaster, the Bede, got to know that the school basement (where the boys' trunks were kept) was beginning to resemble the Houses of Parliament in the time of Guy Fawkes. He made an announcement; there would be an amnesty provided all was surrendered. I was in a dilemma. It was a sad thought to give up all of my trophies, but unfortunately my reputation was such that the Bede would never believe that I had nothing. He had been a bombardier in the First World War and I already had experience of the strength of his grenade-throwing arm.

I appeared at the eleventh hour and he greeted me with a beam; he knew he could rely on me. The police were exceedingly impressed with the size of the collection, which included machine-guns, and several anti-tank rocket-launchers, complete with missiles.

Back home in the holidays, Mike and I broke into an unexploded bomb dump and recovered a Blacker Bombard, which we strapped to the carrier of his bicycle and rode home in daylight without a soul saying a word. Perhaps everyone was getting punch-drunk towards the end of the war. My father discovered it and said it would have to go. He simply telphoned the police. 'I have a bomb. Would you please come and collect it.'

In order to liven things up we started making our own bombs with calcium chlorate and sulphur. Every Saturday, the quarry behind the Isolation Hospital resounded to the crashes of our endeavours. On the way home people would be standing in the road trying to make out where the bombs had been dropped from.

My last acquisition was a 9mm automatic pistol, but I had trouble getting satisfactory ammunition for it and sold it to somebody for a fiver.

I have always been grateful I wasn't a parent in those days. When my wife read this she said didn't I realize I was stealing?

I had to admit we thought of it as the spoils of war.

Boy , aged twelve to fifteen, Northants

CHAPTER 13 THE AMERICAN INVASION

1941 AMERICA I LOVE YOU

'JAPANESE PLANES have attacked Pearl Harbour.' I spent the whole weekend in a daze. *Ridiculous* that America and Japan should fight! I'd read an American comic only a month before, in which American fighters were defending San Francisco against Japanese bombers (they all had open cockpits and fixed wheels with *spats – jokes* by comparison with Spitfires); and I thought: how silly – how can they fight when they're on opposite sides of the world? Science fiction, like the Martians fighting the Venusians . . .

Then Hitler declared war on America, and I *knew* he was mad. Yes, I spent a whole weekend wandering in a daze, and one American song kept running through my brain.

America I love you, you're like a mother to me . . .

From ocean to ocean, this sudden emotion . . .

And America became magic. The things we heard of! Bulldozers that could build a whole airfield in twenty-four hours. Liberty ships built in a week, from the first plate being laid. The Americans were going to build 25,000 planes a year . . . there had only been 3,000 on *both* sides in the Battle of Britain. The war had become, as we soon learnt to say, 'a different ball-game'.

American comics flooded in; new heroes like Superman and Dick Tracy, the cop with the two-way wrist-TV and nose like a rectangular kite. And jazz records we learnt to listen to the American way, heads neck-breakingly on one side, nodding wisely in time with the music, clicking our fingers to the rhythm and, if possible, chewing gum. They seemed all about travel, those records. We were urged to 'Take the "A" Train' or the 'Chattanooga Choochoo', especially on 'Route 66'. Americans were always arriving or departing.

We learnt that Betty Grable had the best legs in the world, and had them insured for a million dollars (the word 'million' was on every lip). Better still, she was married to Harry James, who could play 'The Flight of the Bumble Bee' on the trumpet, faster than it had ever been played before.

There came a dreadful rumour (the first one not concerned with the war for two years) that she had died in childbirth.

Our other hero was Fats Waller, the huge negro who invented Boogie Woogie. Every kid who was allowed near a piano could play the left-hand roll of Boogie Woogie. Fats talked to himself as he played, a shocking thing till you got used to it. We had just got used to it when he died of pneumonia. It seemed a very serious blow to the War Effort.

There were two gods of the clarinet, Benny Goodman and Artie Shaw. (I refused to believe that the American 'Artie' was only a shortening of the mundane English name 'Arthur' – I had a fight with another kid over that.) Both had their supporters, who argued interminably about their virtues, as if they were Arsenal and Tottenham Hotspur. For a while, we quite forgot the War.

But even there, the Yanks were tops. We abandoned our faithful Hurricanes and Spitfires, which had only won the Battle of Britain. The American fighters had much more exciting names, even *swearing* names, like the Grumman Hellcat. Above all, there was the Flying Fortress, that carried so many guns and flew in such tight groups six miles high, that no German fighter would dare come near it. And it had a bomb-sight so accurate that it could drop a bomb into a pickle-barrel from 20,000 feet . . .

And the American troop carriers, huge four-engined monoplanes called 'Stratocruiser' and 'Constellation' that made our old biplanes look like rubbish from the Science Museum.

I made an impassioned speech in our school debating-society, about the superiority of all things American. My beloved English teacher kept tripping me up, stopping me for saying things like 'Th' Americans' instead of 'The Americans'. I couldn't understand it, he'd always been sympathetic to me before . . .

Of course, the gilt eventually got knocked off the gingerbread. The Hellcat, for all its name, didn't do too well against the Japanese Zero. And the Americans kept on shortening their line, and making strategic withdrawals, just like we'd been doing ever since 1940 . . . Then some Americans got stationed at Whitley Bay, and people started saying there were three things wrong with them: they were 'overpaid, oversexed and over here'. They had a fight with the Australian Air Force on the sea-front, and the Australians threw several of them through the plate-glass windows of shops.

Boy, aged thirteen, Tyneside

BOYFRIENDS

MY FATHER WAS POSTED TO INDIA with the RAF. In early 1940, the Army took away the family's two cars. While my dad was away my mum had lots of American and Polish boyfriends. In this way we got a little more food. I used to grease my pedal-car with butter.

Boy, aged nine, Liverpool

AN AMERICAN BOYFRIEND

WHEN I FIRST GOT INTERESTED in men, I brought an American boyfriend home. I really liked this man, and I think he liked me. At the same time, my cousin (who was only a baby) was living with us. He picked the same day as I brought my boyfriend home to 'poo' all over the hall. When my boyfriend came in he slipped on it, went head over heels and landed on his face in it. I've never seen him since.

Girl, aged sixteen, Liverpool

This is how they will always be to us: jeep-driving, gum-chewing, physically arrogant, infinitely more glamorous even than the RAF's 'Brylcreem Boys'. Adults and males loathed them. The kids and girls loved them.

THERE WAS AN AMERICAN air-base near where I lived and my aunty was courting an American called Mike. One night a German plane was shot down at Hooton Airfield and the pilot escaped and was on the run. A car drove down the road with a loudspeaker; a man was telling everybody to lock their doors and stay inside.

My mother decided we should all go down the shelter! But as we were leaving the house there came a knock at the front door. She opened the door a little bit and saw a man panting. He had his head halfway through the doorway when my mother tried to shut the door. He had his head trapped in the door and he was trying to say who he was. He finally made himself under-

stood. He was Mike. The next day we heard the German had been caught. When Mike used to visit my aunty he used to bring boxes of sweets for me and Pat.

Girl, aged fourteen, Liverpool

1942–3 AN AMERICAN GIFT

I REMEMBER THE KINDNESS and generosity of the American GIs, our horror at the Free French sailors who would crack open and eat raw mussels on the beach at Barmouth, and a visit I made to the Polish army camp on the other side of the estuary. Just before Christmas I was collecting holly in the Arthog area. I missed a train to Barmouth, and after trudging through woods and swamps, knocked on the door of the Polish army camp near the far end of Barmouth viaduct.

The Polish troops must have thought I looked a cold, wet, pathetic sight, and handed me a pint mug of tea and a doorstep of bread and cheese, which seemed to be the only food they were having for their tea. Cold and wet that I was, I remember feeling sorry for the spartan rations that the Poles seemed to have and could hardly finish eating the thick chunk of bread.

There were servicemen of many nations in Barmouth, and we besieged them with requests for foreign stamps and coins.

By some means my London evacuee pal, Peter Adamson, or myself had come by the princely sum of sixpence and were debating how to best expend this when my youngest brother came on the scene. I'm afraid that we could not include him in our plans with only sixpence. He followed us down the road to Barmouth, bawling his head off.

A lone American soldier who was strolling along, called him over and presented him with half-a-crown. I'm afraid we immediately descended on my brother and had a three-way split – chips at 2*d.* a bag, fish at 6*d.* and lemonade 5*d.* from the local chip shop.

 Boy, aged nine, Barmouth

CHAPTER 14 PRISONERS OF WAR

1940 RELUCTANT HEROES

WE WENT FOR A COUPLE OF DAYS' holiday in a village near Bethesda in North Wales.

A German bomber came over our heads and crashed into the mountainside. The crew got out, and in good English they explained how they had just eaten in a Paris restaurant which was very nice.

They said that the war was tragic and useless and would result in decadence, if we did not accept a 'Plan' for Europe.

Both seemed to become prisoners quite gladly, once the soldiers arrived, saying it was all over, no one would care for you, if you died fighting or not.

Girl, aged seventeen, Liverpool

1940 GERMAN CHOCOLATE

WE ONLY HAD ONE BIG RAID on Chester, in daylight. A German pilot came down by parachute. My father, who was a special constable, went to arrest him. A big crowd had gathered and were just watching him, not knowing what to do. I think the pilot was quite glad to be arrested; he gave my father some chocolate. My father gave it to me. It was in a little round tin box. I didn't eat it, because the Germans were rumoured to poison that kind of thing. We've still got it . . . I think it was part of his survival ration.

Boy, aged seven, Chester

1942–3 TRAINLOADS OF POWS

AS THE TIDES OF WAR swayed in our favour, trainloads of German POWs arrived at Northwich Station. They were lined

How the Government wanted the public to imagine the prisoners of war – obedient and well guarded.

up four abreast and marched to Marbury Hall. I and hundreds of other youths often went to watch their arrival, to hoot, jeer and shout at these our enemies, whole lines of unkempt men, with few possessions, unshaven, weary, red-eyed and in some cases ill-clad, these once-proud remnants of Hitler's armies, escorted by perhaps a dozen or so armed troops, as they marched the two or three miles to their camp.

Gradually people became used to these arrivals, and feelings towards them gradually tempered. The Italian POWs were the first allowed out of camp to work on farms and in local factories, including ICI.

My Dad was in the lorry business. We had two Germans to help him. They had to eat outside in the barn. My mother was always soft-hearted; she came in one day and said, 'Have you seen what they've given those poor lads for their dinners? A scrap of dry bread and a scrap of sausage. You can't expect a man to do a day's work on that!' Soon she was giving them their dinner. In the end, we had them in for Sunday dinner. One of them had been the only tiger-tamer in Europe before the war – he said there were plenty of lion-tamers but only one tiger-tamer. He pulled open his shirt and showed me where a tiger had mauled him – a terrible scar from his neck all the way down to his belt. Captain Something, he called himself, when he was a tiger-tamer. We became great friends. We still send Christmas cards at Christmas.

Boy, aged thirteen, Cheshire

1943–45 CAMP ORCHESTRA

SOME HUNDREDS of prisoners, not considered a high security risk, came to Marbury Hall.

I remember practising the piano one afternoon, and seeing a German POW, who was engaged in hedge-cutting for the local farmer, spending a long time on the piece immediately in front of our house. When we got into conversation with him it turned out he had been a cathedral organist in Germany and he was delighted to listen to anyone playing Bach, even a beginner like me.

He always lingered after that, when we played classical 78 records, with the window open.

A music teacher in Hartford and her husband invited home a German musician, August Wusterbecker, captured at Ostend. By this time, Wusterbecker, who was not only a violinist but also a conductor, had formed a camp orchestra. Instruments were loaned by local musicians. Paul Voigt, a violin-maker and restorer, supplied a cello and one or two double-basses were actually made in the camp. The problem of dress was overcome by blackout material being used to make a rough type of evening-dress. My family were invited to concerts and it was a great treat for me, because travel to Manchester to hear the Hallé wasn't possible due to petrol-rationing.

Boy, aged fourteen, Cheshire

1944 'WOPS' AND 'JERRIES'

WHEN I WENT TO HELP my friends in Cumberland with their harvest in 1944, I was outraged to see POWs helping as well. No security; an army lorry with canvas top pulled up at the farm gate, the driver banged on his door and shouted 'Out, you idle Wops' and three woebegone figures in brown leapt down from the tailgate and stood clutching bundles and shivering in the morning air.

They were know as 'Alfonso', 'Luigi' and 'That Useless Begger' none of which were their real names. To the farmers, the first one you got was Alfonso and the second Luigi. Not knowing a word of English, they had learnt to answer to these names, like pet dogs. It helped *us* distinguish them. 'You Useless Begger' answered his name as cheerfully as the rest.

Alfonso and Luigi were very small – five foot four. Swarthy, hook-nosed, big-brown-eyed, they might have been twins, though they were not related. They did everything together – never more than four feet apart. The farmer had learnt not to separate them – they got miserable and their work went off. Even in the heat of midday, they kept on their greatcoats and rolled-up balaclava helmets.

The farmer said they were good little workers, because they came from the North – car-workers in Turin before the war. All the ones from the North were hard workers. Those from the South were totally idle; no farmer wanted them, but they had to accept one Southerner for every two Northerners. Rationing!

That Useless Begger (always uttered with total contempt) was from the South. Bigger – about five foot seven, slender, with a trim black moustache and arrogant air. He'd stop work the moment the farmer's eye was off him; drift away to where the two land-girls were working like, as the farmer said 'a tom-cat on heat'. Very handsome, like Douglas Fairbanks, with a flashy smile and perfect white teeth. But as far as the land-girls were concerned, he didn't exist. He had learnt one English phrase – 'I can see the top of your bra!' The land-girl turned to him, broad Lancashire:

'An' I can see the top o' thy underpants an' all – and they're mucky!'

Wet lunchtimes, we sometimes shared the back of the army wagon. Embarrassing. The English farmhands discussing the Italians as if they weren't there – really intimately, as if they were cattle. And the Italians discussed us similarly, in Italian. Had there been an interpreter, there'd certainly have been a fight.

One evening I hitched a lift back to the village in the POW truck. Getting off, over the tailgate, I caught myself awkwardly in the crotch. As I lay doubled up in agony on the road, the truck drove off to enormous Italian cheering and laughter. They seemed to think that for once they'd won a victory. Then I realized how much they really hated us.

The German POW was different; a tall thin dignified scarecrow figure in Afrika Korps uniform that grew daily more like a farmhand's gear. He fastened up his trousers with binder-twine, just like they did. He had a little English, very slow, but all the farmhands listened to him patiently. He had owned his own farm in Bavaria, before the war. All he wanted was to get back to it. He was allowed to do any job on the farm, and was allowed to go off on his own. He had shown the farmhands several agricultural tricks they didn't know, and when they were stuck, they would send for him and ask his opinion. He was very loving with animals, especially the dogs. He wouldn't leave any broken thing unmended; spent one lunch-hour mending a drystone wall that had fallen down. He was called 'Fritz' like all German prisoners, and was content to answer to it.

He worked a fiddle with the farmer, who was charged so much an hour for his services. But however hard Fritz worked, he only got five shillings from the POW camp people. So when he'd worked eight hours, he and the farmer would sign his work-card as having worked only four. Then the farmer would give Fritz a packet of fags instead.

Once, when Fritz's camp-lorry broke down and didn't come for him in the evening, he walked back to camp alone. He wished Hitler was dead, so he could go home to his farm. He was the only one allowed inside the farmhouse, for a meal or a bath.

Boy, aged fifteen

1943 INSIDE A POW CAMP

'LET'S GO TO SLATERS'!'

Our last port of call was the farm, where they'd acquired new pigs. We were both intrigued and disgusted by these creatures wallowing in their filth.

Two brothers ran the farm; how could their late industrious father have sired such lazy incompetents? At potato-picking time – *if* they'd remembered to sow – they forever had difficulty recruiting labour because of their inability to reach into their

Potato picking. This photo has some of the starkness of Russian peasants. Even before the war, women picked potatoes for less than sixpence an hour, while the older children minded the younger.

money-pockets. But with luck we could avoid them and still see their latest acquisitions . . .

'Who's that?'

'Never seen *him* before.'

'Pity anybody who works for them.' The object of our pity was a lad not much older than us, busy filling a wheelbarrow with the product of the pigs. He nodded, smiled a greeting.

'Is there some new pigs?'

'Yes, in *that* place. Till I have cleaned out *this* place.'

We'd become used to foreign accents invading our village since war began; thought nothing of it. Climbed up, leaned over the wall and saw, to our delight, a sow of gigantic proportions, ministering to her six-strong litter.

'Is she not big?'

'A whopper!'

'She and her little ones arrived yesterday with me.'

'Did you bring them?'

He smiled, shaking his head. 'Me . . . no. I come at same time.'

We were curious . . . but curiosity would have to wait.

'Watch out – Slaters coming!'

We vanished in the opposite direction.

Two days later, having made sure all the village industries were functioning satisfactorily, we returned to view the pigs, making sure the hated brothers were in a distant field.

'Hullo, boys! How are you today?'

Why was he so formal? But his smile was genuine. 'What are your names?'

We told him, adding our nicknames. He didn't seem to understand about nicknames. 'My name is Klaus.'

'That's a funny name!'

'Not in my country.'

'Where's that?'

'Ich bin . . . I am a German.' He looked hard, for our reac-

 tion. Two pairs of eyes as wide open as equally open mouths

would allow. Where were the jackboots, the swastika, the monocle?

'You're kidding!'

'Kidding? What is that?'

'Go on, talk German, then!'

He smiled, retreated to an adjacent cow-byre.

'Let's go,' said Dennis; no glory in unmasking imposters. Klaus reappeared, jacket over arm. His grin widened as he slipped it on, did a sudden about-turn to display on his back the tell-tale yellow patch.

Our picture of the typical German, conjured up by films, was shattered. How could this young lad be the enemy, who we'd played at killing for four years? Our minds couldn't grasp it. Our friend was now our enemy – or vice-versa? Were tears forming in Dennis's eyes? My heart was beating like mad. I had a lump in my throat.

'Come, see the pigs. I have them in their new place.' We followed, scared to stay but reluctant to go. Wanting to ask so much, but silent, while Klaus, aware of our dilemma, chattered away about the pigs and the names he'd given them.

We visited daily – provided the Slaters weren't in evidence. We supplemented his prison fare with what titbits we could procure. He didn't smoke, but in the camp cigarettes were used as currency. The few Woodbines we managed helped to make his lot easier.

Until the day he didn't appear.

'He might be ill.'

But a week elapsed without a sign.

'Shall we ask the Slaters?'

'Mebbe they've murdered him and hidden the body?'

Knowing the Slaters, I didn't doubt the possibility but . . . 'Let's go down the camp and try and see him.'

The camp entrance was separated from the church by the graveyard. The gate had been replaced by a rickety contraption of barbed wire. Inside was a lone sentry-box. Beyond, two rows of huts. We passed by, uncertain, recrossed the road.

'We've come this far – let's ask!'

But what to say . . . ? We approached the sentry. Rifle in hand, he was shuffling from foot to foot; glanced through the wire, glad of this slight diversion.

'Can we see Klaus Shuster?'

It shook him. 'A prisoner? What you want one of the prisoners for?'

'Got a message for him,' Dennis offered.

'What kind of message? Who from?' He was getting too nosy; we couldn't cope. We tried pleading. 'We've *got* to see him!'

His duty was to stop prisoners getting out; he couldn't cope with people trying to get in. 'Wait here!'

We stood, only waiting for each other to turn tail.

'What's this then, lads?' The voice, loud and strong, belied the tiny man now accompanying the sentry. We stumbled explanations, together and separately. How could a man hardly bigger than us have attained the exalted rank of sergeant? But he listened, not unkindly.

'Do we know him, Jack?'

The sentry shook his head.

'Well, lads, we've got a problem. We don't know the feller you want. You're not supposed to be here, you know!'

I pointed vaguely and desperately to the huts on the left. 'He's just in that hut there, he told us.'

We'd never understand his reasons. He mumbled something to the sentry. The sentry took a keen interest in some far distant object in the opposite direction. The sergeant glanced up and down the road, placed one foot on the lowest strand of barbed wire, and raised the higher one. 'Quick!'

We were in.

'You've got ten minutes. Never seen you, don't know you, and if I catch you I'll kick your arses.'

We had no idea what hut Klaus was in.

A POW appeared at the door of the first hut. Called to us. We didn't understand a word.

'Klaus Shuster?'

He made some reply, disappeared inside. We waited. But the door remained tight shut.

'Let's go home' said Dennis. But we moved along to another open door, and an elderly prisoner with ruddy complexion.

'Klaus Shuster, bitte?'

With a surprised smile, and a pat on the head, he pointed to the hut opposite. We gave him our best 'Danke gute!'

He said something as we retreated; we hadn't a clue.

Hubbub from the hut. We knocked. 'They can't hear us – there's another door inside.' The second door was ajar.

'Go on, knock!'

'You. I asked the soldier on the gate.'

Dennis rapped lightly.

'That's no good – like this!' My puny fists pounded the door, which swung open to disclose an ill-lit, fuggy-atmosphered mass of humanity. The nearest was sitting darning a large grey sock. He looked up, astounded.

'K – K – Klaus Shuster?'

Tall, lank blond hair, blue eyes. It was lucky we understood little German, for his face contorted as he swore, before abruptly turning his back.

The whole room went still. Two lines of faces, gazing down at us from the rows of bunks.

An older man spoke to the blond – perhaps admonished him. Then called down the hut 'Klaus, kommen sie hier.' He pointed to the far end. Through fug and fear, we couldn't recognize our friend, but headed down the room. The centre aisle was clear, apart from two iron stoves. The heat from the stoves and the packed humanity couldn't dispel the cold fear that gripped us, as a heavily built figure leapt from his top bunk to block our way. Between his teeth he muttered something that wasn't friendly.

We stood rooted. He continued to stand threateningly before us, till a companion took him by the arm and drew him back.

'Kinder! – Children!'

From the far end, a familiar figure appeared. Klaus, arms protectively around us, led us to his bunk.

The older man in the bunk above was introduced as Sep. The younger man next door was Vitus. We'd heard about Sep and Vitus. We asked Klaus about the blond, and the thick-set man. They, and one or two more, were glaring in our direction.

'Do not let them trouble you. They do not like the English – they do not like anyone.'

Vitus added quietly: 'They are Nazis.'

'They are few,' said Klaus. 'Most are good, very good, men. No one will allow you to be harmed.'

Our fears disappeared. We could now relish the idea of being in a POW camp, right in the middle of our enemies.

Klaus told us the Slaters had disagreed with the authorities, as they did with everyone. He'd been transferred to a larger farm, with Sep and Vitus. No facilities existed for post between prisoners and the civilian population, so he couldn't let us know.

Our ten minutes were up. How could we evade the English sergeant? We didn't want to test his veiled threat to kick our arses . . .

'Don't worry,' said Klaus. 'There is a secret way out of the camp.'

Behind the huts, out of sight of the road, the field was only surrounded by a hedge and fence, relics from 1939. And although the gate was festooned with barbed wire, to reassure civilians, the sides and rear were not.

We were proud to be the first civilians to enter the camp (doctors and clergy didn't count). Only later, Klaus disclosed we'd been pipped at the post by a girl not much older than ourselves. We knew her; but all she would say was that she hadn't entered by the gate, like us, and that her visits were for a vastly different purpose . . .

We found a gap in the hedge. Down the narrow lane to meet the main street, and the road for home.

CHAPTER 15
D-DAY

THE MOST CRITICAL DAY

DEAREST MUMMY
Can hardly contain myself now the invasion has started and I want to congratulate Daddy. We had the RAF march-past today and can see the planes roaring over and hear the guns. Could you please cut out anything of interest about the invasion and send it? We are going to have regular 'news' here and we are getting jolly excited. Hooray for Churchill, but it's not all glorious. We are praying hard. Please write.

Best of love, Jill

I put my picture of Daddy up last night, and everyone going past had to salute it . . . great fun. One of the other girls' father is also in the RAF.

Today, I have the urge to write about the most critical and moving day of our history. At last, after the dark anxious days we can hit back, while thousands of our troops are moving into action across the Channel. 'The End of the Beginning' at least! But how many anxious mothers are thinking of their sons who might never return but are proud to be the first to suffer in the great and glorious cause of the invasion which means peace. The world goes on as usual, as it must, but in everyone's heart there is a conscious feeling of victory but we must never forget the men who are fighting for us and their country. The British Lion is certainly very awake and his jaws are crushing the mighty weight of the German war machine. In the quietness of the chapel we pray for the valiant men. The Tommies who loved peace but can move in anger to war for their country and loved ones.

Girl, aged fifteen, Hampshire

CHAPTER 16 FLYING BOMBS AND V2S

1944 FLYING BOMBS

ON 16 JUNE we woke early in our dormitories to hear a peculiar sound in the sky – a phut, phut – with machine-gun fire. Eventually it was announced that the long-awaited Flying Bomb offensive had started. We became very blasé with these little jet-planes streaking overhead, only making a dive under the table when it cut out, and there was that long ominous pause before it crashed and exploded. One sunny afternoon, before the AA gunners, planes and barrage balloons had sorted themselves out, we had the remarkable sight of a Hawker Tempest chasing one of the buzz-bombs straight down the playing-field firing cannon-shell at it. Regrettably the V1 crashed on a residential area beyond Epsom. The school authorities became worried about the constant interruption, so we were sent home, except for those taking exams, many of whom did far better than expected, since allowances were made for their having to dive under the desks several times during each exam.

Boy, aged sixteen, Sussex

1944 V2S

ON 8 SEPTEMBER I was standing in our lounge when the windows shook violently. First accounts said a gasometer had exploded, but eventually censors released the news that the first of the V2 rockets had landed at Chiswick. Fortunately Putney was spared the devastation caused by these 'whispering giants' – sometimes one could just hear the rush of air before the explosion. But by the time the last rocket fell on Orpington on 27 March 1945, 2,700 people had been killed and 6,500 seriously injured. While less accurate than the Flying Bomb, it was more deadly, leaving a crater 30 ft. deep.

Boy, aged sixteen, Sussex

1944 RESCUE WORK

THE TERRACE HAD FALLEN like a pack of cards. These were terraced houses (with an area at the front), reached by a bridge to the front door, one storey up. This front wall was supporting the remaining structure. The entire back walls had collapsed. The floors therefore hung down on one another.

One family, husband, wife and two girls, had taken shelter that night (at the back) when the husband returned to make tea. He heard the bomb approaching and ran to the front of his house to see where it went. It struck the back of his house, completely destroying it, leaving him unhurt on the remains of the small concrete bridge to his front door. Unfortunately his good fortune was not shared by his family. We found them all dead from the blast in their Anderson shelter. The demented husband was taken to hospital for sedation.

The remaining houses in the terrace had to be searched. A check on the shelters indicated approximately four people unaccounted for. The floors had to be carefully jacked-up, and holes made through each, to enable us to enter and search. As I was young and slim, I was asked to go in. The first house offered nothing. We moved next door. A hole was made and I slid in with my torch. Up ahead I could hear a moan and I cleared a way through each floor. I uncovered a middle-aged woman lying on a sofa. She was still alive and apparently unhurt, although her body was supporting the timbers above. Beside her, on the floor and free of debris, lay her sister. She was dead. I signalled the rescue squad and withdrew. They were able to extricate them, the first going to the hospital, the second to the mortuary.

The next house I slid into, the situation was similar. In this one I found a young woman crouching over her child. Both

The awful moment of silence when the putt-putting engine cut out, and you counted, waiting for the bang. June 1944.

were dead, though the child was still warm, indicating that the mother's protective instinct had saved the child from the blast, only for it to suffocate.

Boy, aged sixteen, London

1944 RUNNING REPAIRS

DAD SAID HE WOULD have a go at the upstairs ceiling tomorrow, and we retired exhausted.

The next day dawned bright and hot. We opened those window-frames that were openable, and Dad mounted the step-ladder in the middle bedroom. Placing both hands to the centre of the ceiling he gently eased the whole area back to the rafters. Having achieved this, he released one hand to locate a nail to hammer in and secure.

Suddenly there was a roar and the whole ceiling collapsed, filling the room with dust and debris, which billowed through the window apertures to envelop the house completely.

Neighbours came running, thinking another bomb may have fallen. When the dust cleared, I was able to see my father still standing on the step-ladder and still holding a small piece of ceiling in place. He was completely covered with dust, looking like a statue. I'm afraid that we found it absolutely hilarious, a complete break to the tension we were all subject to. We fell about laughing, much to my father's annoyance, until he too saw the funny side of the incident.

Boy, aged seventeen, London

1944 AFTER THE DOODLEBUG

OVERHEAD CABLES had fallen across the barbed wire and I received a nasty shock on contact.

All around were bits of the girls to whom I had waved so often. Military personnel arrived with large baskets, into which they placed the remains. It was a fearful sight which filled me with rage at such senseless slaughter.

The tension was relieved when a milkman with his horse and float came jogging up. Seeing the road blocked by debris, he attempted to turn his vehicle too sharply and in doing so turned the cart over. Milk bottles were rolling in all directions and milk flowed into the gutters. Many of the rescuers left their life-saving task amongst the ruins to try to retrieve this foolish man's load. Some people have funny priorities.

Boy, aged seventeen, London

1944 FLYING BOMB

IN THE EVENINGS I sometimes rode my bike to the top of Plum Lane, where I could view most of east and south-east London. From this point of view it was possible to see the flight-patterns of the bombs and where they fell. It was a macabre sight, knowing that when the mushroom cloud of smoke came up people were dying in horrible circumstances. I never felt myself at risk – the optimism of youth, no doubt!

Once, on returning along Red Road on a day when there was a low cloud base, I was suddenly confronted with a flying bomb coming straight at me through the clouds. It happened so quickly I was unable to get off my bike before it exploded in an allotment 50 yards away. I was thrown through the air to land further up the road from my bike. The soft earth of the allotment had saved me, as the blast was mainly upward. I was dazed and suffered some concussion.

Boy, aged seventeen, London

1945 THE END OF THE FLYING BOMBS

AS THE NEW YEAR 1945 progressed, the attacks diminished. People came to ignore the occasional explosion.

I recall one day seeing a vapour trail cross the sky, followed shortly by a double bang. That rocket, I was to learn, fell behind Selfridges in London.

Another memory was of a rocket which had failed to explode and was stuck in a garden in Abbey Wood like a gigantic dart.

People you knew were no longer around. Schoolfriends had been killed. Familiar buildings destroyed.

Things started to return to normal. Repairs were being made to houses. Glass was being put back into window-frames, ceilings were being replaced, new doors and casements fitted. Houses began to recover their pre-war look.

However, with this relaxation came the return of the Englishman's reserve and isolation. People who had shared misery and laughter only six months previously now hardly acknowledged each other when they met. This was also felt acutely by the Civil Defence, which had once again become a 'burden on the rate-payer'.

Our armies were streaming across Europe and 'our war' seemed to be nearly over.

I regret the Civil Defence organization had to die; it just faded away. Although it was officially stood down on 8 May 1945, it was by that time virtually non-existent. All the local wardens were unpaid volunteers, except two lady wardens paid by the council. They were exhausted by the demands made on them over previous years and would not report when there was no likelihood of their being needed.

Boy, aged seventeen, London

CHAPTER 17

VICTORY!

VE DAY

OUR STREET HAD A GREAT BIG PARTY and everyone painted their houses red, white and blue. We had nice things to eat, even a cake.

My Aunty Al got her piano out and played in the street and everyone was dancing and singing. The party went on all through the night. Everybody had a great time. In school next day we all got an apple from Canada each; it was beautiful, big and red.

Girl, aged six, Liverpool

DANCING IN THE STREET

WE HAD A DANCE IN THE STREET. I was in great demand, being fifteen and big, and able to dance. It felt quite delightfully wicked, dancing with all the young wives of the soldiers, sailors and airmen, who weren't there. It was hot, and they only wore thin dresses,and they danced very freely that night, and didn't seem to care.

There was a big bonfire, afterwards. I got the whole incendiary bomb, that I'd kept all during the war, and threw it on the bonfire, but it still didn't go off.

Boy, aged fifteen, Tyneside

VE NIGHT IN EDINBURGH

ON VE NIGHT my father was still away in the Army. My mother said 'C'mon, let's go riding on the tram.' We went right across Edinburgh to Corstophine for 1*d*. There were people climbing up the outside of the tram – you couldn't see out of the windows, it was smothered in drunks. Every vehicle moving was covered with people drinking from bottles. Even high up on the trams, near the sparkling electric high-tension wires. Dozens of American sailors with a girl on each arm. You went up to them and said 'Got any gum, chum?' They always gave you some; their blouses were full of packets of gum.

Boy, aged ten

A BONFIRE

MY GRANDMOTHER had five sons coming home, who she called the Royals, as they were in the Royal Navy, Royal Air Force and Royal Liverpool Regiment. She said she would have a bonfire. She did have one, and she was dancing all round it until she found that my grandfather had put all her furniture on the bonfire.

Girl, aged eleven, Liverpool

'UP WEST'

I WAS STAYING with a maiden aunt in London and was taken 'up West' with many thousand other, cheering, laughing, crying, singing people. I had never seen anything like it, and so was totally unprepared for a bear-hug from an American soldier, who lifted me right off my feet and swung me round, and landed me a smacking kiss. Hallelujah!

Later, we gathered outside Buckingham Palace. Who cares about the rain? We began to chant 'We want the King! We want the King!'

I was yelling down the ear of a Canadian soldier. He turned to me. 'Some of us don't,' he said.

'What you want to come here for, then?' I asked.

He shrugged and made no reply, just went on standing in the rain.

Girl, aged fourteen, London

I SMELL PINEAPPLE

Daily Mail

NO 15,290 ONE PENNY FOR KING AND EMPIRE TUESDAY, MAY 8, 1945

VICTORY EDITION

TUESday FIELD-DAY

3-POWER ANNOUNCEMENT TO-DAY; BUT BRITAIN KNEW LAST NIGHT

VE-DAY—IT'S ALL OVER

All quiet till 9 p.m.—then the London crowds went mad in the West End

PM put off the big speech

UNTIL TO-DAY

By WILSON BROADBENT, Diplomatic Correspondent

GERMANY surrendered unconditionally to the Allies yesterday. But there will be no official announcement of victory until 3 p.m. to-day—officially described as VE-Day—when Mr. Churchill will give the news to the world.

He will follow this with a[n] ... address to the House of Commons, and at 9 p.m. the King will speak to Britain and the Empire.

CZECHS TOLD TO 'SMASH GERMANS'

TARAKAN NEARLY CUT IN TWO

Victory lunch

U.S. made it VE-Day all the same

Work walk-out

From DON IDDON, Daily Mail Correspondent

New York, Monday.

THIS was VE-Day in the U.S.—official or not.

Jammed roads

SYMBOL of the mood of London ...

The war still goes on here—

PRAGUE BOMBED AS SS SHOOT CZECH CIVILIANS

GERMAN bombs are falling on Prague for the first time as the war in Europe enters its last hours. In defiance of surrender orders, German forces in Czecho-Slovakia are fighting on. They are venting their last spite on the Czechs, shooting them down ruthlessly in the streets of the capital.

Pilsen kisses

Beacon chain begun by Piccadilly's bonfires

BY GUY RAMSEY

LONDON, dead from six until nine, suddenly broke into victory life last night. Suddenly, spontaneously, deliriously. The people of London, denied VE-Day officially, held their own jubilation. "VE-Day may be to-morrow," they said, "but the war is over to-night." Bonfires blazed from Piccadilly to Wapping.

The sky once lit by the glare of the blitz shone red with the Victory glow. The last trains departed from the West End unregarded. The pent-up spirits of the throng, the polyglot throng that is London in war-time, burst out, and by 11 o'clock the capital was ablaze with enthusiasm.

Processions formed up out of nowhere, disintegrating for no reason, to re-form somewhere else. Waving flags, marching in step, with linked arms or half-embraced, the people strode down the great thoroughfares—Piccadilly, Regent-street, the Mall, to the portals of Buckingham Palace.

They marched and counter-marched so as not to get too far from the centre. And from them, in harmony and discord, rose song. The songs of the last war, the songs of a century ago. The songs of the beginning of this war—"Roll out the Barrel" and "Tipperary"; "Ilkla Moor" and "Loch Lomond"; "Bless 'em All" and "Pack Up Your Troubles."

ROCKETS AND SONGS

Continued in Back Page, Col. 6

SCHACHT SAVED BY 'FIFTH'

Niemoller, too

Daily Mail Special Correspondent

'Evil Hitler'

WEATHER

GOEBBELS' BODY IN A SHELTER

GOEBBELS, the German Propaganda Minister, his wife, and five children have been found dead in Berlin.

MONTY MEETS ROKOSSOVSKY

4 toasts at lunch

Home by searchlight

ARRESTED POLES MAY BE TRIED BY LUBLIN

FATHER'S RETURN

I WENT TO LIME STREET STATION to meet 'The Picture on the Wall'.

Because the only thing I had seen of my Dad was the photo that hung on the wall. And when I played tig and ran across the tables, I always felt guilty in front of that picture.

Boy, Liverpool

WAR CRIMINALS

THEY ARE GOING TO TRY old Fatty Goering and Rudolf Hess too, as war criminals. All the ones who didn't kill themselves in May, before the surrender. It doesn't seem fair. All the wicked ones *killed* themselves – Himmler, Hitler, Goebbels. Old Fatty Goering was only a laugh – he was in the *Beano* and the *Dandy* – no one ever took him seriously. Hess flew to this country, at the risk of his own life, to try for peace. They wouldn't even *talk* to him. Was that *his* fault? And poor old Lord Haw-Haw, too. I mean, old Haw-Haw kept us laughing, in the worst times of the war. You might as well try Tommy Handley as a war criminal and traitor. Besides, Haw-Haw can't be a traitor to the British, he was an American citizen, and broadcast when America wasn't even at war . . .

We had a debate about war criminals in the Sixth Form and they were all being so pious and righteous – it made me sick. So I got up and really let loose.

What about *our* war criminals? What about Butcher Harris of Bomber Command, who burnt 100,000 women and children alive, in the Hamburg Fire-typhoon? What about Churchill and Truman, who atom-bombed Hiroshima and Nagasaki? They were all war criminals too. But I suppose you only get tried as a war criminal if you're on the losing side. Otherwise you are a hero!

I expected to get slammed to hell by the rest of the class. But one or two more spoke up the same way, and there was a lot of clapping, and then suddenly a lot of excitement and cheering, and we passed a motion to have Churchill and Roosevelt and Truman and Harris tried as war criminals. Somebody said Harris would say he was only obeying orders.

Old Puggie Anderson, our English teacher, gave me a funny look. Then he said it was about time I went to university, because I had this need to discuss.

Boy, aged sixteen, Tyneside

HER MAJESTY THE QUEEN: ONE OF THE MOST MEMORABLE NIGHTS OF MY LIFE

I REMEMBER THE THRILL and relief after the previous day's waiting for the Prime Minister's announcement of the end of the War in Europe. My parents went out on the balcony in response to the huge crowds outside. I think we went on the balcony nearly every hour, six times, and then when the excitement of the floodlights being switched on got through to us, my sister and I realized we couldn't see what the crowds were enjoying. My mother had put on her tiara for the occasion, so we asked my parents if we could go out and see for ourselves. I remember we were terrified of being recognized, so I pulled my uniform cap well down over my eyes. A grenadier officer amongst our party of about sixteen people said he refused to be seen in the company of another officer improperly dressed, so I had to put my cap on normally. We cheered the King and Queen on the balcony and then walked miles through the streets. I remember lines of unknown people linking arms and walking down Whitehall, all of us just swept along on a tide of happiness and relief. I remember the amazement of my cousin, just back from four and a half years in a Prisoner of War camp, walking freely with his family in the friendly throng. And I also remember when someone exchanged hats with a Dutch sailor, the poor man coming along with us in order to get his cap back. After crossing Green Park we stood outside and shouted 'We want the King', and we were successful in seeing my parents on the balcony, having cheated slightly because we sent a message into the house to say we were waiting outside. I think it was one of the most memorable nights of my life.

The Queen talking to Godfrey Talbot, broadcast in a BBC radio documentary The Way We Were, *transmitted on Radio 4, 8 May 1985*

8th June, 1946

TO-DAY, AS WE CELEBRATE VICTORY, I send this personal message to you and all other boys and girls at school. For you have shared in the hardships and dangers of a total war and you have shared no less in the triumph of the Allied Nations.

I know you will always feel proud to belong to a country which was capable of such supreme effort; proud, too, of parents and elder brothers and sisters who by their courage, endurance and enterprise brought victory. May these qualities be yours as you grow up and join in the common effort to establish among the nations of the world unity and peace.

George R.I.

ACKNOWLEDGEMENTS

Photographs: Bodleian Library: page 21, Hulton Deutsch: pages 25, 27, 29, 32, 33, 36, 67, 68, 94, 98, 123, 126, 128, 129, Imperial War Museum: pages 37, 71, 75, 81, 93, 102, 130, 139, 143, 147, 151, Popperfoto: page 104, Solo Syndication: pages 62, 64, 114, Syndication International: pages 50–51, 78, 88–89, 105, Topham Picture Source: pages 14, 22–23, 24, 39, 69, 82, 148, 150, 161, 178–179, 185, 191, University of Reading: pages 164, 169.
Map on page 47 redrawn by Raymond Turvey.

Grateful acknowledgement is made to the following for permission to reprint previously published or broadcast material
The British Broadcasting Corporation: two excerpts from 1939 radio broadcasts (pages 36–37, 71).
An excerpt from *Living through the Blitz* by Tom Harrison (Penguin Books, 1978, first published in the UK by Collins), copyright © The Trustees of the Mass-Observation Archive, 1976. Reproduced by permission of Penguin Books Ltd. (pages 100–106).
Sheil Land: excerpt from *The World is a Wedding* by Bernard Kops. (McGibbon and Kee, 1963, now published by Valentine Mitchell) (pages 91–96).
© H M Queen Elizabeth II: memories of VE Day given to Godfrey Talbot, broadcast in *The Way We Were* on BBC Radio 4, 8 May 1985 (pages 187–88).
Norman Longmate: two excerpts from *How We Lived Then* by Norman Longmate (Hutchinson 1971) (pages 118–119, 152).
Macdonald and Charles Scribner's Sons: excerpt from *The Hardest Day* by Alfred Price, copyright © 1979 Alfred Price (page 77).

Every effort has been made to trace copyright holders.
We would be grateful to hear from any copyright holders not acknowledged here.

DEAD IN THE WATER

July, 1923, and Daisy has been invited by an American magazine to cover the Henley Regatta. But unknown to her, she steps into a class war between two members of the Oxford rowing team. Cox Horace Bott – a shopkeeper's son, has always hated rower Basil DeLancey – younger son of an earl and all-round cad and bully. And after a particularly brutal public humiliation by DeLancey, Bott swears revenge – so when DeLancey keels over and dies mid-race, it would seem he's made good his promise.

DEAD IN THE WATER

DEAD IN THE WATER

by

Carola Dunn

Magna Large Print Books
Long Preston, North Yorkshire,
BD23 4ND, England.

British Library Cataloguing in Publication Data.

Dunn, Carola
Dead in the water.

A catalogue record of this book is
available from the British Library

ISBN 978-0-7505-3397-3

First published in Great Britain in 2010 by Robinson
an imprint of Constable & Robinson

Published in Large Print 2011 by arrangement with
Constable & Robinson Ltd.

Magna Large Print is an imprint of Library Magna Books Ltd.

Printed and bound in Great Britain by
T.J. (International) Ltd., Cornwall, PL28 8RW

ACKNOWLEDGMENTS

My thanks to Todd Jesdale, rowing coach of the Cincinnati Juniors and the National Junior Team Boys, and to Phil Holmes, University of Oregon rowing coach, for information and technical advice on rowing and racing boats in general.

Thanks also to Richard S. Goddard, Secretary of the Henley Royal Regatta, for detailed information on the Regatta of 1923, including the experimental course, the names of every rower in every race, and the disasters that overtook several crews. No one, I hasten to add, was murdered.

Any errors, omissions, inventions, or alterations of fact are entirely mine.

CHAPTER 1

Daisy paused at the top of the brick steps leading down from the terrace. The negro butler had said Lady Cheringham was to be found in the back garden, but there was no sign of Daisy's aunt.

On either side of the steps, roses flourished, perfuming the still air. From the bottom step, a gravel path cut across the lawn, which, shaded in part by a huge chestnut, sloped smooth as a bowling green to the river. The grey-green Thames slid past around the bend, unhurried yet relentless on its way to London and the sea.

Upstream, Daisy saw the trees on Temple Island, hiding the little town of Henley-on-Thames. Downstream, the white buildings of Hambleden Mill and the pilings dividing the boat channel from the millrace marked the position of the lock and weir. Beyond the towpath on the far bank of the river, the Berkshire side, Remenham Hill rose to a wooded crown. On the near side, at the foot of the lawn, was a long, boat-house half-hidden by shrubs and a rampant lilac-flowered clematis. From it, a plank landing-stage ran along the bank, with two bright-cushioned skiffs moored there side by side. On the landing-stage stood two hatless girls in summer frocks, one yellow, one blue.

Daisy took off her hat with a sigh of relief. The water-cooled breeze riffled through the honey-brown curls of her shingled hair.

The two girls were gazing upstream, hands shading their eyes against the westering sun, still high in a cloudless sky. From her vantage point, Daisy followed their gaze and spotted a racing eight emerging from the narrows to the north of the island. Foreshortened by distance, the slender boat crawled towards them like an odd sort of insect, oars rising and dipping in unison on either side. The cox's voice floated across the water.

'Got you!' The triumphant exclamation came from nearby, in a female voice.

Looking down, Daisy saw a spotted brown-linen rear end backing cautiously out of the rosebed, followed by a broad-brimmed straw hat.

'Hullo, Aunt Cynthia.'

'I keep telling him chopping off their heads won't kill them.' Lady Cheringham, straightening, brandished a muddy-gloved hand clutching a dandelion with a twelve-inch root. Her lean face, weathered by decades of tropic climes, broke into smile. 'Hullo, Daisy. Oh dear, is it past four already?'

Daisy started down. 'Only quarter past.

The train was dead on time and your man was waiting at the station.' On the bottom step, she nearly fell over a garden syringe.

'Careful, dear! I was spraying the roses, dealing death to those dratted greenfly, when I noticed the dandelion.'

'Not deadly poison, I hope? It seems to have dripped on your blouse.'

'Only tobacco-water, but perhaps I'd better go and wash it off. It does stain horribly,' Lady Cheringham dropped the dandelion's corpse by the sprayer. 'Bister simply won't admit that hoes are useless against these brutes, but that's what comes of having a chauffeur-cum-gardener-cum-handyman.'

'I rather like dandelions,' Daisy confessed.

'Never fear, however many we gardeners slaughter, there will always be more.' She stooped to pick up a trug, loaded with pink and yellow cut roses, which lay on the grass at her feet. 'As a matter of fact, I really just came out to deadhead and cut some roses for your room – you're sure you don't mind sharing with your cousin? The house is packed to the rafters.'

'Nor at all. In fact it's spiffing. It will give me a chance to get to know her better. Now that Patsy's grown up, that five-year gulf between us won't seem so vast.'

'Tish, dear. Patricia insists on being called Tish these days, Heaven knows why. I dare say I should be thankful they don't address each other by their surnames, she and her friend Dottie.' Lady Cheringham waved at the two girls by the river. 'I gather that is the custom at the ladies' colleges, apeing the men. So unsuitable. I can't help wondering if it was quite wise to entrust Patricia's upbringing to Rupert's brother while we were abroad.' She sighed.

'I suppose being brought up in the household of two Oxford dons must have inclined Pat ... Tish to academic life.'

Daisy hoped she didn't sound envious. Neither family nor school had prepared her for university studies. In fact, the idea had never dawned on her until the newspapers reported Oxford University's admission of women to degrees, just three years ago, in 1920. Already twenty-two and struggling to earn a living, she had recognised that her chance was past.

Her aunt said cheerfully, 'Oh, Patricia has to swot like mad. She isn't really any more intellectual than I am. Luckily – since I suspect she has an understanding with Rollo Frieth. A charming young man but not brainy, though he's an undergrad at Ambrose College.'

'That's the crew you're putting up for the Regatta, isn't it?'

'Yes, Rupert's nephew rows for Ambrose. Christened Erasmus, poor boy, but everyone calls him Cherry.'

'I've met him, I'm sure, more than once but years ago.'

'Very likely. He's practically a brother to Patricia. You'll see him at tea, and meet the rest.'

'I think I saw them rowing this way.'

They both turned and looked at the river. The boat was a couple of hundred yards off, drifting downstream towards them, the rowers in their white shirts and maroon caps resting on their oars. Sounds of altercation reached Daisy's ears, though she could not make out the words.

'I must go and change, and deal with these flowers.' Lady Cheringham said hastily. 'Do go on down and say hullo to Patricia, since she stayed home especially to welcome you. That's Dottie Carrick with her.'

Daisy walked down to the landing-stage. At the sound of her footsteps on the gravel, Patricia – Tish – and her friend looked round.

Tish was a pretty, fair-haired girl, just turned twenty. Slim in pale blue pique, a dark blue sash at the low waist, her figure was admirably suited to the bustless, hipless fashion of the day, Daisy noted enviously.

She didn't know her cousin well. Sir Rupert Cheringham, in the Colonial Service, had left his only child to be brought up by his brother and sister-in-law, both lecturers at Oxford University. Visits between that academic family and Daisy's aristocratic family had been few and fleeting, though Lady Cheringham was Daisy's mother's sister.

To Daisy, Oxford was a railway station, or a place one motored through, between London and her ancestral home in Gloucestershire, now the property of Cousin Edgar. Daisy's brother, Gervaise, might have gone to Oxford had the War not intervened. His death had eliminated that connection. The death of her fiancé had left her uninterested in any men who might otherwise have invited her to May Balls after the War, when demobbed officers flocked to the universities.

Gervaise and Michael were five years gone. The new man in Daisy's life had taken his degree at the plebeian University of Manchester.

'Hullo, Daisy!' Patricia greeted her. 'You haven't brought Mr. Fletcher with you? Alec Fletcher is Daisy's fiancé.' she explained to her friend.

'He can't get away till Friday night. He's booked at the White Hart.'

'Just as well. Mother would have to stuff him into the attics. Half the men are on camp-beds already, sharing rooms, with the cox in the linen-room because he's the only one short enough! Oh, you don't know Dottie, do you? Dorothy Carrick, a college friend – and she's engaged to Cherry. Dottie, my cousin, Daisy Dalrymple.'

Miss Carrick, round-faced, bespectacled, rather sallow, her painfully straight, mousy hair cut in an uncompromising short bob, looked every inch the female undergrad. A frock printed with large, yellow cabbage roses did nothing for her stocky form. Daisy, always at odds with her own unfashionable curves, felt for her.

'How do you do, Miss Carrick,' she said. 'Mr. Cheringham's rowing, isn't he?'

Dottie smiled, a boyish grin revealing even, very white teeth. 'That's right. In both the Thames Cup and the Visitors' – the eight and the coxless four, that is.' Her voice was a beautiful, mellifluous contralto. 'The four won their heat this morning, and we're waiting to hear about the eight. You're here to write about the Regatta, Tish said?'

'Yes, for an American magazine. Harvard and some others often send crews over so the races get reported, especially when an American boat wins, but my editor wants an article on the social side of things.'

'Champagne and strawberries in the Stewards' Enclosure?' said Tish.

'Yes, that sort of stuff. Ascot hats, and watching the fireworks from Phyllis Court. A friend of my father's is a member, and the husband of a friend of mine is a member of the Stewards' Enclosure, and they've both kindly invited me. I'm going to throw in a bit about the fun-fair, too.'

'Hoi polloi's share of the social side,' Dottie observed. 'Jolly good. I'll help you do the research. I've been dying to go on the Ferris wheel.'

Tish shuddered. 'Rather you than me! But I'm a dab hand at a coconut shy. Let's talk Cherry and Rollo into going with us after tea.'

'Rollo?' said Daisy disingenuously.

'Roland Frieth.' Tish's fair skin flushed with delicate colour, as good as confirming her mother's report to Daisy. 'He's Cherry's chum.'

'And the Ambrose captain.' Dottie put in. 'Here they are now.'

'Keep out of their way while they get the boat out,' Tish advised. 'It's serious business.'

Head bobbing, a solitary moorhen scurried for the safety of the middle of the river as the boat nosed gently in alongside the landing-stage, behind the two skiffs tied up there. The cox, short and wiry, with bare, suntanned knees knobbly beneath his maroon rowing shorts, jumped out. He held the stern steady while his crew counted off.

'Bow.' Daisy recognised Tish's cousin, Erasmus 'Cherry' Cheringham, a fair, serious-looking young man much larger and more muscular than she remembered him.

'Two.' Another large, muscular young man, dark-haired. He gave a quick, cheerful wave. Daisy assumed they had won the heat.

'Three.'

'Four.'

'Five.'

'Six.'

'Seven.'

'Stroke.' In contrast to the rest, the stroke looked sulky. Otherwise, apart from varying hair colour, they could have been septuplets for all the difference Daisy could see.

On the cox's command, eight large, muscular, perspiring young men stepped out onto the planks, making them bounce beneath Daisy's feet. She hastily moved backwards onto solid ground.

Bow and stroke held the boat while the other six laid the oars out on the grass. Then all eight oarsmen bent to the boat.

'Hands on,' ordered the cox. 'Ready. Up!'

With one smooth motion, the boat rose from the water and swung upside-down over their heads.

'Ready. Split!'

The elongated, many-legged tortoise tramped towards the boat-house. 'We took the trick,' it called gaily as it departed. 'Be with you in a minute, ladies.'

Tish and Dottie each picked up one of the maroon, green, and white banded oars and followed. Eyeing the twelve-foot length and dripping blades of the remaining sweeps, Daisy decided against lending her aid.

The cox also stayed behind, staring after the rowers with a scowl on his face.

'I thought you won,' Daisy said with puzzled sympathy.

'What? Oh, yes, we won all right.' Orotund Oxfordian contended uneasily with a flat, nasal whine straight from the Midlands. 'We may be a small college and we wouldn't stand a chance in the Grand, but we've a good shot at the Thames Cup.'

'You don't look very happy about it. Oh, I'm Daisy Dalrymple, by the way, Patricia's cousin.'

'Horace Bott. How do you do, Miss Dalrymple? Of course I'm glad we took the heat,' he went on gloomily, 'but even if we win the final, I'll still be an outsider.'

'Because you don't row?'

'Because I haven't got the right family, or accent, or clothes, or instincts. When I won the scholarship to Ambrose, I thought all I had to do was prove I'd earned it, but I could take a hundred Firsts with Honours and my father would still be a small shopkeeper.'

'There's nothing wrong with being a shopkeeper.' Daisy encouraged him. 'Napoleon said the English were a nation of shopkeepers, but we beat him all the same.'

'Nothing wrong as long as we know our

place,' Bott groused, 'which isn't at Oxford competing with our betters. "Betters," my foot! Half the stuck-up snobs who treat me like dirt only got into Ambrose through their family connections, and with all the private tutoring in the world they'll be lucky to scrape by with Pass Thirds.'

Daisy didn't care for his peevish tone, but she suspected he had reason for his disgruntlement. If Gervaise had gone up to Oxford, it certainly would not have been on the basis of academic brilliance, nor with the intention of excelling academically. She rather thought he would have scorned those who did, and he had certainly not shared her willingness to hobnob with the lower classes.

'Do you join in the other stuff?' she asked, adding vaguely, 'Acting, and debating, and rags, and sports, and so on... Oh, sports, of course.'

'I thought sports'd do it, coxing, and I play racquets – got my Blue in that last year, actually.'

'You play racquets for the university, not just the college? Congratulations.'

'All very well, but the toffs still don't choose to hoist a pint with me after a match,' Bott said resentfully.

His lack of popularity might have less to do with his birth than with the way he wallowed in his grievances, Daisy guessed.

She nearly said so, then thought better of it. He would be sure to take advice amiss, however well-meant, and though she felt sorry for him, she did not like him.

He took a packet of Woodbines from his shirt pocket. 'Smoke?' he offered.

'No, thanks.'

He lit up the cheap cigarette, flicking the match into the river. 'I suppose you never touch anything but Turkish.'

'As a matter of fact, I don't smoke at all. I don't care for the smell of cigarettes.' Pipe smoke was another matter, especially Alec's pipe.

Bott moved a step away, wafting the smoke from her with his hand. 'Sorry. My girl doesn't like it, either. She's coming down this evening – booked a room in the town – so once I've finished this packet, I won't buy another for a few days.' His momentary cheerfulness at the prospect of his girl's arrival faded and gloom returned. 'Can't really afford them, anyway.'

Tempted to start listing the things she couldn't afford, Daisy was saved by the return of the others from the direction of the boat-house. Beside it, the racing shell, too long to fit inside, now rested upside-down on supports.

Three of the men started up the lawn towards the house, a Georgian manor built of age-mellowed red brick with white sash windows. A shout followed them: 'Don't hog all the hot water!'

Tish, Dottie, Cherry, and four others came towards Daisy and Bott.

'Daisy, you remember Cherry?' said Tish.

'Yes, of course.'

'How do you do, Miss Dalrymple?' the fair-haired bow-oarsman greeted her.

'Daisy, please. We're practically cousins, after all.'

A grin lit his, face. 'Daisy it shall be, if you promise never to call me Erasmus.'

'I promise!'

During this exchange of social amenities, two of the men picked up a pair of oars each and returned towards the boathouse, while Daisy heard the dark number two rower say to the cox, 'Jolly good show, Bott.'

'Thanks to St. Theresa's hitting the booms,' the fifth oarsman said sarcastically. He was dark-haired, like Number Two, but his hair was sleeked back with pomade. Daisy thought he was the sulky stroke.

'Lots of boats are hitting, with this experimental course being so deucedly narrow. Bott's steered us dead straight. We'll beat the tar out of Richmond tomorrow.'

'Not if we're all poisoned by those filthy things he smokes.'

Bott gave the stroke a malevolent look, then turned and headed for the house.

'Oh, come on, DeLancey, pack it in,' said

Number Two. 'Not everyone's so frightfully keen on those foul cigars of yours.'

'It sticks in my gullet taking orders from that beastly little pipsqueak twerp,' DeLancey fumed.

'All coxes are small...'

'Bott's no twerp!' Dottie interrupted, flaring up. 'He's brainier than the rest of you put together.'

'Oh, I say,' Cherry protested.

'Well, nearly,' his fiancée affirmed, unrepentant. 'You've got a good mind, my dear old soul, but his is tip-top.' Cherry looked chagrined.

'Better watch it, Miss Carrick,' DeLancey said nastily, 'or you'll be an old maid after all.'

'Here, I say!' Cherry stepped forward. 'You mind your tongue, DeLancey!'

Tish put a hand on his arm. 'Don't come unbuttoned, old thing. The best way to make him eat his words is to stay engaged to Dottie.'

'I shall!' her cousin snapped, 'but I'd like to stuff his rotten words down *his* gullet, all the same.'

'This isn't the time for a dust-up. You've got a race to row tomorrow,' Tish reminded him.

'Common sense and pretty, too,' DeLancey applauded mockingly. 'A girl with your looks is wasted on books and lectures. I'd be glad to show you how to have a good time.'

Tish turned her back on him.

Number Two, his face red with suppressed fury, said through his teeth, 'Didn't I tell you it's your turn to help with the oars, DeLancey?'

'So you did, Captain, so you did.' With insolent slowness, DeLancey strolled towards the remaining two oars.

Captain – so Number Two was Tish's Rollo, as Daisy had already surmised. Fists clenched, he stared after DeLancey, then shrugged and turned back to the others.

'I'm so sorry, Daisy.' Tish apologised unhappily. 'What a welcome!'

Daisy murmured something soothing.

'Oh, didn't introduce Rollo, did I?' The ready blood tinted her cheeks. 'Roland Frieth, the crew captain.'

'And a pretty sorry specimen of a captain you must think me, Miss Dalrymple,' Rollo said ruefully. 'Unable to squash dissension in the ranks.'

'I thought you squashed it very neatly,' Daisy said with a smile. 'The oars are on their way to the boat-house, aren't they?'

They all glanced at DeLancey's retreating back.

'I ought to have introduced him, too.' Tish worried.

Dottie snorted. 'He hardly gave you much opportunity.'

'One of these days,' said Cherry darkly, 'he'll go too far and get his teeth shoved down his precious gullet.'

Rollo shook his head. 'I doubt it. He's a boxing Blue, remember. What I'm afraid of is that one of these days he'll biff Bott.'

'Oh, Bott! He can scramble Bott's brains with my goodwill, as long as he waits till after the Regatta.'

'But, Cherry, he's twice Bott's size!' Dottie protested.

'I can't see that stopping him,' said Rollo. 'For all his pater's an earl, the way he goes around insulting ladies proves he's no gentleman, and he's really got his knife into Bott.'

'Bott's no gentleman either,' Cherry muttered, 'even if he is a bloody genius.'

'Oh darling!' Standing on tiptoe, Dottie kissed his cheek. 'Bott's brains are absolutely the only thing about him I admire. I wouldn't marry him for a million in cash. I mean to say, how could I bear to be called Dottie Bott?'

Laughing, they all moved towards the house.

CHAPTER 2

Afternoon tea was served on the terrace. All the crew were present. Their donning of flannels and blazers seemed to Daisy to reduce them to manageable proportions. Still, even after being introduced to those she had not yet met, she wasn't sure she'd know one from the next if she met them on the river-bank.

Cherry and Rollo stood out not only in their relationship to her cousin, she realised. They were older than the others, about her own age, having fought in the War before going up to Oxford. They were third-year men, as were Horace Bott and Basil DeLancey, the rest being first and second.

Some on garden chairs and benches, some sprawled on cushions on the crazy paving, they lounged about the terrace. Tish presided over the urn and teapot, as her mother had not turned up.

'Shall I go and find Aunt Cynthia?' Daisy offered, suddenly anxious as she recalled the splotches of insecticide on Lady Cheringham's blouse.

Tobacco-water didn't sound very dangerous, however noxious the fumes from cheap cigarettes. But it must contain nicotine and that, she had a feeling, was a deadly toxin in certain circumstances. She had read a book on poisons after the Albert Hall affair, though she couldn't remember the specifics.

'I saw Lady Cheringham out in the front garden when I came down,' Rollo said, 'taking a pair of shears to one of the topiary swans.'

'Mother's so thrilled to have a proper English garden, she finds it hard to drag herself away,' Tish explained.

Cherry grinned. 'And Uncle Rupert can't be pried from his manuscript. You know he's writing his memoirs, Daisy? It seems to be *de rigueur* for retired colonial administrators, a sort of tic, like giving their houses frightful names like "Bulawayo." I'll take him a cup. The servants are run off their feet with this heathen lot to cater to.' He waved a careless hand at his guzzling crew-mates.

'I'll go,' said Daisy. 'I haven't said hullo to Uncle Rupert yet. He's keen on cucumber sandwiches, isn't he?'

She started to pile a plate with the thin-cut, crustless triangles, but Tish, momentarily distracted by handing cups to two suppliants, turned back to stop her.

'I'm afraid Daddy's made a bolt for it,' she said, as guiltily as if she was personally responsible for her father's dereliction of his duty as host. 'He said he couldn't hear himself think with dozens of galumphing athletes in the house, so he packed up the great work and departed for his club. Bister took him to the station when he met you, Daisy. You must have just missed him.'

Cherry laughed, but Rollo looked dismayed.

'Dash it, I'm most frightfully sorry, Tish,' he said. 'You should have told me. I'd have made them shut up.'

'It's all right, you great oaf,' Tish told him lovingly. 'Mother says it's his own fault for agreeing to put up the crew. She's used to accommodating any passing Europeans, of course. To tell the truth, I don't think Father was listening when I proposed inviting you all, so perhaps it will teach him to pay attention to his daughter's words in future!'

'Typical man!' said Dottie, and added something Daisy didn't understand.

Cherry responded in what sounded like the same language.

'Greek,' said Tish, seeing Daisy's blank look, as Dottie and Cherry moved away together to stand by the balustrade, obviously engaged in all-absorbing debate. 'Ancient Greek, not modern. I don't understand it either, just recognise it.'

'It's all Greek to me, too,' Rollo admitted, looking modestly pleased with his little joke. 'I had to do a year of it at school but I never quite got the hang of it. Latin was bad enough.'

'I take it your degree isn't in the Classics,' Daisy said, laughing.

'Not me! Modern Languages. I picked up French like billy-oh when we were over there, and then German in the Army of Occupation. I ended up in liaison, in fact.'

'That must have been jolly interesting.'

'Frightfully. I was really keen. The trouble is, speaking 'em isn't the same thing as writing 'em, let alone reading and discussing the literature, and all that guff. I'd never have got into Ambrose if it weren't for the allowances they made for ex-service men. That and my father having been an Ambrose man. And now I've been ploughed for Schools,' he finished disconsolately.

'Rotten luck,' said Daisy.

'Not really. I should have dropped rowing and concentrated on exams. I know I'm not clever, not like Cherry, who managed to row *and* swot enough to get a decent First in Greats.' Rollo glanced round and lowered his voice. 'Let alone that beastly little squirt Bott, who sailed through with a brilliant Double First without even trying.'

Daisy saw the unfortunate Bott sitting all alone on a bench on the far side of the terrace, moodily sipping his tea. Though once again she was sorry for him, she had no desire to join him. She turned back to Rollo.

'Are you going to try again?' she asked.

'Yes,' said Tish at the same time. They

exchanged a glance.

Before Daisy could request an explanation, DeLancey came up and presented his cup to Tish for a refill. 'Be so kind, fair lady.' he said, his insinuating tone stripping the words of their innocence.

Stony-faced, Tish complied.

With a mocking laugh, DeLancey turned away from her, picked up a nearly empty plate of macaroons, and offered it to Daisy. 'Better have one of these before the ravening hordes finish them off. Sweets to the sweet,' he said unoriginally.

Daisy might not be learned, but she knew her *Hamlet*. 'Do you propose to strew them on my grave, Mr. DeLancey?' she enquired sweetly. 'I assure you, I'm not going to drown myself for unrequited love.'

She took a macaroon – they were, after all, one of her favourites – deliberately with her left hand, making sure her sapphire engagement ring flashed in the sun. The stone was not large, but it was exactly the colour of her eyes, Alec said, the guileless blue eyes which led people to confide in her, including him. Their depths had more than once led him to indiscreet revelations about his cases.

Not an hour ago, Bott had unbosomed himself to her after two minutes' acquaintance. Daisy hoped DeLancey was not going to bare his soul. She didn't want to see it. He was as disagreeable as Bott, and without that miserable little man's excuse.

DeLancey looked rather nonplussed by her riposte. Whatever his course of study, it had presumably not included Shakespeare. He did, however, comprehend the sapphire's significance.

Casting a derisive glance at Dottie, still deep in discussion with Cherry, he said, 'You're engaged too, Miss Dalrymple?' At least he didn't sound insultingly surprised.

'To a policeman.' Daisy informed him.

'To a...! But I thought... That is, isn't Lord Dalrymple your brother?'

'No,' she said baldly, awaiting his reaction with interest.

'Oh, don't tell me you're just another of these bally would-be intellectual women, are you?'

'I'm a writer.'

'Heaven help us! Where did I get the idea you were the Hon. Gervaise's sister?'

'I was.'

'What? Was? I say, he didn't buy it, did he?'

'Yes.' Daisy paused to allow some expression of regret, in vain. 'But you can't have known him. You were only a little boy.' And a very spoilt one, she suspected.

At her dismissive tone, DeLancey flushed. 'Cedric – my brother – knew him in France and used to talk about him when he came home on leave. But Ceddie was invalided out before the end, so I didn't hear... He's staying at Crowswood Place for the Regatta.'

'He's keen on rowing, too?'

'Not particularly, nothing more than messing about in a punt or a skiff on the Isis. But it's quite a social occasion, after all. I say, he and I and some of the others are going dancing at Phyllis Court Club this evening. Would you like to come?'

'No, thanks,' said Daisy. A pity, for though she wasn't keen on dancing, it was just the sort of do she ought to write about. But nothing could induce her to go out for the evening with DeLancey.

Rollo broke in. 'You're not going either, DeLancey. Our Thames Cup heat's first tomorrow. No larking about tonight for anyone. And I want the four in the boat in quarter of an hour to practise a few starts. Tell the others, will you?'

'Oh, I wouldn't care to break up such a charming tête-à-tête,' the stroke said sarcastically.

'I'll tell Cherry,' said Daisy standing up, 'and I'll take a cup of tea to Aunt Cynthia, since it doesn't look as if she's going to turn up.'

As she approached the pair by the balustrade, she heard Dottie say vehemently, 'And in the ninth place...'

'My apologies for nipping your ninth point in the bud,' Daisy interrupted with a chuckle, 'but your captain calls, Cherry. A practise for the four in fifteen minutes.'

'I'm on my way.' He dropped a kiss on Dottie's cheek. 'Don't lose track of number nine, darling. You may persuade me yet.'

Looking after him, Dottie said affectionately, 'The oaf would have conceded by now if I wasn't a year behind him. I'll say this for him, he doesn't refuse to take my arguments seriously just because I'm a woman.'

'He wouldn't dare, would he?' Daisy observed. 'What with his mother being a don.'

Dottie laughed. 'True. He's been properly brought up. Blast, my tea is stone-cold and I've barely had a sip. I hope there's some left.'

They returned together to the tea table. Daisy hunted in vain for a biscuit, a slice of cake, or even a sandwich to take to her aunt. Every last crumb had vanished.

'And what's more, guzzling now won't spoil their appetites for dinner,' said Tish, presiding over the ruins. 'Here's a cup of tea for Mother, Daisy. She'll have to make do. Oh, by the way, no funfair today, I'm afraid, as they're taking the four out now.'

'Never mind. I'd as soon wait for Alec. As for going dancing with that beast DeLancey – catch me! Do you know his brother?'

'Lord DeLancey? No, I've never met him, but I know he's the Earl of Bicester's eldest son, quite a bit older than dear Basil, and

Cherry told me...' Tish stopped and smiled coolly at Bott as he marched up to the table, cup and saucer in hand.

'More tea, Mr. Bott?' she offered. 'You prefer Indian, don't you?'

'What if I do?' the cox growled belligerently.

Daisy escaped. She found Lady Cheringham at the front of the house, tying a delphinium to a stake. Nearby Bister, erstwhile smart chauffeur, dressed now in shirt-sleeves, distinctly disreputable trousers, and a dilapidated straw hat, mowed the circle of lawn enclosed by the carriage-sweep. The green smell of fresh-cut grass vied with the flowers' mingled scents.

'Oh dear, have I missed tea again?' Lady Cheringham gingerly picked her way out of the herbaceous border. 'Thank you, Daisy dear.' She gulped tea.

She still had the tobacco-stained blouse on, probably irremediably stained by now, though its wearer seemed to have suffered no ill effects. The wet patches must have dried fast on such a warm day, Daisy thought. It might be an idea, though, to see if she could find any information about the toxic effects of nicotine, so as to warn her aunt to take care.

After chatting for a few minutes, she went into the house and invaded Sir Rupert's library. Opposite the drawing-room at the back of the house, it had a long library table down the centre, with several straight chairs. Comfortable leather-covered armchairs were grouped about the windows at this season, with small tables beside them. A large walnut kneehole desk stood between the windows, where the light from both would fall on it. Except for the fireplace, the two walls opposite the door and windows were entirely lined with bookshelves.

Though the books were well organized by subject. Daisy had no idea where to start looking and searched the shelves for some time without success. About to give up, she glanced at the volumes lying on the library table. There was Henslow's *Poisonous Plants*, the section on tropical poisons bristling with bookmarks.

Consulting the index, Daisy found tobacco, turned to the page, and skimmed through the details. *Nicotiana* was related to deadly nightshade, she discovered. The long list of horrible symptoms of nicotine poisoning included headache, nausea, dizziness, incoherence, and convulsions, leading to death. Most alarming, as she had vaguely remembered, the stuff was highly dangerous when absorbed through the skin.

She ran to find her aunt.

'Yes, dear,' said Lady Cheringham absently but not at all incoherently, stooping without apparent dizziness to pull an intrusive groundsel from among the pinks, 'I'll go and change. And I'll remind Bister to be sure to keep the shed locked, though I'm sure he already does. Arsenic, you know, for rats, and cyanide for wasps' nests, I believe. Nasty stuff.'

Daisy felt she had done what she could to preserve Aunt Cynthia from a dreadful death.

Even more than tea-time, dinner was devoted to refuelling the crew. Daisy was astounded by the amount of food that disappeared. In the circumstances, conversation was vestigial.

By now, aided by one slight stammer, one fair, wispy moustache, and one set of altogether enviable long, dark, curling eyelashes, Daisy had put names to faces. The four second-year men were Poindexter (the stammerer), Wells (eyelashed), Meredith (moustached), and Leigh.

Daisy sat next to Fosdyke, the only fresher in the crew – in both crews, in fact. A first-rate oarsman, according to Rollo, he had rowed for St. Paul's School before going up to Oxford, and he was a member of the Ambrose four as well as the eight. The double exertion and the presence of his elders no doubt accounted for his being the most taciturn of a taciturn company.

'Please pass the salt,' was the longest

speech Daisy got out of him throughout the meal.

However, as they rose at the end, he stifled an enormous yawn, apologised, and went on, 'I'm for bed. You can't get these chaps to do any serious training, but I like to run a few miles before breakfast.'

'Good for you,' said Daisy with a smile and a suppressed shudder. While she admired those who excelled, she considered sports a torture to be avoided if at all possible.

She felt much the same about bridge, though her mother's passion for the game had forced her to learn. When, as they headed for the drawing-room, Leigh, Meredith, and Wells invited her to join them in a rubber, she shook her head in feigned regret.

'It's kind of you to ask, but I don't play.'

'We'll teach you.' Meredith proposed.

'I'm hopeless at cards. I'm afraid my partner would murder me.'

They protested, but weakly. She held firm, so they shanghaied Poindexter, who wanted to write a letter, promising him the first dummy hand.

Lady Cheringham had already settled down with a gardening book. Daisy strolled out through the French windows onto the terrace. The sun had set, but the western sky was a blaze of colour, reflected in the shimmering pink river, and it would be light for an hour or more yet.

Tish and Rollo, Dottie and Cherry were all on the terrace, very plainly paired off. Daisy didn't want to disturb them. She ambled down to the river-bank, missing Alec.

Tomorrow evening she'd have him to herself, for the whole weekend. Fond as she was of his daughter, Belinda, the prospect was heavenly. He had promised not to give Scotland Yard a telephone number for contacting him. Only one thing could spoil their weekend: a vital case arising tomorrow, before he got away. Daisy knew and accepted that marrying a detective was not going to be easy. She didn't have to dwell on that aspect of things, though. She started to plan their time together.

A single-sculler slid by up-river with long, lazy-looking strokes, setting a family of grebes bobbing on the V of dark ripples on the rosy water. Then a motor-launch *put-putted* round the bend from Hambleden Lock, bound for a mooring in the town. Its whistle shrieked a warning at the sculler. As the engine noise died away, the raucous music of a steam calliope, mellowed by distance, floated down the river from the fair-ground. Daisy was glad they hadn't been able to go this evening. Now she had an excuse to get Alec onto the Ferris wheel, where a kiss at the top was practically *de rigueur*.

'Damn!' She slapped her bare arm, squishing a mosquito. Too late – it left a bloody splodge.

A couple more whined about her head. Scrubbing her arm with her spit-dampened handkerchief she hastened back towards the house.

Two figures stood at the balustrade, at opposite sides of the steps, darkly silhouetted against the drawing-room windows. Two red points of light glowed in the growing dusk.

The form to Daisy's right was rather smaller than the other. Horace Bott, she thought, and his Woodbines. A whiff of cheap cigarette smoke fought its way to her nostrils through the heavy perfume of the roses.

She sighed. She couldn't very well march past without exchanging a word or two, but at least the smoke would keep the mosquitoes at bay.

As she ascended the steps, the other man turned slightly to watch her. By the light from the windows, she recognised Basil DeLancey, and a moment later the choking stench of his cigar hit her. An expensive cigar, no doubt, but the smell was perfectly beastly, quite capable of slaying mosquitoes in flight by the thousands.

She coughed. Instantly, two red-glowing points arced down to land among the rose-bushes.

'Oh *blast!*' Daisy muttered to herself.

It looked as if both of them wanted to

speak to her. If she paused at the top and let them converge on her, she'd find herself acting as a shield against DeLancey's Bott-shots. Perhaps she could sail through between Scylla and Charybdis with a 'Heavenly evening! Goodnight.'

'Heavenly evening,' she managed.

'The forecast for tomorrow's on the hot side for rowing,' Bott got his word in first. 'But it's better than rain or a crosswind,' he conceded.

Daisy turned towards him. He was in many ways the lesser of two evils, and he would be hurt if she ignored him, not just offended. 'I suppose a crosswind must make steering fearfully difficult,' she said.

'With the experimental course a mere seventy-five feet wide, a wind vector of only...'

Daisy laughed. 'Don't get technical on me. My schools idea of science education was "What you can't see won't hurt you." Your degree is in science?'

'And maths,' drawled DeLancey, joining them. 'What would you expect of a shop-keeper's brat?'

'Better manners than I can apparently expect of an earl's brat!' Daisy snapped.

To her intense relief, footsteps on the terrace behind them announced the arrival of Poindexter and Leigh, one with a lit cigarette, the other tamping his pipe.

'Marvellous evening.' observed Leigh.

'Easy for you to s-say, you won. I s-say, DeLancey,' Poindexter continued, 'you're a whisky man, aren't you? Lady Cheringham had her butler bring in a perfectly s-splendid S-scotch. You ought to try a nip, Bott,' he added with kindly condescension.

'I don't drink spirits.'

'Beer is the drink of the lower classes,' said DeLancey. 'Anything stronger goes straight to their weak heads.'

'Oh, I s-say!'

Leigh turned a laugh into a cough.

Furious, Daisy took Bott's arm. 'Shall we go in, Mr. Bott? There seem to be a lot of irritating insects out here.' She tugged him towards the French windows.

'You see,' he muttered angrily, 'I can't do anything right. They even despise me for studying mathematics and physics instead of dead languages. I'm going to accept the fellowship I've been offered at Cambridge, where they take maths and the sciences seriously.'

'Going to relieve Oxford of your presence, eh?' said DeLancey, coming up on Daisy's other side as they stepped into the drawing room.

Wells and Meredith were sprawled in chairs with glasses in their hands. They struggled to their feet when Daisy entered.

'Miss Cheringham said to tell you she and

Miss Carrick have gone up, Miss Dalrymple,' said Meredith of the moustache.

'Thank you. I'll be on my way, too. Good-night.'

'Good-night,' came a chorus, with a 'Sweet dreams,' from DeLancey.

Daisy hoped Bott would follow her example. She glanced back when she reached the door. He had crossed to the drinks table. Behind him, DeLancey looked on, sneering.

With a set expression, Bott poured whisky into a tumbler. Daisy was very much afraid he was going to drink it.

CHAPTER 3

The mosquito bite had begun to itch in earnest. Rubbing the skin around it, fighting the instinct to scratch, Daisy turned right on the landing at the top of the stairs.

Cherry emerged from the bathroom at the end of the passage, blue-striped pyjamas protruding from beneath his blue dressing-gown.

'Wrong way,' he said, coming towards her. 'You're in with Tish, aren't you? Her room's that way, first on the right past the stairs. Aunt Cynthia put all us men in this wing.'

'Oh yes, I forgot. Last time I stayed I was in here.' She indicated the nearest door.

'You don't want to go in there. That's Fosdyke and that bast ... blighter DeLancey. Fosdyke sleeps like a log. I wouldn't count on him to wake up and defend your virtue.'

'Is DeLancey really so bad?'

'Well, there was a nasty story about him and a shop-girl, but I don't suppose he'd actually force his attentions on a viscount's daughter. Still, I'd steer clear of him in dark corners if I were you. Tish had some trouble with him at the Ambrose May Ball.'

'And Rollo still put him on the crew!'

'He's a damn good oarsman, and the crew was already picked by then. Dropping him would have caused no end of a dust-up. The invitation to stay here had been issued and accepted too, worse luck.'

'What a frightful mess.'

'Isn't it? I swear I'll do the rotter in if he's rude to Dottie one more time. But not till after the Regatta.' he added hastily.

'Of course not,' said Daisy, laughing. 'You have a pretty good chance of winning, do you?'

'Pretty good. Bott's a pill but he's a first-rate cox, and that counts even more than usual with this narrow course, though at least it's straight. The four has a better than even chance in the Visitors', too. I really hope we win one or the other. I mean, it doesn't matter so much to me, but it would buck Rollo up a bit. The poor chap doesn't show it much, but he's frightfully cut up over being ploughed for Schools.'

'I'll be out there cheering for you. I'd better get to bed, now.' she said as footsteps and a burst of laughter approached below. 'Nighty-night.'

'Good-night, Daisy. I'm glad you're here. Dottie and Tish don't feel quite so outnumbered!'

Smiling, Daisy turned back. The men were now noisily ascending the stairs.

'Hush!' said a cautionary voice.

She resisted the urge to glance over the banisters. If Bott had allowed himself to be goaded into drinking more whisky than he could cope with, no doubt she'd find out in the morning.

At least he could no longer complain that the others refused to drink with him.

Daisy found Tish seated at her dressing table, cold-creaming her face. 'I'm glad to see intellectual pursuits don't preclude a touch of vanity,' she said.

'I'm not really frightfully intellectual.' Tish admitted, echoing her mother's view, 'but my aunt – Cherry's mother – would have been madly disappointed if I hadn't gone up. I'm determined to get my degree if it kills me.'

'As bad as that?'

'No, not really. I can manage, as long as I don't fall behind. But oh, Daisy, I'm desperately worried about Rollo.'

'Cherry told me he's more pipped about failing his exams than he seems.' Foreseeing a lengthy exposition, Daisy plumped down on the bed, glad to see Tish's pink cotton pyjamas laid out on the camp-bed.

'He feels he's let me down by spending time rowing when he should have been swotting. You see, he'd planned to go into the Foreign Service right away and save up so that we could marry when I go down next year. He's frightfully keen on the Foreign

Service, but he'd never be more than a clerk without his degree.'

'I suppose not.'

'I want him to stay on at Ambrose and retake his Schools, but he's talking about leaving and trying to find some sort of work that will pay enough to marry on. It doesn't help that he's older than most undergrads.'

'Haven't his people any money?'

'There's an older brother, and two younger. They'll pay for another year of college, but then he's on his own. *We're* on our own,' Tish said fiercely. 'I *will* marry him. The fathead refuses to be properly engaged because he doesn't want to tie me down. I'll have some money from Father, and I'd be happy to get a job too, but he refuses to "sponge" on me. He's so damned *noble!*' she said with a sort of half sob.

'If he stayed and got his degree, then...'

'Then he'd go into the Foreign Service and I suppose we'd have to wait another year or so. But maybe not. After all, we'd have another whole year together in Oxford and I'd have a chance to work on him.'

'I dare say you'd prevail. What does Cherry think?' Daisy asked.

'Oh, he's all in favour of Rollo staying on, but he doesn't really understand how Rollo feels, especially about the Foreign Service. The university is Cherry's whole life, you see.'

'He's more or less been brought up in it, hasn't he?'

Tish nodded. 'He and Dottie are all set to follow in his parents' footsteps, and you simply can't *imagine* how much I envy them!' Tears welled in her eyes and rolled down her woebegone face. She swiped them away. 'I'm sorry, I'm being a rotten hostess. Would you like a bath? I'm sure there's enough hot water left.'

'That's all right, I had one this morning. A wash will do me.'

Her cousin summoned up a wavering smile. 'Just as well. To be perfectly truthful, I should have said I *hope* there's enough hot water. You've no idea how much the men use. Bister swears he spends all his time stoking the boiler.'

'Just think how unbearable the house would be if they stopped taking baths!' Daisy exclaimed, slipping down from the bed and picking up her sponge-bag from the bedside table.

'Ghastly thought. Thanks for listening, Daisy. I couldn't talk to Mother or Dottie about it, and I feel better just for getting it off my chest.'

'Good. I'll think about it and see if I can't give Rollo a tactful shove in the right direction. Back in a minute.'

When she returned to the bedroom, Tish was already half asleep on her camp-bed.

'Breakfast from nine on,' she mumbled. 'G'night.'

'Night, Tish.' Even the mosquito bite and the grievous discovery of three new freckles on her nose could not keep Daisy awake. '*Must* wear a hat.' she told herself as she drifted off.

Lady Cheringham wisely avoided all the 'early' morning heartiness by taking breakfast in bed. Tish, Dottie, and Daisy were made of sterner stuff. They went down to the dining room together.

Young Fosdyke, pink-cheeked and horrifyingly bright-eyed for the time of day, was already halfway through a plateful of eggs and sausages. Rollo and Cherry had also started on their breakfasts, while Wells and Poindexter were at the sideboard, investigating the contents of the covered dishes on the electric hot-plates.

When the girls appeared, the latter two stepped aside. 'After you, ladies.' Wells said gallantly.

'Go ahead,' said Tish. 'You need to digest yours before your race.'

'Bott's not going to be digesting much this morning,' announced Leigh, coming into the room. 'He's not feeling too chipper. Meredith's holding his head under the cold tap.'

'Sick as a dog.' DeLancey followed Leigh

in. 'I told the ass he couldn't hold his liquor.'

'What?' Rollo jumped up. 'Bott got plastered last night?'

'Bott got blotto,' DeLancey confirmed smugly.

Rollo started for the door. 'Just let me get my hands on the little swine!'

Daisy sped after him. When she reached the hall, he was already at the foot of the stairs. Pulling the dining-room door shut behind her, she called, 'Rollo, wait!'

'What is it?' he said impatiently, turning with one foot on the bottom step.

'Bott's not to blame, at least not entirely. He was provoked into drinking whisky when he's used to beer. 'It would have taken a saint not to rise to the bait.'

'DeLancey?'

'Who else?'

Rollo groaned. 'Bott's a prize chump not to see he's only playing DeLancey's game.'

'Actually, the way DeLancey put it, he won either way. That man seems to delight in causing trouble, even if it means cutting off his own nose to spite his face, though of course he's in the four, too. Will it wreck your eights race?'

'I can't tell till I see how bad he is. Will you ask Tish to send up buckets of black coffee?' Rollo continued on his way, taking the stairs two at a time.

Daisy relayed his request, then helped herself to bacon, toast, and tea. Joining Dottie and Cherry, luckily at the far end of the table from DeLancey, she quietly explained the extenuating circumstances of Bott's hangover.

Fosdyke continued to munch placidly. Leigh, Poindexter, and Wells, all to some degree implicated in the cox's downfall, were rather shamefaced. They said nothing to the purpose, however, their sidelong glances at DeLancey suggesting that they did not care to risk becoming targets of his malice.

DeLancey, for a wonder, appeared slightly uncomfortable. Could he be having second thoughts about jeopardizing the eight's chances? Perhaps he had not thought so far ahead when he wreaked his mischief last night.

The door opened and Meredith came in, followed by Bott. Rollo brought up the rear, holding Bott's upper arm supportive or custodial, or both. Bott was greenish-pale and walked as if on eggshells.

'You'll feel twice the man after a spot to eat,' said Rollo heartily.

Bott groaned and turned greener as the smells of breakfast assaulted his nostrils. 'I can't,' he moaned, stepping backwards. 'Let me go back to bed and die in peace.'

'Pull yourself together, old man. We've a race to row in a couple of hours.'

'I can't do it, I tell you.' He clutched his

head with both hands. 'My head's going to explode. I can't see straight, let alone steer.'

Rollo's lips tightened. 'Then I'll phone up the stewards and see if they'll put our heat back till this afternoon. The schedule's pretty tight, though. I doubt they can manage it.'

'Trust a pleb to let the side down,' said DeLancey contemptuously. 'I always said it was a mistake picking him to cox. That sort of mushroom not only can't hold his liquor like a gentleman, he has no sense of loyalty.'

'All right, damn you, all right! I'll do it. Now just let me get out of here!' His hand to his mouth now, Bott fled. 'Hair of the dog?' Wells suggested.

'Aspirin and dry toast,' Cherry advised.

'We'll give it a try,' said Rollo grimly, with a black look at DeLancey. 'I'd hate to scratch.'

'You come and eat your breakfast,' said Cherry. 'Leave him to me.'

Daisy, Tish, and Dottie wanted to see the end of the race, so, with the river to cross and a mile and a half to walk, they departed well before the scheduled starting time. They left the oarsmen warming up with physical jerks on the lawn, watched by the limp, still-pallid cox, sprawled in a deck chair on the terrace.

Tish and Dottie rowed Daisy across the sparkling river in one of the skiffs. Daisy sat in the rear seat, clutching the rudder-lines and doing her best to steer. Last time she had been on a boat, ages ago, she had steered with a wooden tiller, which meant pushing left to turn right. The memory of that clung, confusing her, though it was actually quite easy: pull on the right rope to turn right, left rope to turn left.

Fortunately, the other skiffs, dinghies, motor-launches, canoes, and punts on the water, heading upstream towards the race course, were all under better control. They were shouted at, hooted at, and whistled at, but they made their erratic way safely to the Remenham bank.

Red-faced, Tish tied the painter to a post. 'We'll leave the rudder out on the way back,' she said severely, 'and steer with the sculls.'

'Please do!' said Daisy, fanning herself with her hat, then, mindful of the fresh crop of freckles, quickly putting it back on. It was new, and for once not from Selfridge's Bargain Basement. Her always smart house-mate, Lucy, had found a real treasure, a little milliner in the King's Road whose prices were low because she was just setting up in business for herself.

The hat was navy straw, cloche-shaped but widening to a shady brim, with a circlet of daisies around the crown to match Daisy's blue voile frock, which was patterned with daisies. She was rather pleased with it. She didn't aspire to compete with the splendid headwear created for the Royal Ascot meeting a fortnight ago, which ladies of fashion showed off again at Henley.

Besides, Daisy thought, a picture hat would look less than professional. She glanced down at her frock. Ought she to have worn a tailored costume? The day was far too fine!

Her clothes had nothing to do with her credentials, she reassured herself. Her press pass from the Regatta office was safe in her handbag with her notebook. She wondered whether the American magazine's prestige had obtained it, or the 'Honourable' before her name, which often proved useful in gaining access.

They walked along the towpath, past marshy meadows splashed with shiny yellow kingcups. Few people were about as yet.

'There's the new starting line.' Tish pointed out as they approached the downstream end of Temple Island. 'It used to be on the Bucks side.'

Halfway up the island's length, a small knot of people had gathered on the bank. A stewards' launch was already there, but neither the Ambrose boat nor their opponent, Marlow Rowing Club, had yet arrived.

As they passed the upstream tip of the island, Daisy glanced back at the so-called Temple, hidden till then by the trees. The small building was an enclosed summer-house topped with an open, pillared cupola and fronted by a wide landing-stage, sheltered on the north by a weeping willow – a delightful place for a picnic. It was private land, of course, belonging, Daisy assumed, to Crowswood Place, where Lord DeLancey was staying, over there on the Buckinghamshire bank.

Or was it Oxfordshire at this point? The Cheringhams' address was Bucks but Henley-on-Thames was Oxon.

The town was visible now, beyond the Phyllis Court grandstand. Mellow red brick and brown tile roofs stretched along the river, dominated by the square grey tower of St. Mary's. The eighteenth-century bridge was hidden by the bend at Poplar Point. There, on the Berkshire bank, overlooking the finish line, grandstands and marquees sprang from the water-meadows like monstrous mushrooms.

A good half-mile to go. Daisy consulted her wristwatch. Still plenty of time to get there before the first heat started.

Past Remenham Club they came to the fairground. The calliope was silent now, the merry-go-round horses still, the booths shrouded. Over it all loomed the Ferris wheel, a steel spider's web, the gaudy cars exotic insects trapped in its toils. A few sleepy-eyed men with cigarettes dangling from their lips lounged about doing odd jobs.

'It looks frightfully tawdry without the crowds, doesn't it?' said Tish a trifle nervously. 'It needs people and chatter and music.'

A cuckoo called from the woods on Remenham Hill. They all laughed.

They reached the general Enclosure. Dottie and Tish had the Ambrose crew's guest passes. Daisy presented her press card and was waved through the gate with them.

'Whew!' she exclaimed in relief. 'I've never had one of these before. It really works!'

'Open Sesame,' said Tish. 'Come on, let's go up in the stands. Have you got Cherry's binoculars, Dottie?'

Dottie opened the small satchel she carried over her shoulder, rummaged, and produced the glasses. 'Here. Don't lose the lens caps or he'll have your blood. Or mine.'

They climbed up into the grandstand.

Only dedicated rowing enthusiasts were present so early in the day, gentlemen from eighteen to eighty, most in caps and blazers. The vivid – not to say vulgar – salmon-pink of the Leander Club predominated, their premises being just along the bank beyond the Stewards' Enclosure, by the bridge. Eavesdropping on a disgruntled conversation, Daisy gathered the Leander eight had been knocked out in the first heat of the Grand. However, they had good hopes for a pair in the Silver Goblets and a single-sculler in the Diamond.

The starting gun sounded in the distance. Instantly, binoculars sprouted, and a bright-hued flock which had been chatting on the ground hurried up into the stands.

'So Bott came through!' Dottie sighed, releasing unacknowledged tension.

'Damn good view!' commented the Leander man in front of them to his companion. 'Wasn't too sure about this new course, but having the start south of Temple Island is a definite improvement.'

Tish had the glasses trained downstream. 'I can't see much,' she said. 'They're just dots. You can't tell who's ahead.'

'Let me see,' Dottie took her turn. 'We are the Berks side, aren't we? There's a terrific glare off the water with the sun so bright. Gosh, they hardly seem to be moving at all.'

'They do look slow at this distance.' Tish agreed.

'Here you are, your turn, Daisy.'

Daisy peered, adjusted the focus, and peered again. There they were, the two boats, crawling up the river. She swung the glasses to gaze at Phyllis Court, where the grandstand was even less populated, and then to the flotilla of small craft crowding the river. Racing boats threaded between, heading downstream to the start.

She turned back to the race course. Now she could clearly make out the individual men hauling on their oars. Her angle of vision distorted the view, but she thought Marlow was nosing ahead.

The Ambrose crew visibly speeded their stroke. They crept up on Marlow, inch by torturous inch.

Then, without warning, Bott doubled up over the side and was violently sick.

'Oh gosh!'

'What is it?' Tish demanded. 'Look, they're veering all over the place. What happened?'

'They've hit the boom,' said Dottie resignedly, as Daisy passed the binoculars to Tish. 'They'll never make it up now.'

'The cox is sick as a dog,' said one of the Leander men. 'Just like the Oriel crew on Wednesday.'

The other nodded. 'They're out of it, dead in the water. Damn shame. What's the next heat?'

Daisy watched the Marlow boat drawing swiftly away from their floundering opponents. The Ambrose crew had pulled themselves together enough to make way against the current, but barely. Soon she could see with the naked eye Bott curled in a miserable ball in the stern. He must be holding the rudder straight, at least, so that Cherry, in the bow, could give the rowers appropriate orders to keep them more or less on track.

'Let's go down to the finish line,' Tish proposed, long-faced.

They reached the floating jetties, just beyond the finish, as the Marlow boat crossed the line to a smattering of applause and a tactful lack of cheers. Marlow would advance to the next round, but it was scarcely a victory to be proud of.

Glum Ambrose struggled in. Current and former Ambrose men in maroon blazers crowded around offering commiseration. Two of the youngest crouched to hold the boat as Rollo led the crew in the disembarking drill. Disconsolately, the eight oarsmen clambered out. Cherry and Rollo pulled wry faces at the three girls.

Rollo and numbers three to seven, accompanied by Tish and other well-wishers, set off with the oars to the racks by the tents.

'There's always next year,' said Meredith philosophically. 'And you've got the four s-still to come, Frieth,' Poindexter consoled Rollo.

Ignored, Bott still crouched, head in hands, in the stern. With plenty of willing hands to hold the boat, Cherry went along to him.

'Come along, old fellow. It can't be helped.' He offered his hand.

Accepting his aid, Bott clambered rockily out. He stood swaying on the jetty, eyes shut, his face drained of colour. 'It was the motion,' he mumbled, 'and the glare of the sun on the water. I told you I wasn't fit enough.'

'Not fit!' exploded DeLancey, swinging round from the men he had been talking to. 'You're not fit to associate with gentlemen, you ghastly little oik! Bounders like you shouldn't be allowed out of your filthy hovels.'

He pushed past Cherry and gave Bott a mighty shove in the chest. The cox toppled backwards into the river.

CHAPTER 4

Bott surfaced, spluttering. 'Help me,' he cried in a panic. 'I can't swim.'

Daisy reached for a nearby boat-hook. Rollo thundered past her, the jetty bobbing beneath his tread. Cherry was already on his knees, reaching for Bott's waving arms.

'It's all right,' he said calmingly, 'it's only three or four feet deep at most. You can't possibly drown. Put your feet down, man. Stand up.'

Flushed with humiliation, Bott rose to mid-chest above the water. He waded a step forward and Rollo and Cherry hauled him out. Murky river water streamed down his face from his hair. His sodden shirt and shorts clung to his wiry, shivering body.

'A drowned rat,' DeLancey mocked.

Someone snickered. Two or three men grinned openly; Rollo and others turned away to hide their mirth. But one or two, including Cherry and Dottie, looked at DeLancey in disgust.

'You're responsible for the whole bloody mess,' Cherry said angrily.

'*Filthy* mess,' said DeLancey, eyeing Bott, 'but I can easily make the disgusting little wart a bloody mess.' He moved forward, fists clenched in a boxing stance.

'Shame!' someone cried.

'Whoa, there!'

'Hold on, he's half your size!'

'I s-say, not the thing!' Poindexter and the others were back.

Cherry and Rollo moved to intervene, but they were forestalled by a newcomer, a man of about thirty in a navy blazer. As tall as DeLancey but slightly built, he grasped the stroke by the arm.

'For pity's sake, Basil, don't be a blithering idiot.' Harassed and furious, he gestured at the bystanders and the overlooking grandstands. 'Half the world's watching. You're creating a thoroughly vulgar scene.'

'The only vulgarity here's that swab who's supposed to be our cox,' DeLancey said sulkily, shaking off his hand.

'Leave the fellow be. You're making a spectacle of yourself, lowering yourself to his level. The pater will be livid. Come away.'

'Please, do take him away, Lord DeLancey,' begged Rollo. 'We'll manage the boat without him.'

'I'll get back at you for this, DeLancey,' Bott swore venomously, as Cedric DeLancey dragged away his protesting brother. 'Just you wait! You're going to find out you can't ride roughshod over people without suffering the consequences.'

Seeing he was losing whatever sympathy his plight had elicited, Daisy moved to hush him. She reached his side at the same moment as an attractive girl with a snub nose and dark red, bobbed hair under a jaunty buttercup-yellow hat.

'Do shut up, Horace,' said the girl. Beneath a superficial refinement, her voice had the same touch of the Midlands as Bott's.

'Did you see what that cad did?' Bott spluttered.

'Yes, but you're just drawing more attention to yourself now. Least said, soonest mended, say I. You'd better come back to my room and dry off.'

'I quite agree,' Daisy put in. 'The whole business is best forgotten, and, unwell as you've been, Mr. Bott, you'll very likely catch a chill if you don't change.'

'Thank you.' The girl gave her a friendly smile. 'I'm Susan Hopgood.'

'Daisy Dalrymple. The Ambrose crew is staying at my cousin's.'

'Pleased to meet you, I'm sure.'

'The *Honourable* Miss Dalrymple,' said Bott in a doom-laden tone.

'Don't be silly, Horace,' Miss Hopgood said severely, 'and come along, do. My landlady's ever so nice. She'll dry your clothes and give us a cuppa.'

She took his dripping elbow in a white-gloved hand and urged him along the now deserted jetty towards the bank. Under Rollo's orders, the rest of the crew and a volunteer had lifted the boat from the water, and crying, 'Mind your backs!' they wended through the spectators towards the boat-tent. All eyes were now directed down-stream, where the next heat was in progress.

Daisy walked along with Bott and Miss Hopgood. The girl was obviously strong-willed and a good influence on him, but she might need further support to make her awkward swain behave sensibly, especially if he happened to catch sight of his tormentor.

Heading towards the bridge, they passed the Leander Club, aswarm with pink blazers, caps, ties, and socks, like a flock of flam-ingoes. Daisy saw the DeLancey brothers going into the club house with one of the flamingoes, perhaps Lord DeLancey's host at Crowswood. She hoped Cedric would succeed in reining in the Hon. Basil.

Hastily, she directed Bott's attention in the opposite direction. 'You see the keystone in the centre of the bridge?' she said. 'I was reading up on Henley before I came down. The heads – there's another on the upstream side – were carved by an eighteenth-century woman sculptor.'

'Fancy that,' said Miss Hopgood brightly. 'Look, Horace.'

He growled.

'They represent Isis and Tameses, the spirits of the river, I suppose you could call them, but I can't honestly remember which is which.'

'Didn't you tell me the Thames is called the Isis in Oxford, Horace?' Miss Hopgood persevered.

'That's right. A typical attempt to separate those in the know from the ignorant masses.'

'You *are* an old bear today, really, and me coming all the way down to see you! Well, you'll feel a sight better once you're dry and comfy.' Without abandoning her firm grip on his elbow, Miss Hopgood turned to Daisy and enquired, 'D'you always read about places you're going, Miss Dalrymple? I must say, I think it's ever such a good idea.'

'Only when I'm going to write about them.' Daisy had meant to turn back when they reached the bridge, but she didn't want to throw fuel on the fire of the thin-skinned Bott's resentment by seeming above her company. Besides, she rather liked Miss Susan Hopgood. 'I write for magazines, you see,' she explained.

'Gracious, you mean you're a working girl?'

'For fun,' grunted Bott.

'For a living,' Daisy said firmly. 'Do you have a job, Miss Hopgood?'

'I'm a bookkeeper. The pay's quite a bit

better than typing, or even stenography, and I always was good at numbers in school. Not like Horace, here, of course,' she said with affection. 'He's a real genius, he is. Oh look, Horace, isn't it nice?'

She stopped in the middle of the bridge and leaned on the parapet, admiring the view. Downstream was all the bustle of the Regatta, framed by green, wooded hills. Marquees and grandstands hid most of the funfair, but the Ferris wheel was clearly visible.

'Oooh, Horace, you didn't tell me there's a fair!'

'We'll go this evening,' Bott smiled at her, for the first time, but then a burst of cheering greeted the winners of the heat after the disastrous Ambrose race, and he added sombrely, 'Since I won't be coxing.'

If he was willing to contemplate the fair, Daisy reflected, at least his ducking must have relieved his hangover!

No one they encountered as they walked on took much notice of his bedraggled state. Sodden boaters were no uncommon sight in the river town.

They passed the picturesque Angel Inn, on the riverbank at the end of the bridge, and St. Mary's Church with its stone and flint chequerwork. Just beyond the church was the Old White Hart, the ancient inn where Alec had booked a room.

Surreptitiously, Daisy crossed her fingers, entreating Providence not to allow a sudden spate of heinous murders, dope fiends, or Bolshevik bombers to spoil their weekend together.

Miss Hopgood's room was in a tiny brick terrace cottage in a back street – half the population of Henley made a little extra by renting out rooms for the Regatta. The lady of the house clucked over Bott's condition. Shooing him upstairs, she promised his shorts and shirt would dry in no time on the line in the back garden. In the meantime, she'd bring a cup of tea to him in Miss Hopgood's room, while Miss Hopgood and her friend had theirs in the front parlour.

The minuscule parlour was stuffed with furniture to the bursting point, its usual couch and easy-chairs augmented by a small table and chair for the lodger's meals. Daisy and Miss Hopgood shared a pot of tea so black that milk barely turned it mahogany. With it came huge slices of Victoria sandwich cake.

Miss Hopgood took a bite and a sip and turned to Daisy. 'Well, now, Miss Dalrymple, d'you mind telling me what all that nasty fuss was about? And what you meant by saying Horace was unwell? I know something happened in the middle of the race, but I couldn't see much from the bank.'

Deciding the girl was sensible enough to

hear the whole thing, Daisy explained about the taunts, the Scotch, the hangover, and the disastrous effect of the boat's motion.

'I see.' Miss Hopgood sighed. 'I've told him time and time again not to let that De-Lancey bloke get his goat. He's a nasty piece of work, he is, if you don't mind me saying so.'

'Not at all. He's no friend of mine. He's rude to everyone, you know, not just Mr. Bott.'

'What Horace heard is he's the baby of the family, with three sisters a whole lot older than him who spoiled him to death. They prob'ly thought anything the dear little boy said was clever or funny.'

'Or both.' Daisy agreed.

'But all the same, however much he provoked him, Horace ought to know better than to drink whisky. He's always had a weak head, he has. Hardly ever drinks more than a half of pale ale.'

'You've known him a long time?'

'We were neighbours in Wolverhampton when we were kids. His dad owns the news-agent's on the corner. We went to the same Board School, him on the boys' side, me on the girls' and started keeping company soon as we were old enough to walk out together.'

'But – forgive me for being nosey – you're not engaged?'

Miss Hopgood spread her bare left hand,

glancing at Daisy's ring as she said bluntly, 'I wouldn't. He's going up in the world, going to be a professor at least, maybe win one of those Nobel Prizes. I'd only hold him back. He needs a posh wife that can help him get on.'

'You may be right,' Daisy acknowledged, 'except that the way he feels he's been treated at Oxford, a "posh" wife might just increase his inferiority complex. I think you'd be jolly good for him. You'd support him and stop him dwelling on his grievances.'

'He always did take things personal, if you know what I mean – take things to heart, like.'

'I wouldn't give up too quickly if I were you.'

'Really?' Miss Hopgood looked pleased but dubious. 'Well, I wouldn't give him the push anyway, but who's to say what he'll be wanting once he gets to this here Cavendish Laboratory at Cambridge. Who's *your* fella, then? A lord, is he?'

Daisy laughed. 'No, a policeman.'

'Go on, you're having me on! A bobby?'

'Not exactly an ordinary bobby. He's a Detective Chief Inspector at Scotland Yard.'

'Coo, you'll have to mind your p's and q's, you will,' said Miss Hopgood, giggling. 'But if you're an Honourable, that means your dad's a lord, doesn't it? I shouldn't be calling you "my lady" should I?'

'No, Miss Dalrymple is right, but do call me Daisy.'

'Oh no, I couldn't. I mean, your auntie's a Lady, isn't she? Sir Rupert and Lady Cheringham, Horace said. It's ever so nice of them to invite the whole crew to stay.' Her face fell. 'Oh dear, d'you think your auntie'll mind Horace stopping on another two nights now his college is out of the race?'

'I'm sure Aunt Cynthia expects them to stay, to cheer on the four. Most of them probably will.'

'Yes, but Horace... The rest's all nobs, aren't they? Real gentlemen, I mean. The thing is, I've already paid Friday and Saturday nights, but I wouldn't want to stay without him, and he can't afford to get a room, even if he could find one, which isn't likely. I s'pose he could sleep in his tent.'

'I'm quite sure he can stay at my aunt's till Sunday,' Daisy assured her. 'Why did he bring a tent? Don't tell me he expected to be made to sleep on the lawn?'

'Oh no!' Miss Hopgood laughed at the thought. 'That nice Mr. Frieth, the captain, he said they'd have to double up but there was room for everyone, and Horace had a room of his own in the end. No, Horace is going on a walking tour after the Regatta, so he brought his tent and knapsack and all. He likes...'

She stopped as the landlady came in with

Bott's crumpled shirt and maroon shorts over her arm.

'What'd I say, dry near as makes no odds and I'll just run a hot iron over 'em to finish 'em off so's the young gent don't catch cold.'

Miss Hopgood jumped up. 'Oh, thanks ever so. I'll iron them, though. I'm sure you're busy.'

'Well, there's my man's dinner to get...' She looked doubtfully at Daisy.

'I must be on my way,' Daisy said at once. 'My cousin will be wondering where on earth I've got to. Thanks most frightfully for the tea. I've enjoyed talking to you, Miss Hopgood. I expect we'll run into each other again down by the river.'

By the time Daisy reached the general Enclosure again, the crowd had thickened. It was still nothing like the crush it would be tomorrow, when the fashionable set arrived for Finals day, but there was a scattering of bright frocks and morning suits among the blazers.

Thirsty after walking from the town under the now hot sun, Daisy headed for the refreshment tent. With its sides furled, it was shady without being stuffy, and allowed a view of the river.

There she found Tish, Dottie, Rollo, and Cherry, the girls with lemonade, the men with beer tankards.

'Where *have* you been?' Tish greeted Daisy.

'We were contemplating calling in the police,' said Dottie, 'but we weren't sure whether to get the local chaps or go straight to Scotland Yard.'

'Oh, Scotland Yard, of course. Alec *would* have wrung my neck!'

The others laughed. Cherry went to get lemonade for Daisy while Rollo asked her anxiously how Bott was.

'I had to get the boat out of the way, with the next two on their way,' he explained, 'and it looked as if you and his girl – or his sister, was it? – and Lord DeLancey had things under control between you.'

'His girl, and a very sensible girl she is. She calmed Bott down, and he seemed to have got over the headache and tummy trouble.'

'Shock treatment,' said Cherry, returning with Daisy's lemonade. 'A ducking'll do it every time. We should have chucked him in before the race.'

Rollo shook his head. 'I should have asked for a postponement, and scratched if we couldn't get it. At least we'd have avoided that appalling scene with DeLancey playing the...'

Tish elbowed him in the ribs. The DeLancey brothers were approaching. They would have made a handsome pair were it not for the elder's tight lips, the thundercloud of resentment on the younger's brow.

'Sorry about the shindy,' said the Hon. Basil stiffly. As a gracious apology it was a dud. 'I shouldn't have gone off half-cocked in front of the ladies. But that wretched little pleb made me see red, ruining the race for us!'

'As to whose fault...'Cherry snorted. Tish used her other elbow on his ribs.

'Least said, soonest mended.' Lord DeLancey put in smoothly, unknowingly echoing Miss Hopgood, to Daisy's amusement. 'A regrettable incident on both sides.'

His brother was not so easily hushed. 'Did you hear Bott's threats? He swore revenge. If he's not too yellow to stand up and fight, I'll thrash the living daylights out of him.'

'That's easy to say,' Dottie exclaimed. 'You're twice his size and a boxer to boot.'

'Don't be an ass, Basil,' said his lordship with asperity. 'A hundred years ago you might have horsewhipped the fellow, but these days that's not on.'

'More's the pity. I suppose the snivelling wretch would haul me up before the beak.'

'He may yet,' Dottie observed, not without a touch of malice. 'I imagine he has a very good case for assault if he chooses to pursue it.'

Both DeLanceys stared at her in high-nosed outrage.

'I'll have a word with him,' said Rollo pacifically. 'DeLancey, our Visitors' Cup heat this afternoon isn't till after five. I'm still not happy with our starts. See if you can round up Fosdyke, will you, and we'll meet back at the boat-house in an hour for some practice.'

'The four!' Dismay chased outrage from the Hon. Basil's face. 'I bet that's it. Bott's planning to sabotage the boat to get back at me. What does he care if the coxless four doesn't win?'

'What rot!' Cherry said in disgust.

'No, think about it. He has no sense of loyalty to Ambrose. I shouldn't think he's likely to try anything in daylight, but I tell you, I'm going to stand guard over that boat tonight, even if you fellows won't join me.'

'We shan't,' Rollo assured him.

'Nor will you!' Lord DeLancey snapped.

'Why the deuce not, Ceddie?' Basil said insolently.

'Don't call me that. Spend the night on sentry-go in the boat-house? All you'll accomplish is to make yourself and the family a laughingstock. It's a dashed good job your race this morning was so early, before the crowds arrived, but even so you've caused more than enough talk!'

Oddly enough, Daisy received the impression Lord DeLancey was quite as much apprehensive as angry. In particular, the sidelong glances he cast at Rollo and Cherry as he berated his brother seemed almost fearful.

Now what could he possibly have to fear?

CHAPTER 5

'I'm frightfully glad the four won their heat,' said Tish, cautiously climbing into her bed, which was liable to tip up if approached unwarily. 'I think Rollo would be happier about another year at Ambrose if he had won a cup for the college.'

'I like him.' Yawning, Daisy scratched her mosquito bites. A new one had made the old one start to itch again. 'I hope things work out for the two of you, win or lose.'

'Just one more elimination before the final. Keep your fingers crossed. Daisy, you don't suppose there's anything in what Basil DeLancey said, do you? About Bott sabotaging the boat?'

'I shouldn't think so. Lord DeLancey was rather queer about the whole affair, wasn't he? Practically in a blue funk. Admittedly, it must be pretty foul having a brother like dear Basil, but people can hardly blame him for it.'

'No.' Tish hesitated. 'Actually, Dottie said much the same and Cherry explained to us. I shouldn't be surprised if it gets about anyway, but I wouldn't want to be the one to start the talk.'

Intrigued, Daisy protested, 'Have a heart! You can't tell me so much and no more. If Scotland Yard can trust me with its secrets, you jolly well can, too?'

'Does he? Does Mr. Fletcher tell you things?'

'Sometimes. As a matter of fact, I've helped him with one or two cases. But we're not talking about that now. Tell me about Cedric DeLancey, or I'll tip you out of bed.'

'Don't! I'd have to make it up again. All right, Cherry said Lord DeLancey is scared to death of arousing any gossip about the family in case his war record comes out. It seems he panicked and lost his head and led his company into a massacre, only he led it from behind, like the Duke of Plaza Toro...'

'"He led his regiment from behind,"' sang Daisy. '"He found it less exciting. That celebrated..."'

'Hush!' Tish hissed, glancing at the door. 'There were only three survivors and he was the only one to come out with a whole skin. He was cashiered, but it was hushed up, his father being an earl and in the government. The family put it about that he was invalided out. But Cherry and Rollo were both in the same battalion so they knew what really happened. Cherry said if it got out – society gossip, or even worse, the press – he'd be ostracized.'

'Gosh, he'd probably be blackballed at his

clubs and not received at Court. I dare say his father might even be eased out of his post as an embarrassment to the government. Not,' said Daisy austerely, 'because anyone would care two hoots that he got his men massacred. After all, the generals did that by the thousands. But people won't forgive his panicking, which seems to me an altogether natural reaction to being caught in the middle of a battle.'

'I would,' Tish agreed with a shudder, 'but men aren't supposed to show they're afraid, let alone act as if they were. Maybe that's why they start wars, to prove to each other how brave they are.'

'Like little boys daring each other. Are you ready? I'll turn out the light.'

In the dark, Tish said, 'I almost forgot to ask how your research is going.'

'Very well. I met an American who rowed in the Harvard crew which won the Grand in 1914. He brought his wife over to see the Regatta. Their views will interest American readers. And my friend Betty – her husband, Fitz, is a member of the Stewards' Enclosure – has offered to present me to the Duke of Gloucester tomorrow, Isn't it too spiffing? The Americans adore British royalty, don't ask me why.'

'You're going to meet Prince Henry?'

'Tomorrow afternoon. Alec told me some of his plainclothes colleagues will be circulating in the crowds to keep an eye on things. Alec has to pretend not to recognise them, but of course they'll recognise him. I just hope nothing happens to make them need his help.'

'Let's hope not. It's a pity he reached Henley too late to go to the fair with us.'

'It was too sweet of Fosdyke to escort me, but he made me feel like an aged aunt! At least Alec has arrived. You never can tell with policemen. He's going to pick me up in the morning in time to watch the start of the Ambrose four's heat.'

'Dottie and I decided to watch the start, too. If they lose, the finish will be too depressing for words, and if they win, we'll watch the finish of the final.' Tish was silent for a moment, then said, 'I *do* so hope they win. Do you think Basil DeLancey will go and guard the boat in spite of his brother telling him not to?'

'I don't know,' Daisy said sleepily, 'but he hasn't much self-control at the best of times and that was a pretty stiff whisky-and-soda I saw him put away, not to mention starting on a second. If he does, I hope Bott doesn't take it into his head to go down there, or there'll he murder done.'

Startled into wakefulness, Daisy lay for a moment straining her ears. Heavy, blundering footsteps, harsh breathing – someone was in the room! She snapped on the bedside lamp.

Basil DeLancey stood there, swaying, one hand to his head, the other held out as if groping for support.

Tish lay wide-eyed, terrified, clutching the bedclothes to her chest. DeLancey took a staggering step forward. With a squeal, Tish sat up. Her camp-bed collapsed and DeLancey tripped over a protruding corner.

Jumping out of bed, Daisy ran to extricate Tish from the tangle of sheets and blankets.

'He came after me!' Tish whimpered.

But DeLancey lay sprawled on the floor, groaning, making no attempt to rise and ravish.

Daisy frowned. 'Perhaps. I suppose he might have drunk enough to try to seduce you, forgetting I'm sharing your room. But I suspect he's just drunk enough to have turned the wrong way at the top of the stairs. His room is the first on the other side, isn't it?'

'Oh yes.' Tish said thankfully. She was white as a sheet, and she stared at the recumbent intruder like a rabbit fascinated by a stoat.

DeLancey was fully dressed in a pullover and flannels. Daisy glanced at the clock on the mantelpiece. Past two o'clock! He must have stayed downstairs drinking by himself. Or perhaps he had fallen asleep downstairs, she thought, trying to be charitable, and was as much fuddled by sleep as drink. She hoped so, or tomorrow's race would be another disaster.

Either way, she and Tish could not manage him. She grabbed her cousin's dressing gown. 'Here, put this on and go and wake his roommate. It's Fosdyke, I think. He'll get him to bed.'

'You can't stay alone with him.' Tish's voice trembled.

'Of course I can. He's in no state to attack, and anyway, it's you he's been making up to. Don't for pity's sake wake Rollo and Cherry. They'd have his blood without waiting to ask questions. Just Fosdyke. Go along now.'

Tish left. Daisy put on her own dressing-gown and turned back to DeLancey. He looked more like victim than villain now, trying ineffectually to push himself up.

Distastefully, Daisy helped him to roll over and sit up with his back to the wall.

'C-can't see straight,' he mumbled, thick-tongued. His eyes had an unfocussed look and his face was livid, his dark, pomaded hair sticking out in all directions as if he had run his hands through it. His breath smelled of spirits. 'God, my head hurts. Wha' happened?'

'Whisky happened,' Daisy informed him severely, wishing the room had an old-fashioned wash-basin, 'unless you went on to something else. Don't you dare be sick in here.'

'Not going... Where...'

If he was unaware of being in Tish's bedroom, Daisy was not about to enlighten him. With luck, by morning he'd have forgotten his detour on the way to bed.

Tish returned with Fosdyke, sleepy-eyed and blushing in a daffodil-yellow dressing-gown over daffodil striped pyjamas, his feet bare.

'Awfully sorry,' the youth muttered, turning a brighter red when he saw Daisy. 'Miss Cheringham said not to dress.'

'She was quite right. Do you think you can get Mr. DeLancey to bed without waking anyone else to help you? The fewer people who know about his mistake the better.'

'Crikey, yes! Not a word to a soul. He looks as sozzled as a sucking pig.' Fosdyke stared down disapprovingly at DeLancey, who squinted back in apparent confusion. 'Doesn't look too good for the visitors' heat, does it? Yes, I'll manage him all right, Miss Dalrymple. Come along, old chap.'

He heaved DeLancey up onto his feet. Tish wouldn't go near them, but Daisy arranged DeLancey's arm across Fosdyke's shoulders. With Fosdyke's arm around his waist, DeLancey stumbled out.

'Gosh,' said Daisy with a sigh, shutting the

door behind them, 'to think I expected all the drama of my visit to come from the boat races! Come on, let's get your bed put back together. Fosdyke's a dear, isn't he? And luckily the strong, silent type.'

'It took forever to wake him. I had to go in and shake him,' Tish said, fumbling at the bed frame with still-trembling hands. 'It was awful.'

'I assume you're referring to DeLancey's incursion, not to waking Fosdyke. Cheer up, no harm done, as long as you don't go and let it out to Rollo or Cherry.'

'Oh no!'

'As for the race, I can't believe he's such an ass as to drink enough to risk wrecking his performance, not after the way he blasted Bott. I expect he's one of those people who sleeps it off and never suffers the morning after. There's your pillow, in you hop – I mean slither.' She tucked her cousin in. 'Sleep well.'

Daisy hopped into bed herself and turned out the light. She had every intention of following her own advice, but sleep failed to come.

Had DeLancey taken into account his capacity for absorbing alcohol? He hadn't shown much in the way of common sense so far, and he had seemed awfully rocky. At least he hadn't been sick. More confused than anything else, she thought.

Confusion – one of the chief symptoms of nicotine poisoning. Could Bott, rather than harbouring designs on the fours boat, have put nicotine in the whisky?

Bosh, Daisy told herself. Not without risking poisoning everyone in the house, all the men, anyway. Nor had Bott any reason to be aware of the tobacco-water insecticide in the garden shed. Besides, vomiting was another symptom and DeLancey – thank heaven – had not vomited.

No, Bott and poisoning was out. But what about Bott and the boat? Suppose DeLancey had in fact gone down to guard it, and Bott had come and...

She had said herself that would lead to murder. She had been exaggerating, of course, but suppose DeLancey had been drinking to ward off the chill and attacked Bott with more force than he intended. He outweighed the cox by a good couple of stone. Might not the shock of having killed a man, added to the whisky, bring on just such a state of confusion as DeLancey had displayed?

Bosh! she told herself again, uneasily. It was two in the morning – more like half past now – the time when all sorts of horrors tend to descend on the wakeful mind. On top of that, in the past few months she had found herself caught up in investigating several murders, so her brain was bound to run on those lines.

And run and run, round and round in circles.

If Bott was dead, there was nothing she could do to help him. What if he was badly hurt? Even Basil DeLancey surely wouldn't have abandoned an injured man; but perhaps he thought he had killed him.

Daisy wished she knew where Bott's linen-room/bedroom was. She couldn't go peeking into everyone's rooms just to reassure herself that the cox was sleeping peacefully.

But she could go down to the boat-house.

An electric torch was kept on the table on the landing in case of a current failure, she remembered as she wrapped her dressing gown around her and tied the sash. Feeling her way, she tiptoed from the room.

On the landing a faint light from the window, where the curtains had not been closed, enabled Daisy to find her way across to the table. Light gleamed on the torch's metal casing. She reached for it, then hastily drew her hand back. If there had been dirty work at the crossroads, it just might have significant fingerprints on it. Alec would kill her if she messed them up.

Kill her? She really must stop thinking in morbid clichés!

Fortunately, she found a hankie in the pocket of her dressing gown. This she wrapped around the end of the torch, careful not to smudge potential dabs, as Alec's Sergeant Tring called them. Picking it up, she started down the stairs, step by step, holding the banister and her breath, waiting for a creak loud enough to bring everyone running. What a frightful ass she'd look!

The house was still. Undiscovered, she reached the front hall. It was pitch-dark down here, but she shuffled across to the drawing room door without using the torch. The door closed safely behind her, she switched on the electric light.

The curtains at the French windows were drawn apart, and one door was open.

Fear clutched Daisy's heart. Though she had come so far, she had practically convinced herself she was on a fool's errand. But someone had been out. Why, and who, if not DeLancey to the boat-house? He was muddled enough to have left it open when he came in.

DeLancey or Bott. DeLancey *and* Bott? She had to go and see.

A gibbous moon was setting as she crossed the terrace. Down the steps, across the dewy lawn, silver in moonlight augmented by its reflection off the river. A plank squeaked as she set foot on the landing-stage. A scrabble and a splash – a water rat, she assured herself, not a house rat. Think of *Wind in the Willows*, and nice, friendly Ratty.

The boat-house door was open. Daisy

stood outside, listening. The river gurgled around the landing-stage piles, lapped the bank with a soft and constant plash. *Sweet Thames, run softly, till I end my song.* Had Bott's song ended forever? *Old Father Thames keeps rolling along, down to the sunless sea.* No, that was Alph, the sacred river, wasn't it? In Xanadu:

A savage place as holy and enchanted
As e'er beneath a waning moon was haunted...

How sinister everything seemed by moonlight!

Not a sound from the boat-house. Daisy pushed the torch's button with her knuckle. The click made her jump.

A wide, comforting beam sprang out. She moved to the doorway. Something brushed her cheek and she jumped again, then realised it was only a stray tendril of clematis.

'Chump,' she apostrophized herself. If anyone was here, they were certainly no threat to her.

She played the torch's beam around the boat-house. It seemed much larger inside than its foliage-camouflaged outside suggested. The light scarcely plumbed the furthest corners. Her view was obstructed by a rack of oars, too, and by the fours boat, apparently undamaged, upside-down on its chocks. The boat barely fitted in, its sleek hull stretching the entire length of the opposite wall.

No body hidden in that, at least. But she would have to go in to search the building properly.

The large doors onto the river were closed and barred. The torch beam gleamed on the still, dark water of the channel in the centre, where the boats entered. No floating body.

No moans or groans, no sound of breathing reached her straining ears. On tiptoe, swinging the torch from side to side, she passed the gaily striped pillows from the skiffs, piled on the plank floor just inside the door. Nothing beyond the oar-rack but a coil of rope or two, iron hoops and canvas to turn the skiffs into floating tents, and odds and ends of less identifiable boating clutter. Nothing in the shadow behind the fours boat.

Daisy returned to the black water. The torchlight could not penetrate its surface. If Bott was at the bottom, he was beyond help. She was *not* going to start fishing with a boathook!

CHAPTER 6

In spite of her disturbed night – or because of it – Daisy was one of the first down to breakfast, joining Cherry and Leigh. Fortunately for her peace of mind, Bott was not much after her.

His face bore no sign of having collided with DeLancey's fist. Though morose, he was no more so than usual. He bade Daisy good morning and told her he was going to walk into Henley to meet Miss Hopgood.

'There's no public towpath on this side, and it's a long way round by road,' Cherry said good-naturedly. 'I'll run you across to the other side in one of the skiffs.'

Bott gave him a somewhat suspicious glance, but thanked him politely enough.

Rollo, Poindexter, and Wells came in.

'Tish not down yet?' said Rollo. He was looking rather careworn. His duties as crew captain had been unexpectedly onerous, Daisy thought, and there was the worry about his future, too.

'She was still asleep when I came down,' Daisy told him. 'She was a bit tired last night. Aunt Cynthia has rather left the host-essing to her, and she's not used to it. Buck up, I'll see she's up in time for your race.'

Surely one of the others could take DeLancey's place if necessary? He was not indispensable, like the cox.

Fosdyke arrived next, returning from his morning run. He carefully avoided meeting Daisy's eyes. While he was serving himself at the sideboard, she said casually, 'I think I'll have a sausage after all,' and went to join him.

She raised her eyebrows at him.

'Still asleep when I left,' he hissed from the corner of his mouth. 'Half an hour ago. I'll wake him if he doesn't come down soon.'

'You're a trump,' said Daisy, and he blushed.

Bott left, with Leigh, who had volunteered to row him across the river in Cherry's place as he was not racing that morning. Dottie and Meredith came in. Still no sign of Tish or DeLancey. There was plenty of time yet, Daisy told herself, regarding the mountain of food Fosdyke was methodically ploughing his way through.

Then DeLancey arrived. He stood for a moment in the doorway, holding the jamb, gazing around bleary-eyed. Then he advanced unsteadily into the room.

Rollo jumped up, glaring at him. 'What's wrong with you?'

'Nothing,' he said, thick-tongued. 'Got a bit of a headache, but nothing a cup of coffee and a spot of breakfast won't cure.'

'It'd better not be! If you're not fit to row...'

'Perfectly fit,' said DeLancey irritably. He could hardly say otherwise with everyone staring at him and remembering how he had taunted Bott.

'Sit down,' Rollo ordered. 'I'll get your breakfast.'

Rather to Daisy's surprise, DeLancey ate heartily. She had thought nausea was an invariable component of a hangover, and he certainly showed other signs of that disorder, quite apart from his behaviour last night. Presumably his was an idiosyncratic reaction to overindulgence. In that case, he appeared to know his own capabilities, so if he believed he'd be able to row, he was probably right.

His hearty appetite calmed her last remaining fear, that of Bott having poisoned him with nicotine. She could not recall all the details of the symptoms, but she was quite certain nausea was one of them.

Finishing her breakfast, she went up to see how Tish was doing.

Her cousin had just crawled out of bed and was listlessly putting on her dressing-gown. She looked as if she wished she hadn't woken up.

'You'd better stir your stumps,' Daisy advised her, 'if you're going to eat before the race.'

'I'm not hungry. Daisy, last night...'

'I'm afraid it wasn't a dream. But DeLancey came down to breakfast. He neither met nor avoided meeting my eye, and he said nothing – not even dropping nasty hints – about his intrusion, so I suspect he's forgotten it. What's more, he swears he's fit to row.'

'Really?' Tish cheered up no end. 'He's really all right?'

Daisy decided not to tell her the Hon. Basil had been less than steady on his pins. 'He must have a head of granite. Or, no, not quite that, considering how he behaved last night, but he doesn't seem to be susceptible to morning-after-itis. When I left, he was eating like a ... like an oarsman, actually.'

Tish gave her a weak smile. 'Thank heaven. Perhaps I am a bit hungry, after all, but I don't want to see him, even if he's forgotten. Could you ask one of the maids...'

'I'll bring you up something. Tea and toast and a rasher?'

'Spiffing. Thanks, Daisy. I'm glad you're my cousin.'

With that unexpected testimonial she departed for the bathroom.

Alec arrived dead on time. Daisy wasn't exactly hanging about looking out for him, she told herself. She was in the front garden because that was where she had found her aunt, and in order to say good-morning to that elusive lady one had to track her down wherever she happened to be.

Which clever rationalisation did not prevent a thrill of delight when the little yellow Austin Seven turned into the drive.

'...too chalky for rhododendrons to flourish in this ... Daisy, you're not listening to a word. You really must stop me when I bore on and on about the garden. Oh, that's your young man's motor, is it?'

'Yes, Aunt Cynthia. You were telling me how your rhododendrons flourish.'

'They don't. Run along with you, dear. Bring him over to say hullo, and I promise I shan't tell *him* about rhododendrons.'

Alec had the hood of the Austin Chummy down. When Daisy waved madly, he turned his dark, hatless head, waved back, and brought the motor-car to a halt. Daisy abandoned the dignity of her twenty-five years and raced across the lawn to jump in beside him.

The grey eyes, capable of transfixing the guilty with a coldly piercing glance, smiled at her warmly. The heavy dark eyebrows, capable of expressing scepticism or displeasure with equal ease, were at rest. His hair still sprang crisply from his temples in that delicious way that begged her to run her fingers through it.

She did. 'You haven't changed.'

Alec laughed. 'I seem to remember spending all day last Sunday with you, taking Belinda to the Zoo.'

'But I haven't seen you all week.'

'We have two whole days.' Alec simply could not resist those candid, hopeful blue eyes. He kissed her, becoming aware even as their lips met that the woman she'd been talking to was watching with what he hoped, though he could not be sure at that distance, was amused indulgence.

The kiss became perfunctory. He raised his head with a cough and returned the woman's wave. 'Your aunt?' he whispered.

'Yes. Don't look so terrified, you'll find Aunt Cynthia *much* easier than Mother.'

'I'm not looking terrified, wretch. Detective Chief Inspectors don't know how.'

'You gave a jolly good imitation, then. Drive on up to the house, then we'll walk back and I'll introduce you.'

Obeying, Alec parked beside a green Lea-Francis, a cheapish vehicle, but sporty. Already insecure – he could arrest an erring duke with aplomb but quailed at the prospect of meeting Daisy's aristocratic relatives – he felt his other source of doubts bubbling up. Shouldn't Daisy be with a dashing young gentleman in a two-seater instead of a staid, middle-class copper ten years older than herself in a staid, middle-class family car?

She didn't seem to mind, fondly smoothing his hair where she had ruffled it. He straightened his tie – the Royal Flying Corps one he generally wore when consorting with the upper classes – and went round to open the passenger-side door.

Daisy took his hand as they crossed the lawn. Her warm little hand in his both gave him confidence and added to his doubts. When he was her age, before the War, even an engaged couple would never have approached a relative hand-in-hand. Not in his class, at least. Who knew what the nobs did?

Lady Cheringham did not appear to take it amiss, smiling at him and taking off her grubby gardening glove to shake his hand as Daisy presented him: 'Aunt Cynthia, this is Alec Fletcher.'

'How do you do, Mr. Fletcher? Or – oh dear! – should I call you Detective Chief Inspector?'

'Great Scott, no, please! I'm here strictly in mufti, Lady Cheringham. What a splendid display of phlox!'

'They are looking good, aren't they?' her ladyship agreed, regarding the colourful herbaceous border with complacency. 'But I promised Daisy I wouldn't delay you with garden-talk. You'll want to be off to the river to catch the race.'

As they returned towards the house, Daisy

said indignantly, 'You dark horse! I didn't know you could tell a phlox from a foxglove.'

'Modesty is my middle name. My father was quite a gardener. I'd do more if I had the time.'

'I would have warned you garden-talk was the way to Aunt Cynthia's heart.'

'My dear, my darling girl, you are engaged to a detective, remember. When I saw Lady Cheringham in rubber boots and muddy gloves, trowel in hand, grass stains on her skirt about the level of her knees, I said to myself either she's been burying a body or...'

'Idiot,' said Daisy, laughing. He loved to hear her laugh.

He was besotted, he recognized ruefully, not for the first time. He wouldn't give her up for the world, in spite of the opposition of both their mothers, and the appalling tangles she all too frequently inveigled him into.

They went through the front door, standing hospitably open, into an attractive hall, parquet floored. Alec, who had specialised in Georgian history at university, approved the pale blue-grey, white-striped Regency wallpaper and the inlaid half-moon table.

'Roses,' he said, pointing at the vase of flowers on the table, reflected in the mirror hanging above.

Daisy laughed again. 'Stop showing off and come and meet everyone. Everyone but the crew, that is.'

She led the way through a pleasant, comfortable drawing-room and out through French windows onto a terrace overlooking the river. Four young men in maroon blazers jumped to their feet, as did a pretty blond girl, who turned out to be Daisy's cousin, Patricia Cheringham.

Miss Cheringham came to greet him. She was as welcoming as her mother, though she looked rather tired. The strain of a houseful of hearty oarsmen must be telling on her. She introduced her friend, Miss Carrick, a plain young lady with a voice like warm honey, and the four undergrads. The latter were deferential, no doubt because of his age, he thought ruefully. His rank would not impress them, even if they knew it. To such privileged scions of the aristocracy and the gentry, no policeman was quite 'one of us.'

At least they did not seem to hold his lack of the proper accent against him. Not for the first time, Alec blessed his mother for not allowing him to pick up the slightest trace of North London speech patterns. He spoke the King's English, better in fact than they did, with their university slang and the plummy voices which made them sound like pompous fools.

Eton and Oxford did not automatically

make a man a pompous fool, Alec reminded himself charitably.

They all went down to the river-bank together. Two double-scull skiffs were moored there. Each had a forward-facing seat in the stern, a V-shaped seat fitting into the bow, and two benches for oarsmen amidships.

'I hope you're not expecting me to row you over,' Alec said to Daisy in a low voice, regarding the swarm of small craft heading upstream. 'I might manage the current or the traffic, but not both. The Serpentine is the limit of my experience.'

'I've rowed on the Severn.'

'Then you can row me over.'

'Not likely! It was years ago, and a much smaller, quieter river. Luckily, we have four stalwart oarsmen to hand.'

In fact, the Ambrose men took it for granted that they would man the sculls. Miss Cheringham and Miss Carrick embarked with Meredith and Leigh, Alec and Daisy with Wells and Poindexter.

'You do know how to steer, don't you, Mr. Fletcher?' Miss Carrick called as he settled on the well-cushioned rear seat with Daisy.

Daisy put the tiller-lines in his hands.

'I think so,' Alec said cautiously.

Miss Carrick and Miss Cheringham exchanged a glance. 'There are an awful lot of boats out,' said Miss Cheringham. 'I'll come with you.'

Though there was plenty of room for all of them, Daisy didn't want to leave Miss Carrick on her own, so she took her cousin's place in the other skiff.

'I thought I'd better ask,' Miss Cheringham said apologetically as Alec pushed off with the boat-hook. 'Daisy steered us all over the place yesterday. I expect you would have managed perfectly well.'

Alec smiled at her. 'Or I might have steered into someone else and upset a couple of boatloads into the river. You were quite right not to trust me, Miss Cheringham.'

'Do call me Tish. After all, we'll be cousins soon. Unless you prefer Patricia.'

Reciprocating, Alec intimated that Tish would do very well. Her suggestion that he might prefer to use her proper name once again made him feel his age. He was beginning to wonder if his hair had greyed overnight without his noticing.

Daisy was five years older than her cousin, he reminded himself. Not that she looked a day over eighteen in her pretty summer frock and daisy-garlanded hat.

Two whole days with nothing to do but enjoy her company.

They reached the opposite bank and disembarked. As they set off along the towpath, Alec and Daisy lagged behind the others, who were anxious not to miss the start of the Ambrose four's heat.

'Your cousin is charming,' Alec said. 'Do I gather *her* cousin is rowing? Tell me a bit about this crew I'm to cheer.'

'Yes, Cherry's one of them.' Daisy tucked her hand under his arm. 'He's more like a brother, really. His parents pretty much brought her up, my aunt and uncle being abroad so much. He's engaged to Dottie. They're both brainy types, heading for academic careers. But nice, not a bit condescending to us mortals with merely average minds.'

'Speak for yourself!'

'I do.' Her eyes danced as she glanced up at him. 'I'm quite aware of your brilliance, even though you don't toss around ancient Greek quotations like Jove tossing thunderbolts.'

'Zeus. Do they?'

'Rarely, but they can. Rollo Frieth, on the other hand, failed his exams, poor chap. He and Cherry are older than most undergrads, having fought in the War. Rollo's the crew's captain, Cherry's friend, and Tish's young man, in whatever order you prefer. Thoroughly good-natured, and good at smoothing ruffled feathers, which is an excellent qualification for the captain of this crew.'

'A quarrelsome lot?' Alec asked. He waved at the men tramping ahead. 'These seem pretty placid.'

'Most of them are, especially young Fosdyke, who lives to row, run, eat, and sleep. A nice, obliging boy, though. He's in the four, too. Then there's the Hon. Basil.'

From her tone, he guessed, 'The fly in the ointment?'

'Mosquito.' She rubbed her arm reminiscently, explaining, 'I was bitten the other evening. Don't look so horrified: by a real mosquito, not Basil DeLancey. I don't *think* he actually bites, but I wouldn't be prepared to swear to it.'

'A Don Juan?'

She frowned. 'No, not exactly. At least, Cherry said he got a shop-girl into trouble, and he's been pestering Tish like billy-oh, but that's as much to annoy Cherry and Rollo as... No, it's not even that. He just says exactly what comes into his head, and what comes into his head is rude as often as not, as he seems to despise most people. He was horribly insulting to poor Dottie. I honestly don't believe he realizes how obnoxious he is. No one could want to make enemies right and left as he does, could they?'

'I've known a few who don't care.'

'That's it. He doesn't care. Susan Hopgood told me he was the baby of the family and we decided he grew up under the impression everything he said was clever or funny or both.'

'Susan Hopgood?' Alec queried.

'Horace Bott's girl. He's the eight's cox,

and DeLancey's principal victim.'

'Don't talk to me of victims! I'm on holiday.'

'All right, I won't.' Daisy promised with a chuckle. 'That's Temple Island. Gosh, look at all those people waiting to watch the start! I hope we'll be able to see.'

Concentrating on Daisy, Alec had been only distantly aware of the wooded island in the middle of the river. Now he saw a knot of people ahead, clustered on the bank. Nearby, flags marked the start, beyond which the river was divided by floating booms into two lanes. Officials on board a motor-launch were watching the approach of two fours boats. The oarsmen in the nearer boat wore maroon shorts.

'This side is the Ambrose boat?' Alec asked.

'Yes, the Berks side. The other lane's known as the Bucks side, though by the time they get to the finish it's actually Oxfordshire. Who is it they're racing, Mr. Meredith?' Daisy enquired as they caught up with the others.

'Medway. The Medway Rowing Club. We thought we'd go on a bit farther, Miss Dalrymple, beyond this crowd.'

Miss Carrick looked back. 'We'll be past the start but we should get a better view,' she explained.

'We'll come too,' said Daisy.

Poindexter forged ahead, clearing a way along the path with his, 'I s-say, excuse us, chaps, do.'

Most of those who had gathered at the start were young fellows, who no doubt had friends rowing in this or later heats. There were one or two older men, perhaps fathers, and a few young ladies. A large, middle-aged police constable stood at ease in the meadow a few yards off, keeping a benevolent eye on the crowd.

Though Alec did his best to ignore the officer, to his annoyance he caught the man's eye. The constable stepped a couple of paces forward and said in a confidential tone, 'The young gents sometimes gets a bit excited, sir, if there's a false start called, like, or they mebbe thinks there oughta be.'

Alec smiled and nodded. Moving on, he said to Daisy, 'Do I look so like a policeman?'

'You know you don't. I'm sure he didn't guess. It's just that you have a sort of natural air of authority. I expect you looked as if you wondered what he was doing here, so he told you.'

'As long as he doesn't expect me to wade in on his side if fists start flying,' Alec grumbled, hiding his pleasure. She considered he had a natural air of authority, did she?

Then he grimaced at her oblivious back,

reminding himself that she had never yet let his authority stop her doing exactly as she saw fit.

Tish, in the lead, had stopped level with the upper end of the island, a short distance beyond the start. They all gathered around her. They had an excellent view of the boats manoeuvering into position at the start. This appeared to Alec to be an extraordinarily complicated matter.

Poindexter explained. 'You s-see, s-sir, the idea is that the s-stern should be on the s-starting line, but that gives a longer boat an advantage since the first bow to cross the finish line wins. S-so if one boat is shorter, as in this case, the other is pulled back to bring the bows level.'

Alec forebore to ask why they did not just start with the bows at the line. Every sport, profession, and trade had its own arcane rules, incomprehensible to outsiders.

One of the officials on the stewards' launch raised his arm. In the ensuing hush, Alec heard a cuckoo call. Daisy hung on his arm, endearingly excited.

The starting pistol cracked out. Oars sliced the river's surface. Men heaved with sudden effort. The boats shot forward. In beautiful unison, with the grace of a heron's wings, the oars rose, swept back, dipped again.

On the third pull, the boats drew past.

'That's Cherry in the bow,' said Daisy, 'then Rollo, then Fosdyke, then DeLancey at stroke. He has to steer with his feet and count as well as... Gosh, he looks ghastly.'

Even as she spoke, it became apparent that DeLancey was not bending forward for the next stroke but doubling up in pain. He let go his oar, clutched his head, then leant over the gunwale and vomited into the river.

'Oh Lord, just like Bott yesterday,' someone groaned.

The boat was veering out of control as the other three rowers tried desperately to correct their course, though the race was obviously forfeited. Cheringham shouted orders, but it was impossible to allow for the loss of their steersman as well as one of four oars, not to mention DeLancey's off-centre weight.

The boat wallowed, dead in the water, slipping backwards.

The stroke seemed to make an effort to sit up, but instead he half-rose to his feet with a convulsive jerk, then toppled into the river.

Before the spectators had time to do more than gasp in shock, Cheringham dived in after him. The current swept DeLancey's unresisting body a few feet downstream, then Cheringham reached him and turned him on his back. Swimming strongly, he kicked out for the bank with his burden.

In the few seconds before they reached the

near boom, Alec sprang into action.

'Stand back, please, everyone. Give them room. Officer, over here! Poindexter, Wells, give them a hand. You two, help the constable keep people back.'

One of the older men, a solid, prosperous-looking gentleman, pushed through the gaping crowd. 'I'm a doctor,' he announced, waving a shooting-stick.

'Excellent. Thank you, sir.' Turning, Alec saw Poindexter and Wells haul DeLancey from the water.

They laid him on the grass and the doctor knelt beside him, reaching for his wrist.

Cheringham pulled himself onto the bank, water streaming from his hair and clothes. 'Turn him on his front,' he panted. 'I know artificial respiration.' He dropped to his knees beside DeLancey's still form.

The doctor shook his head. 'No pulse. I'm sorry, young man, there's nothing you can do for him. He wasn't in the water long enough to drown. I've an idea...' He lifted one eyelid and peered at the staring eye.

Cheringham's shoulders slumped.

Alec gave him a hand to rise. 'You did your best. Now stand back, please, the three of you.' As Cheringham and the other two moved back, Daisy appeared, pale-faced. 'Daisy, please!'

'Just a minute. I think it could be nicotine poisoning,' she said apprehensively.

The doctor looked up and shook his head again. 'No. I'm fairly certain it was a subdural haemorrhage. There are contusions on both sides of the skull. In plain English, he's been hit on the head.'

CHAPTER 7

Daisy stared down at DeLancey's body. Lying there in his sodden crew shorts and shirt, he looked pathetically harmless. His poisonous tongue was stilled, but not, it seemed, by poison.

With a shudder, she turned away. Alec's arm went about her shoulders for a quick squeeze.

Releasing her, he glanced around. Daisy followed his gaze. She picked out faces in the crowd: horrified, curious, excited. Cherry was aghast, the other four Ambrose men pale and frozen in place. Further along the bank she saw Tish sitting hunched on the grass with her head buried in her hands. Daisy wondered if she should go to her cousin, but Dottie had her arms around her and seemed to be coping admirably.

The constable stood with his mouth open, looking stunned.

Alec sighed. 'I'm a police officer,' he announced in a resigned voice. 'Detective Chief Inspector Fletcher, Scotland Yard. This isn't my pigeon, but I'll take charge till a local man arrives. Constable...?'

'Rogers, sir.' His relief obvious, the man

saluted. 'Inspector Wishburn's on duty up by the stands. Will I go fetch 'im?'

'No, I need you here.' Alec turned to the Ambrose crewmen. 'Would one of you gentlemen mind going for the Inspector?'

'I'll go.' Leigh stripped off his blazer and handed it to Meredith. 'Here, you'd better use this to cover him.' He set off along the towpath at a fast lope.

Meredith stood still with the blazer in his hands. 'Dead?' he said in a queer voice. 'DeLancey's dead?'

'I'm afraid so.' Daisy took the blazer from him and, trying not to look at the dead face, helped the doctor cover DeLancey's head and torso. The doctor looked vaguely familiar, though she was pretty sure she had never seen him before.

Alec finished talking to Constable Rogers, who started to move the crowd along, dispersing them upstream and downstream. As Alec turned back, Cherry said to him, 'If you don't mind, sir, I'll take the ladies home.' Shivering, he gestured towards Tish and Dottie.

'Yes, you'd better go and get changed. Don't go anywhere, please. They'll need to talk to you. By all means take your cousin and Miss Carrick, but I want Daisy here.'

His tone was not such as to give Daisy joy. She wished she had not burst out with her theory about tobacco poisoning. Thank heaven she was wrong. It would have been simply frightful to discover that an antidote administered last night could have saved DeLancey's life.

Alec requested Poindexter, Wells, and Meredith to stay nearby in case they were needed, then he turned to the doctor, only to be interrupted by a hail from the river.

'Hi, there!' The stewards' launch had pulled up to the boom. 'What the deuce is going on?'

'Police! We've got a body here.'

'What about the next race?' demanded a purple-faced official in a gold-braided nautical cap.

'Go ahead and row it. He won't mind. But I must remind you – you must have seen with your glasses – you have two men rowing a four-man boat up the course, with the rudder swinging out of control. I imagine they have no choice but to go on to the Finish.'

'They can't turn between the booms, nor leave their lane.' another official confirmed. 'We'll give them a few minutes more to get clear. Everything under control here?'

'More or less,' Alec said ironically.

'We'll carry on, then. Sorry, and all that, but we can't very well call a halt to things.'

The launch went into reverse and *putputted* back towards the starting line, where the next two boats waited.

Once again Alec turned to the doctor. 'Thank you, Dr...?'

'Mr. I'm a surgeon. Fosdyke's the name. My boy's one of the two rowing the four-oar boat.'

'Thank you, Mr. Fosdyke. May I ask how sure you are of your diagnosis?'

'I'm not usually concerned with initial diagnoses, but I've operated on a number of patients with subdural haematoma and haemorrhage. Naturally, their physicians discussed their symptoms with me beforehand. This unfortunate young man appeared to suffer from an acute headache, did he not?'

'That's what it looked like,' Alec agreed.

'He vomited, without preceding nausea, one would assume, or he'd not have embarked upon the race. And the pupils of his eyes are of different sizes, a significant indicator. In my view, the contusions on his head virtually clinch the matter. The autopsy – there will be an autopsy, I assume? – will provide definite proof. Or disproof.'

'I see. He couldn't have fallen?'

'Unless he fell twice,' said the doctor quizzically, 'landing first on one side of his head and then on the other, I incline to the opinion that he was hit sufficiently hard to make him fall. I trust I am not unduly influenced by the fact that what my son has told me about the character of the deceased makes such an eventuality not unlikely.'

Alec matched his dryness. 'So I gather. I must assume he was not hit after he got into the boat, as he couldn't have fallen after that. So his death was a delayed reaction to a blow. How long ago could it have happened?'

'Weeks, theoretically. From the condition of the contusions, anywhere from four to twenty-four hours. Two to thirty-two, perhaps. I'm no expert. No doubt a police surgeon will be able to narrow the time period.'

'I hope so! Will you be so kind, Mr. Fosdyke, as to wait until the local man arrives?'

'By all means.'

Daisy scarcely heard the doctor's answer. His previous words had just sunk in. Two to thirty-two hours ago!

'Mr. Fosdyke,' she said, her voice trembling with dread, 'is mental confusion another symptom? And incoherence, and loss of balance?'

'Yes, indeed, Miss…'

'Dalrymple,' Alec put in, seeing Daisy was incapable of speech.

'And disturbances of vision,' the doctor added. 'Symptoms vary according to the areas of the brain affected.'

Daisy sat down rather suddenly on the grass, feeling decidedly queer. 'We thought he was drunk,' she said faintly, as Alec crouched beside her and took her hands in a comforting clasp.

'A most natural assumption,' said Mr. Fosdyke.

'But if we had phoned for medical help – no, Alec, I must know! – if DeLancey had seen a doctor at once, he would have survived?'

'Time is of the essence. However, the prognosis is poor even in cases where the hemorrhage is stopped by prompt surgery, and in those who survive, full recovery is far from assured. You have no cause to reproach yourself, Miss Dalrymple,' the doctor said kindly. 'The symptoms are easy for the layman to confuse with overindulgence in alcoholic beverages.'

Daisy gave a shaky nod. 'Alec,' she said urgently, 'I'd much rather tell you what happened than a stranger. Then you can tell the detective in charge.'

'You know better than that, my love. If you have significant information, you'll have to repeat it to the local people.'

'I suppose so. But you can tell me what is significant?'

'Now, Watson, you know my methods. Any detail may turn out to be significant. You can't withhold anything from the investigators.'

'All right.' Daisy sighed. 'Let me tell you just to help sort out my thoughts. Only I'm afraid, if I'm right, they will probably ask you to take charge.'

'No, this is our weekend!' Alec exploded, rising to his feet and pulling Daisy with him into a bear hug.

The doctor tactfully turned his back, unfolded his shooting-stick, and sat down to watch the start of the next race.

Revelling in Alec's annoyance at the prospect of their weekend being spoilt, Daisy nonetheless said sadly, 'I rather doubt Scotland Yard will agree to send someone else when you're already on the spot and actually witnessed DeLancey's demise. You see, he appears to have died in Berkshire, but I'm pretty sure he was biffed in Buckinghamshire.'

'Damn,' Alec groaned, 'if you'll pardon the expression. You're right, they'll probably call in the Met. And with you involved, the A.C. is bound to insist on my handling it.'

'I don't see why your Assistant Commissioner considers me his *bête noire*,' she said with some indignation. 'I've given you loads of help.'

He grimaced. 'Daisy, how is it you keep falling over bodies? Do people see you coming and promptly decide to do someone in?'

'I can't help it! It's like when one comes across an unfamiliar word, and for the next week, everything one reads – there it is. Or meeting an acquaintance one hasn't seen for years and then one keeps running into them everywhere one goes. It happens to lots of people.'

'Not with bodies, it doesn't, thank heaven! Right-oh, you'd better tell me all.'

'Must we stay here, right on top of *him*?' Though Daisy had her back to DeLancey, whose face was covered, and his eyes closed, she felt his dead, reproachful gaze fixed on her.

'No, just within calling distance. We shan't be interrupted if we move over into the field a bit.'

The towpath was growing busier. The curious stared at the maroon blazer and the bare legs protruding from beneath it, already drying in the sun, but Constable Rogers kept people moving.

'There's been a h'accident,' he repeated stolidly to all questions.

Already a new group of spectators had gathered, somewhat downriver from the start, beyond the constable's range, intent only on a good view of the crews they had come to support.

While Alec had a word with Rogers and asked Meredith, Wells, and Poindexter to move closer and stand guard over DeLancey's body, Daisy moved back into the meadow. The grass had been mowed for hay but already ox-eye daisies and purple knapweed raised their heads. She found a slight bank and sat down.

Alec joined her. 'You'd better sit on my jacket,' he said, starting to take it off.

'Keep it on. You'll want to look professional when the local coppers arrive. The ground's quite dry, and anyway, it's too late for my frock.'

Sitting down, he left a couple of feet between them. She made a moue at him, and he said, 'It won't look professional if we're any closer, and besides, you'll distract me from what you're saying. You are over the worst shock, aren't you?'

'Yes. It was bad enough his dropping dead, but knowing I might have prevented it...'

He took her hand, distraction or not. 'Fosdyke is right, darling, you couldn't have guessed. You didn't see the lumps on his head, did you?'

'No, but I did think he might have been poisoned with nicotine. If I'd called in a doctor for that ... but I couldn't see quite how it could have been done, and it seemed so unlikely, and he *had* been drinking. His breath smelled of whisky.'

'Daisy, what is all this about nicotine poisoning? And when and where did you see DeLancey in his parlous state? And...'

'I'd better begin at the beginning,' said Daisy firmly, 'or I shall get muddled. It started with Aunt Cynthia and the aphids. She was spraying the roses with tobacco-water and I worried about nicotine. I read up on poisons after that horrible Albert Hall affair, you see.'

'Just in case?' Alec suggested.

She pulled a face at him. 'I'd forgotten the details so I looked it up later. There's such a long list of symptoms I still couldn't remember them all, but I'm sure DeLancey had some of them. But I'll get to that in a minute. After talking to Aunt Cynthia, I went down to the landing-stage. The eight was just coming in. I talked to Horace Bott while the others put the boat away.'

'The mysterious Bott?

'He's not at all mysterious, you just haven't seen him because he's the eight's cox and the four is coxless.'

'And he didn't turn out with the rest to cheer the four,' Alec pointed out.

'No, and I can't blame him. The others don't like him. Well, I can't blame them, either. He seems to be in a permanent state of dudgeon. It's a vicious circle, actually. He has a brilliant mind – he won a scholarship to Ambrose and took a Double First in Physics and Maths, and he's been offered a Cambridge fellowship – but he's the son of a newsagent. From Birmingham.'

'Wrong accent, wrong family,' Alec said wryly.

'Wrong instincts, wrong clothes.' Daisy added. 'That's what he told me. I don't doubt he was badly treated, and the result is, he looks for reasons to take offence, and of course he finds them, and so he's permanently up in arms. So even those who'd be willing to take him on his merits can't get past the prickles.'

'And DeLancey was his chief tormentor.'

'His only tormentor, really. The others just ignore him, mostly. Rollo stood up for him when DeLancey was being quite disgustingly rude, and he and Cherry went to the rescue when DeLancey attacked him.'

'DeLancey actually physically attacked Bott?' Alec exclaimed.

'He shoved him into the river.' Daisy explained about the taunts which had led Bott to drink whisky and to attempt to cox next morning, and the sorry result. 'DeLancey didn't accept any responsibility whatever. He blamed the whole thing on Bott. The ducking was only the climax of a whole string of public insults, and there's no knowing what he might have done next if Lord DeLancey – his brother– hadn't taken him away.'

'So Bott had every reason to go for DeLancey.'

'Cherry and Rollo did, too.' Daisy immediately regretted her instinctive defence of the defenceless cox, but Alec's raised eyebrows demanded elaboration. 'Cherry was absolutely livid over DeLancey insulting Dottie and pursuing Tish,' she said reluctantly. 'Rollo only just stopped him going for him once. But Rollo found it hard to restrain himself, as well. He and Tish aren't engaged yet, but he's frightfully fond of her.'

'Bott, Cheringham, and Frieth,' Alec mused. 'What about the rest of them?'

'I didn't hear DeLancey provoking any of them, not to fury. They were pretty fed up with his behaviour to Bott when it made them lose the race. It wouldn't surprise me at all if one of them quarrelled with him over it. Assuming he ignored his brother's wishes, anyone could have gone down to the boat-house and...'

'Hold on! Where do DeLancey's brother and the boathouse come into this? Oh, the dickens, here come Leigh and the local constabulary!' He stood up and reached down to help Daisy up.

'Oh blast!' she said. 'If you're not put in charge, I don't suppose anyone else will be willing to listen to my theory.'

Holding both her hands, he looked down at her with a crooked smile. 'I'll do my best to persuade them at least to listen,' he promised. 'You do occasionally come up with the odd fairly bright idea.'

'You're too kind!' said Daisy.

CHAPTER 8

Leigh had brought Inspector Washburn, two bobbies, and a tall, lean gentleman he introduced as the Chief Constable of Berkshire. Alec blinked at Sir Amory Brentwood's brilliant pink blazer, tie, cap, and socks, a startling contrast to the sober police blue surrounding him.

'Everything under control, eh?' said Sir Amory. 'Hope you've no objection to taking charge, my dear fellow. My men are spread thin, what with the Regatta crowds, and Prince Henry due to pop in this afternoon. Dashing young chappie, wants a bit of watching, what?'

Seeing Daisy lurking not quite beyond earshot, her back tactfully turned as if she was watching the races, but undoubtedly listening, Alec made a last-ditch effort to save their weekend. 'Sir, the Assistant Commissioner…'

'I'll make all right with your A.C., never fear,' Sir Amory assured him. 'Spot of luck your being down here. You can call on Inspector Wishbone here for any help you need, of course, but I hope you'll try not to be too much of a drain on my manpower.'

Alec surrendered. 'I'll send for my own men, sir. There seems to be a Buckinghamshire connection. I don't suppose you could advise me how to get in touch with the C.C.?'

'Old Felter? He'll be at Phyllis Court I expect, old chap, and so will Packington, the Oxfordshire C.C., if you need him. I'm a rowing man myself, you know.' He sighed. 'Or used to be. Well, I'll leave you chaps to get on with it then. Over to you, Wishbone, what?'

'Yes, sir,' said the Inspector resignedly.

Already turning away, Sir Amory swung back. 'I say, it is murder, is it? That young fellow wasn't too sure.'

'Or manslaughter, sir,' Alec temporized, 'but that's up to the courts. For police purposes, all homicides are presumed to be murder.'

'Yes, of course. Homicide, eh? Not a homicidal maniac, I trust?' He laughed nervously. 'Er, who...?' He glanced past Alec at the victim under his temporary maroon shroud.

Alec was glad to see that Poindexter had used his blazer to cover the legs. 'The Honourable Basil DeLancey,' he said.

'Honourable...?' The chief Constable paled. 'Good gad! It couldn't be a Bolshevik plot, could it?'

'I think it highly unlikely, sir.'

'Good, good. Prince Henry coming and

all, what? Be grateful if you could keep it under your hat as much as possible, old chap. Don't want a lot of fuss with royalty around, eh?'

'I'll do my best, sir, but I gather Lord DeLancey, the victim's brother, is in Henley. I can't expect to keep it from him until the Prince has left.' In fact, Alec began to realise, the case was not only going to disrupt his time with Daisy. One way or another, it was going to land him in a thoroughly invidious position.

Sir Amory shook his head gloomily. 'Can't ask more than your best,' he admitted. 'Lord DeLancey, eh?'

Leigh, who had stepped away to join Daisy, returned. 'Sorry to butt in, sir,' he said, 'but I think that's Lord DeLancey coming now. There, in the navy blazer.'

The Chief Constable glanced back along the towpath, his eyes popping. 'I'm off. Least said, soonest mended, eh, Chief Inspector?'

Alec did not waste time watching him go. 'Washburn, isn't it?' he said to the local Inspector, earning a look of gratitude. 'I'd like to keep your two men for the moment, though I'll return them to you as soon as possible. I won't detain you, but will you be so good as to telephone the Yard and ask them to send down my men?'

'Of course, sir.' The Inspector took out his notebook.

‘Sergeant Tring and Constable Piper. They’d better go to the Henley police station. I’ll leave a message there when I know where to have them contact me.’

‘Right you are, sir. I’ve sent for our police surgeon, sir, Dr. Dewhurst, but he has to come from Reading. If you’re going to be working with the Henley force, too, you might want to get hold of their man.’

‘Damn!’ said Alec. ‘I need to speak to the Bucks and Oxfordshire C.C.s. Where’s this Phyllis Court?’

‘It’s an exclusive club – social, not rowing like Leander – over on the other side of the river, sir.’

‘It would be! I’ll have to get to a telephone myself.’ He groaned as he saw complications multiplying. The man Leigh had pointed out as Lord DeLancey was about to add to them. ‘Felter and Packington, was it?’

‘Colonel Felter and Mr. James Packington, sir.’

‘Thanks, Washburn. Forget about the Henley surgeon for the moment. I’ll send one of these fellows if I need your further help.’

Inspector Washburn, turning to leave, was accosted by the man in the navy blazer. ‘Hi, you, I’m DeLancey. What’s all this rot about my brother falling out of his boat? Is he ill?’

‘Detective Chief Inspector Fletcher will assist you, sir,’ said the Inspector, and made good his escape.

Lord DeLancey paled. 'What's going on?' he asked uncertainly. 'Frieth just said he'd puked and fallen in.'

'I'm sorry, sir.' Alec said, 'I'm afraid I have bad news. Your brother is dead.'

'Drowned? The damned fool!' DeLancey said savagely, flushed now with anger. 'No one drowns at Henley! With half the world looking on, we'll never manage to keep it quiet.'

So much for brotherly love. Alec had the fewer qualms as he said, 'Not drowned. It seems Mr. DeLancey died from the delayed effects of a blow to the head.'

'He fell?' His lordship's flush faded. 'Or do you mean someone hit him?'

'Yes, sir. Presumably in the course of a quarrel.'

'A quarrel?' DeLancey's pallor almost equalled his dead brother's. 'What do you mean delayed? How long delayed?'

'At present I have very little information. I shall have to ask you when you last saw your brother and his condition at that time, what you know of his movements, and whether you are aware of anyone who ... disliked him. However, this is hardly the place.'

For the first time, Lord DeLancey looked beyond him, at the blazers covering Basil DeLancey's corpse. 'This is hardly the place to let him lie, exposed to every passer-by,' he exclaimed irritably.

Alec agreed. Nor was there any reason not to move the body before the police surgeon saw it; no need to photograph its position; no need to search the ground for clues. The clues would be found wherever DeLancey was hit and fell, not where he died.

In the boat-house? Alec wondered, glancing at Daisy, still pretending not to listen.

'I hesitate to have him carried through the crowds to the town,' he said to Lord DeLancey.

'No, by jingo!'

'Which doesn't leave much alternative. Daisy!' Alec almost smiled at the alacrity with which she turned. 'How upset would your aunt be if we carried the deceased back to the house?'

'I haven't the foggiest. Not too, I expect. Worse things must have happened in Africa, don't you think? It ... he wouldn't stay long, would he? Gosh, that sounds awful. I'm sorry, Lord DeLancey. Please accept my condolences.'

DeLancey bowed slightly.

'Just until we can get him to the nearest mortuary,' Alec said. 'She won't mind if I make a few telephone calls?'

'No, not at all, I'm sure.'

'We'll take him to the Cheringhams then. You know the house, Lord DeLancey? "Bulawayo," on the Marlow Road.'

‘I know it.’

‘It may be rather awkward managing things in a skiff, but we’ll do it somehow. You can put the stretcher together now, Constable.’

One of Washburn’s men had brought a stretcher, dismantled and rolled up with a sheet inside. Alec took the sheet while the two constables started to assemble the stretcher.

‘I’ll be on my way,’ said Lord DeLancey.

‘You won’t come with us?’ Alec asked, surprised.

‘No. I’m going back to Crowswood Place, where I’m staying – you can reach me there. I must try to get in touch with my people. The Earl and Countess of Bicester, you know. They’re on board ship on their way to visit my sister in America.’

One complication the fewer. Alec breathed a silent prayer of gratitude. ‘As you wish, sir. First, I must ask you to identify the victim. Not that there’s the least doubt he’s your brother, I’m afraid, but the Coroner prefers formal identification by a relative.’

Reluctantly, Lord DeLancey trailed him over to the body. Alec turned back the corner of the blazer from the face. His lordship cast a quick glance, looking sick.

‘That’s my brother, Basil DeLancey,’ he confirmed, beads of sweat breaking out on his forehead.

'Thank you. I'll be in touch.'

DeLancey departed along the towpath at a walk fast enough to be almost a trot.

With the assistance of Poindexter and Wells, Alec quickly and smoothly replaced the blazers with the sheet. Poindexter and Leigh showed a marked distaste for their returned clothing.

'It doesn't s-seem quite respectful to put it on,' said Poindexter.

Leigh merely shuddered and held his at arm's length.

'You might as well wear them,' Daisy said practically, 'because you'll have to carry them back anyway. You can't just drop them here.'

'I should rather say not, fellows,' Meredith agreed. 'We don't want a couple of scavenging tramps wandering around in Ambrose blazers.'

'Here come Frieth and Fosdyke,' Leigh announced. 'Their need is greater than ours.'

He and Poindexter went to meet Rollo and the younger Fosdyke, whose father turned at the sound of his name. The doctor had not stirred since propping himself on his shooting-stick, but now he folded it.

'Chief Inspector,' he said to Alec, now supervising the constables in lifting the sheet-covered body onto the stretcher, 'do you wish me to accompany you to ... er ... Bulawayo?'

'If it's not too much of an imposition, Mr. Fosdyke, I'd appreciate it.'

'Not at all. I shall be glad to be with my boy at such a distressing time.' He followed Leigh and Poindexter.

'What about the police surgeon?' Daisy asked Alec. 'The man's coming from Reading, which is Berkshire...'

'I knew you were eavesdropping!'

She grinned at him. 'But the body's going to be in Bucks.'

Alec groaned. 'And I suppose the Henley surgeon's in Oxfordshire.'

'Marlow's probably the nearest in Buckinghamshire – though it's not a very big town.'

'The Reading man will have to do the job.' Alec said decisively. 'He's on his way, and after all, DeLancey died in Berkshire. Didn't he?'

'Possibly,' said Daisy, 'but the county boundary runs down the middle of the river and I've no idea exactly where. You see why I said they'd want you to take over?'

'I do indeed!' He turned to Wells and Meredith. 'You two won't mind giving a hand with the stretcher, will you? And rowing over to the Cheringhams'?'

They hastened to assure him that Scotland Yard might count on them. The shock of DeLancey's death past, Daisy suspected they were beginning to enjoy the drama of the occasion. It wasn't as if the victim had been beloved of all.

Alec sent one of the constables back to Inspector Washburn with a message for Dr. Dewhurst to proceed to Bulawayo. By then Rollo and young Fosdyke had arrived with their escort. They both looked exhausted and shocked.

'He's really dead?' Rollo asked Alec. 'It's my fault!'

Everyone stared at him.

'Mr. Frieth.' Alec said gravely, 'It is my duty to warn you that...'

'That's not what he means,' Daisy cried, her own feelings of guilt rushing back. 'You didn't hit him, did you, Rollo?'

'Lord, no!' he exclaimed, aghast. 'I saw enough violence in France. Haven't raised my hand to a soul since. But Mr. Fosdyke says it was probably the stress of sudden exertion which made him keel over. I should never have let him row.'

'Fat choice you had.' Wells snorted. 'He insisted he was well enough to go out. And anyway you thought – we all thought – all that ailed him was a hangover.'

'That's right,' the others agreed.

Mr. Fosdyke started to reassure Rollo, but Daisy didn't listen as Alec, after glaring at her, set about organizing the cortege. The remaining seconded constable led the way at the head of the stretcher, with Wells at the foot. Alec thanked Constable Rogers for his assistance, then he and Daisy joined the tail end of the procession, behind Mr. Fosdyke and Rollo.

'You shouldn't have interrupted.' Alec said softly, tightlipped. 'For all you knew, he was going to confess. You made him pull back from the brink.'

'I'm sure he didn't whack DeLancey. He's much too peaceable.'

'You can't be sure. You told me he had a motive, had a hard time restraining his anger at DeLancey's making eyes at Patricia. You can't take him under your wing just because he's your cousin's suitor.'

'I'm not!' Daisy insisted. 'He's just not the sort to biff someone without immediate provocation. Since Tish wasn't at the boat-house to be quarrelled over…'

'Ah, the boat-house! Let's drop Frieth and Tish for the moment while you explain why you keep harping on that. And also how it happened that you and she saw DeLancey in a parlous state when no one else – apparently – did.'

'All right. I told you DeLancey shoved Bott into the river. Bott swore revenge, and DeLancey took it into his head that he was going to sabotage the fours boat. So he – DeLancey – planned to spend the night in the boat-house guarding the boat. Lord DeLancey forbade it, said he'd just make a silly ass of himself and people would talk. Though after his public attack on Bott, a mere vigil would hardly add to the scandal.'

'Lord DeLancey seems to have a strong aversion to being a subject of gossip,' said Alec. 'That was his chief emotion on learning his brother was dead.'

Daisy hadn't actually promised Tish not to pass on the reason. The details were irrelevant, however. 'He had rather a poor war record.' she said. 'It was hushed up, but of course some people know, and he's madly afraid it will come out if there's talk about the family. Anyway, I shouldn't be at all surprised if Basil DeLancey went down to the boat-house regardless of his brother's prohibition, should you?'

'Not at all.'

'Especially as he *had* been drinking, so he very likely wasn't thinking frightfully clearly.'

'Very likely not. We'll have to consider the boat-house as a possible scene of the crime, certainly, but there's nothing to say it wasn't elsewhere.'

'I suppose not,' said Daisy, crestfallen.

'Cheer up, my love. It's worth knowing we need to check the place carefully. "We," I say. I can only hope Tring and Piper turn up, and soon.'

'There are extra trains down to Henley because of the Regatta, and it's not more than an hour's journey.'

'True, but it depends whether the Yard can contact them quickly, and how hard they try, based on a request from a Berkshire Inspector. I'd better ring up myself. I'm going to be spending a long time on the telephone, Daisy, so you'd better tell me the rest before we get to the skiffs.'

'There's not much more. Only that DeLancey woke us up, Tish and me, in the middle of the night. He came stumbling into the bedroom, confused and unsteady on his feet, just as if he were drunk.'

'The middle of the night?' Alec asked sharply. 'Can you be more definite?'

'About two. Just past.' Daisy noted that he expressed no concern for her safety. She could not decide whether to be pleased that he believed she could take care of herself, or hurt by his lack of solicitude. Of course, he could see she had suffered no harm. 'I looked at the clock when I turned on the light to see what was going on,' she added.

'It sounds as if DeLancey was hit before two, then, though I'll have to talk to Mr. Fosdyke and Dr. Dewhurst about the symptoms. They'll probably want a more precise description from you. What did you do about his intrusion?'

'Tish fetched young Fosdyke – they shared a bedroom – and Fosdyke took him away for us, bless him.'

Alec stopped her with a hand on her arm,

so that they fell further behind the next in line, Rollo and Mr. Fosdyke Senior.

'If DeLancey was, in fact, simply drunk at that point,' Alec said in a low voice, 'he could have started a dust-up with young Fosdyke after they left you.'

'You mean it could have been Fosdyke who biffed him?'

'Exactly. Though, come to think of it, surely someone would have heard if they had scrapped in the passage or bedroom.'

'Not necessarily. The rowers sleep the sleep of the dead– Ugh! I mean, they sleep like logs. Tish had a frightful struggle to wake Fosdyke. Rowing seems to be a fearfully *draining* sport,' Daisy remarked in a meditative aside. 'They all eat like horses, too.'

'No one heard DeLancey in your room, I assume,' Alec said impatiently, starting off again after the others.

'No. It's on the other side of the landing from the wing the men are in, and there's a bathroom opposite, and a dressing-room between Tish's room and her parents'. Dottie's opposite Aunt Cynthia's room, diagonally across the passage from Tish's.'

'Miss Carrick heard nothing?'

'She might have if DeLancey had kicked up a row, but actually all he did was mumble and moan. Tish was afraid for a minute that he'd come after her, but he wasn't at all aggressive.'

'He might have become aggressive on being removed. Young Fosdyke has to go on my list. Oh, Daisy, Daisy, I'm afraid our weekend is thoroughly dished!'

'Too maddening,' said Daisy with regret, but she went on philosophically, 'Still, no one can say you didn't warn me about marrying a policeman. And at least you're here with me, not in the outer reaches of darkest Devon or Derbyshire.'

'Daisy, where's Tish?' Rollo asked anxiously, dropping back as Mr. Fosdyke moved ahead to join his son.

'Cherry took her and Dottie home, ages ago. She was fearfully upset.'

Rollo frowned. 'I didn't think she liked DeLancey.'

Glancing at Alec, Daisy was sure he had noted this intimation of jealousy. 'She didn't, you chump,' she assured Rollo. 'Seeing someone die right in front of you is upsetting even if you loathe him.'

'He wouldn't stop pestering her!'

'He's stopped now,' Alec observed.

'Yes,' said Rollo, not troubling to hide his satisfaction. If he was going to be a successful diplomat, Daisy thought, he needed to practise inscrutability. 'I can't say I'm sorry,' he went on, adding earnestly to Alec, 'but I didn't take a whack at him, you know, though I can't deny I often wanted to.'

Alec's nod was as inscrutable as a nod can

be. 'From what I've heard, you had cause.'

Rollo stopped in his tracks, an expression of horror crossing his eloquent features. 'Daisy, what's upsetting Tish isn't that she thinks I biffed him, is it?'

That notion had not crossed Daisy's mind before. 'Of course not. She knows you too well,' she said hastily, as convincingly as she could, but it seemed more than possible that Tish suspected Rollo, or Cherry, or both.

Tish had another reason for her distress, Daisy recalled. Now that DeLancey was dead, no harm could come of Rollo knowing about his intrusion into their bedroom, so she told him.

'You see, Tish and I have as much cause to reproach ourselves as you did.' she pointed out. 'If you hadn't let him row, if we'd realized he wasn't drunk but needed a doctor...'

'Mr. Fosdyke says even if he had not rowed, any exertion could have killed him. And even with medical attention he might have died, or lived on with crippling brain damage. I'll ask him to talk to Tish,' Rollo hurried after the doctor.

Alec sighed. 'He does seem too ingenuous to be lying. What about Cheringham? If I'm not mistaken, you said Frieth once held him back from coming to cuffs with DeLancey.'

'I wish I hadn't told you!' said Daisy. 'Anyway, he pulled DeLancey out of the river.'

'I don't for a moment imagine whoever struck DeLancey intended his death, or he'd have finished him off there and then. But, as you no doubt heard me tell – remind – Sir Amory, from a police point of view, all unlawful deaths are equivalent. It's up to the courts to decide between murder and manslaughter. Cheringham's efforts to save DeLancey would certainly be a mitigating factor.'

'I don't believe he did it.' But Daisy remembered Cherry's aghast face when Mr. Fosdyke pronounced DeLancey dead.

'I suppose I can't expect you to speak ill of your cousin's cousin. Nonetheless, I'm afraid he and Frieth have to be considered prime suspects.'

'What about Horace Bott?' said Daisy.

'Ah, there you have it,' said Alec, 'what about Horace Bott? And, more to the point, where is Horace Bott?'

CHAPTER 9

Alec spent a frustrating but ultimately successful hour on the telephone in Sir Rupert's library.

He had permission from the Chief Constables of Bucks and Oxfordshire to operate on their respective manors as necessary. They were both delighted not to have to deal with a murder, especially one involving the aristocracy.

Alec's Superintendent at the Yard – or rather, run to earth at his country cottage – had impatiently agreed to the three C.C.s' request for Alec's services, as relayed by Alec. With luck, the Assistant Commissioner for Crime need never be consulted. He'd receive the final report, but Alec meant to do his damnedest to keep Daisy's name out of it.

Detective Sergeant Tom Tring and Detective Constable Ernie Piper were on their way to Henley. Alec was sorry to wrest them from a weekend with their respective families, but in a case which promised as many complications as this, he needed men he knew he could rely on.

A Henley constable had been despatched to make enquiries at Bott's young lady's lodgings (Daisy knew the name and address; how the dickens did she manage it?).

The Berkshire officer who had helped to carry the stretcher was ensconced in the drawing-room, keeping an eye on the young men. Three constables had already arrived from the Buckinghamshire police, who were minimally involved in the Regatta. One was guarding the boat-house, one the bedroom DeLancey had shared with young Fosdyke – what else ought to be guarded and searched Alec could not guess. The third stood outside the library door, ready to run errands.

The police surgeon had also arrived. The next item on Alec's agenda was to talk to Dr. Dewhurst and make sure he agreed with Mr. Fosdyke's diagnosis.

Alec gulped the last bite of the sandwiches Lady Cheringham had kindly sent in to him and washed it down with a swig of lukewarm tea. Daisy had made Alec's apologies to her aunt when they reached the house, while he headed straight for the telephone. He was very glad her uncle was in London – though the news might well bring him scurrying back.

Leaving the constable to mind the telephone in Sir Rupert's library, Alec made for the old coach-house and stables, now converted into garages. In one of these reposed the remains of the Honorable Basil DeLancey.

Dr. Dewhurst and Mr. Fosdyke sat on a bench against the sunny brick wall, the former smoking a pipe, the latter a cigar. Crossing towards them, Alec felt in his pocket for his own pipe and the tobacco pouch Belinda had made him, blue, with a crooked monogram.

The medical men saw him and stood up. Fosdyke introduced Alec to the police surgeon, a short, slight, elderly but sprightly-looking gentleman.

'Miss Dalrymple is your fiancée, Chief Inspector?' asked Dr. Dewhurst, shaking his hand. 'A charming young lady. Judging by her description...'

'You have spoken to her?' Alec demanded.

'Why, yes. In such cases, a first-person report is greatly to be preferred, and I understand the young lady of the house, who was also a witness, is indisposed.'

Mr. Fosdyke shook his head gravely. 'I've talked to Miss Cheringham, tried to convince her that no possible fault attaches to her for failing to recognize that the young man was not simply inebriated.'

'That was kind of you, sir.'

'She has taken the matter a good deal to heart, I fear. I prescribed a bromide, and her mother, a sensible woman, has put her to bed.'

'I'm sorry to hear she's so cut up,' said Alec, wondering if Tish might be suffering from knowledge – not mere suspicion – that Cheringham or Frieth was involved.

'Miss Dalrymple is made of stronger stuff,' Dr. Dewhurst said in a congratulatory tone. 'I hope you don't object to my having consulted her.'

Tamping the fragrant tobacco into his pipe with his thumb, Alec bit back a sigh. 'No, of course not, sir.' He should have realized Daisy had already inextricably entwined herself in the case. He wasn't even sure any more whether he'd wanted to keep her out of it to protect her – or himself.

'She gave an admirably clear account of the symptoms of the deceased last night and this morning.' the police surgeon continued. 'Taking it together with Mr. Fosdyke's account of his death and my own preliminary examination, I concur absolutely with his conclusions. I should be exceedingly surprised if the autopsy doesn't show the cause of death as subdural haemorrhage and haematoma resulting from a blow to the head and subsequent fall.'

'Would you say DeLancey might have been drunk when she saw him last night? That is, could he have been struck later?'

'Oh yes, quite possibly. But he could equally well have been suffering already from the effects of the brain injury. To the layman, the two may be virtually indistinguishable. Not more than forty-eight hours; at least four. Not much help, but I might be able to narrow it a bit at autopsy.'

'Thank you, sir. I expect I'd better take a look at the injuries for myself, if you wouldn't mind coming along to help me interpret what I see.'

'I'll be off,' said Fosdyke, 'if you don't need me any more. Here's my card, Chief Inspector. I'm staying at the Catherine Wheel in Henley, at least until tomorrow evening. If, that is, as I assume, you want Nicholas – my boy – to remain here.'

'I can't insist, sir, but it would be more convenient.' Alec applied a third lighted match to his pipe and puffed vigorously.

'He'll stay. Nick didn't do it, you know. A fist to the chin, perhaps, but a blunt instrument to the back of the head, never.'

'That's what it looks like?'

'You'll see.' Fosdyke shook hands and Alec thanked him for his assistance, hoping the surgeon was right about his son.

Examining the contusions on DeLancey's head, Alec found himself agreeing with Fosdyke's analysis, though there was room for disagreement. For a start, neither swelling appeared to be caused by a fist.

'The impact of individual knuckles is observable ninety-nine times out of a hundred,' Dr. Dewhurst said, adding cautiously, 'There is always the hundredth time, of course.'

Which lump came first was less certain. They were both on the sides of the head rather than the top, front, or back. The one on the right was towards the upper rear, that on the left much further forward but well behind the hair-line. The latter had a raw, scraped look in spite of the draining of blood to the back of the head after death.

'This must have bled,' said Alec.

'Yes, but not badly. It's more of an abrasion than a laceration. Blood would ooze, not flow. Enough to leave you a clue, possibly, but not enough to draw attention, matted in his dark hair as it would have been.'

'And those who saw him were half-asleep. This would be the secondary blow, don't you think?' Alec proposed. 'It looks as if he might have fallen and slid across a rough surface.'

Dewhurst agreed. 'Also, the swelling is less pronounced, as if caused by a fall from no great height, not a severe blow. What is more, there is some bruising on the left hip and…'

'I don't need to see it,' Alec said hastily as the doctor started to draw back the sheet. It was difficult enough to keep his professional composure while examining a disembodied head, without the pathetic sight of the naked body. He puffed on his pipe, though this body, unlike many, required no counter-irritant for the nasal membranes. Thank heaven.

The doctor was also puffing away, speaking around his pipe-stem. 'There are several tiny splinters of wood in the secondary contusion and in the left hand.' he observed.

'A wooden floor? Rough plank, not parquet.'

'That's for you to find out, Chief Inspector, but it would seem a reasonable inference. I find it difficult to picture a weapon which would leave such signs, though that, again, is your business. On the other hand, the right parietal contusion appears to have been produced by some sort of blunt instrument, more flat than rounded, I should say, and smooth rather than rough. No bleeding.'

'Hit from behind, by a right-handed assailant,' Alec concluded.

'From behind and slightly above.'

Alec frowned. 'He's quite tall, isn't he?'

'Five foot eleven and a quarter.'

'Tall enough. Crouching?' Lurking low in the boat-house?

'Bruised hip,' countered Dr. Dewhurst. 'He landed on it from more than crouching height.'

'Hmmm. He'd have been knocked unconscious, I assume.'

'Not necessarily. The immediate effect might have been quite insignificant. It was intra-cranial swelling, bleeding, and possibly a blood clot which killed him.'

'So his assailant may not have realized

how badly he was injured.'

'I'd be surprised if he wasn't feeling pretty groggy,' the doctor said, 'but brain injuries are curious things. It's possible he simply got up and walked away.'

DeLancey could have made his own way from the boathouse to the house, then. 'Anything else I ought to consider?' Alec asked. 'Will you do the post-mortem, sir?'

'If you wish. I doubt jurisdiction will be disputed in the circumstances, and I have good facilities in Reading. If you have the body delivered this afternoon, I'll get on to it right away.'

'The sooner the better, I'd say. It's a hot day. If you're doing the post-mortem, perhaps you wouldn't mind notifying your local Coroner? Thank you, Doctor.'

Returning towards the house, Alec was met by the constable he had left at the phone. 'The station rang up, sir.' he reported. 'Henley Police Station, I should say. Miss Hopgood's landlady says she made 'em a picnic, her and Mr. Bott, and they was talking of taking a walk up the river, t'ards Marsh Lock.'

'That's away from the Regatta?'

'That's right, sir. The lock's a mile or thereabouts up from the bridge. They wants to know, did you want summun to go after Bott?'

Alec pondered as they entered the house

by a side-passage. He didn't see how Bott could possibly have learnt of DeLancey's death, so there was no reason for him to attempt to flee. It would not hurt to have more information before confronting him. Things looked black for the cox. Alec could imagine Frieth or young Fosdyke or Cheringham letting fly with his fists, but to attack someone from behind with a weapon would go against the instincts of a gentleman.

All the same, he should not have let Cheringham return to the house with the girls. He had had every opportunity to destroy evidence.

'Alec!' Daisy came up to him as he crossed the hall towards the library. 'I was coming to find you.'

'Ah, Daisy, Bott is expected back here, isn't he?'

A lover-like greeting! she thought, practically trotting to keep up with his stride. 'Yes. He was worried that Aunt Cynthia would expect him to leave once the eight was knocked out of the Thames Cup, but of course she didn't.'

'Good.'

'He wanted to stay on because of Miss Hopgood, of course, and it's impossible to get a room in town. When she goes back to London tomorrow evening, he's going off on a walking tour, camping at night, but he left all his stuff here, I know. Leigh rowed him across the river – the towpath's a shorter walk than by road – and they went off straight from breakfast. Alec, I...'

'Just a minute, darling. Henley Police are expecting me to ring back.'

Daisy glanced at her wrist-watch. She had a few minutes to spare still. Unabashedly she listened as Alec told the officer on duty it was not necessary to track down Horace Bott.

'But have the beat bobby keep an eye on Miss Hopgood's lodgings, please, and report to me when they come in.' He listened, his face relaxing. 'At the railway station? Good. I'll fetch them myself. Can you give me directions and the telephone number?'

'Tring and Piper?' Daisy mouthed at him and he nodded. She waited as he wrote down the number and cut the connection, then she said, 'If you're going to drive into the town, you could give me a lift.'

'A lift?' he asked, already dialling again.

'I have an appointment...'

'Hullo. This is Detective Chief Inspector Fletcher.'

'...to meet my friend who...'

'That's right. Please tell them I'll pick them up in a quarter of an hour.'

'...is going to present me...'

'Yes, thank you.'

'...to Prince Henry, Duke of Gloucester.'

'What's that, Daisy? The Duke of Gloucester?'

'For my article. If I have to walk, I must leave right away or I'll have to hurry and get all hot and sticky. Rollo said he'd drive me, but I imagine you don't want him to leave. It's all right for me to go, isn't it? I'm not a suspect.'

'No?' Alec asked with a grin.

'No.' Daisy said firmly, leading the way back to the front hall. 'DeLancey never insulted me. After all, I'm as Honourable as he was.'

'Rather more so, I hope.'

'Idiot. Will you take me as far as the bridge?'

'Yes, love. Are you ready? Go on out to the car while I make my apologies to the gentlemen for keeping them waiting. Not that I'm particularly sorry. In this case, letting them stew for a while won't hurt and might help, and I want Tring and Piper here when I start asking questions. Where are they all?'

'In the drawing-room and on the terrace. Trying to pretend nothing's happened, not easy with a bobby on watch. Dottie's with them, with Cherry, but Tish is in bed.'

'Yes, Mr. Fosdyke said he had prescribed a bromide. I'm sorry she's taken it so hard, and glad you have more backbone, my love. Be with you in a minute.'

Glowing from the rare compliment, Daisy went out to the yellow Austin. She didn't mind any more that he hadn't noticed how smart she was in the new amber silk-georgette frock. Even Lucy said the narrow pleats all the way from shoulders to hem made her look almost slim. They had also made it frightfully expensive, but after all, she was going to meet Prince Henry, and spruced up with a scarf it would do as a dinner dress afterwards.

The Chummy was standing in the shade, fortunately, or the seats would have been too hot to sit on. It would be unbearably stuffy with the hood up, but the road into Henley, the main road to Marlow, was metalled so she shouldn't get too dusty. She checked in her handbag for her comb.

Alec did not keep her waiting. 'Actually.' he said as he sat down behind the wheel and pressed the self-starter, 'you aren't a suspect. It looks as if the assailant was at least as tall as DeLancey. The blow was struck from above.'

'It wasn't Bott, then.'

'He's short?' Alec did not sound pleased.

'He's a cox. All coxes are small, because of the extra weight in the boat. You were thinking it must be him?'

'Leaning that way,' he grunted, turning left out of the drive into a road between hedges wreathed with traveller's joy and fragrant honeysuckle. 'It seemed to me improbable that anyone raised as a gentleman would strike someone from behind with a weapon, rather than a fist to the face. Not without a more serious motive than a fit of anger, anyway. I suppose I'm being naïve.'

'Gentlemen born and bred don't always behave like gentlemen. Just consider DeLancey!' Daisy pointed out. 'But the rest of the fellows are the real thing. Couldn't someone short have hit him with something long?'

'Hm, that's possible. Which means you are a suspect after all.'

'No, I'm not.' Daisy said indignantly. 'If anything, I insulted him, not the other way around.'

'Darling, did you really?'

'I refused – rather curtly – to go dancing with him, and I as good as told him his manners were worse than Bott's.'

'Great Scott. I'm lucky he didn't biff you over the head!'

Daisy blew him a kiss. 'Aren't you? Alec, could DeLancey have been biffed with an oar? There's a rack for oars in the boathouse. As far as I could see they were all in place when I looked, but...'

'When you looked? Daisy, is there something you haven't told me?'

'Look, that's Crowswood, where Lord DeLancey is staying.'

Though Alec gave the open gates and the lodge a thoughtful glance, as a diversionary tactic it was a failure. 'What were you doing in the boat-house at a time when an oar used as a weapon might have been out of place?' he demanded.

'Looking for Bott, as a matter of fact.'

'Looking for *Bott?* Don't tell me you were so concerned about sabotage...'

'Gosh no. I was concerned about Bott. I thought, if DeLancey was on guard and Bott really did go down there, DeLancey might have hit *him* and left him badly hurt, if not dead. I thought it might explain why DeLancey was in such a state. Shock, you know.'

'So you went down to the boat-house in the middle of the night. Alone, I take it?'

'Everyone was asleep, and I couldn't let Bott just lie there badly hurt, could I? Especially after I found the French windows open, proving someone– Look, there's the entrance to Phyllis Court. I told you we're invited there this evening?'

'You did. I can't promise...'

'I know. But I expect you'll have solved it by then.'

'Your faith is flattering, love.' Alec smiled at her, hastily turning back as the Marlow Road met the main street through Henley. 'But it's equally possible I may be stymied by then and needing to get away from the case for a while. Don't cancel yet, at any rate. You didn't find Bott in the boat-house. What did you find?'

'Absolutely nothing. It was horridly eerie,' she confessed with a reminiscent shudder, though nothing could have been less eerie than the shops and pubs of Bell Street on a sunny afternoon. 'I couldn't be sure he wasn't lying drowned at the bottom of the water, but if he was, it was too late to help him. You can't imagine how glad I was when he came down to breakfast.'

'I can. How did you see? Is electricity laid on?'

'No, I took the electric torch from the landing. I was very careful not to mess up any fingerprints.' Daisy said proudly.

'Tom Tring will be proud of you. Unfortunately, by now anyone could have wiped it, if the housemaid doesn't polish it daily,' Alec observed with callous masculine logic. 'Still, we don't know that the boat-house was the scene of the crime.'

'Anyone going before me might not have needed a torch, anyway. I didn't need it outside – the moon was just setting – and earlier... Oh, here, this is Hart Street. Turn left here, then right at the bridge, and drop me there. Then you can go straight on along the river, turn right at the end, and there's the station.'

'Right-oh. The boat-house has windows?'

'Actually, I didn't notice.' Daisy admitted sheepishly. 'If not, the brightest moon wouldn't help inside, of course.'

Alec turned right and stopped. He couldn't pull the Chummy over to the curb because of all the motors, some with boat-trailers hitched behind, parked along the street, so Daisy quickly hopped out. She turned to say goodbye as a harassed-looking bobby advanced on them.

'That's a very fetching frock,' said Alec. 'Should I be jealous of Prince Henry?'

'It's all right, he's too young for me. See you later, darling.'

The Austin zipped off just ahead of the constable's reprimand. Daisy turned back towards the bridge.

So Alec had noticed her new dress after all. He had been joking about the Prince, of course, but his words reminded Daisy of Rollo's possible motive for getting hot under the collar where DeLancey was concerned.

Rollo had jumped to the conclusion that Tish was upset about DeLancey's death because she was fond of him. Could he be right? Was Tish prostrated because she feared for Rollo and Cherry, or because, though she repulsed DeLancey, she was attracted to him? His obvious lack of serious intent might have led her to reject him with a show of pique, whatever her feelings.

If Rollo had real cause for jealousy, or believed so, he had a much stronger motive for violence than if he was just angry because of DeLancey's persistent pestering.

Bosh! Daisy told herself, nipping across the road between an ancient governess-cart and a royal blue Napier driven by a chauffeur in matching uniform. Alec was right – even the peaceable Rollo might strike out with his fists but he wouldn't biff someone over the head from behind with an oar.

Horace Bott was another kettle of fish. Daisy stopped in the middle of the bridge, gazing down at the bustle of the Regatta on the river and the bank, as she had yesterday with Bott and his girl after his ducking. Bott had far greater cause for resentment than Rollo or Cherry. Grossly outweighed by DeLancey and, as he said himself, without the instincts of a gentleman, he might well have resorted to a weapon if attacked when bent on sabotage.

But if DeLancey was on the attack how did he manage to get hit from behind?

Shaking her head in puzzlement, Daisy walked on.

CHAPTER 10

Attacked with an oar? An oar-blade could be the flat, smooth weapon Dr. Dewhurst described, though Alec was not wedded to the boat-house theory, as Daisy seemed to be.

What the dickens had got into her to go alone, in the middle of the night, to investigate the conjectured scene of a violent crime? Any ordinary female would have wakened one of the myriad young, strong men in the house to accompany her, or more likely to take her place. But Daisy was not ordinary, which was why he loved her and why she drove him to distraction with her foolhardy, infuriating, but occasionally illuminating meddling in his cases.

An oar, in the boat-house?

Coming to the end of the street, Alec turned right on Station Road. Tom Tring, massive in his robin's-egg-blue and white check summer suit, and young Piper were waiting on the pavement in front of the station. Alec pulled up the Austin beside them.

'Hullo, Chief!' Piper dropped his Woodbine, ground it out underfoot, and reached for his suitcase.

'Hullo, Tom, Ernie. No, don't get in just yet,' said Alec, reaching back behind his seat for his umbrella. With it in hand, he climbed out. 'My apologies for wrecking your weekend.'

'All in a day's work, Chief, though the missus was a bit put out about the steak-and-kidney pud,' rumbled Tom. He took off his pale grey bowler, revealing the vast, hairless dome, now glistening with perspiration, which counterbalanced the walrus moustache flourishing on his upper lip. He fanned himself with the hat while wiping the limitless expanse of his forehead with a blue-spotted handkerchief. 'A good job you didn't make us walk to the local copper-shop.'

Piper pointed to the black, rolled umbrella. 'The chief's brought his sunshade for you, Sarge.'

'You can have it for a parasol in a minute, Tom,' said Alec, grinning, 'but first I want to try a little experiment. Piper, move away a few feet. That's good enough. Now, pretend this is solid wood and, oh, about ten feet long. Too heavy to catch in your hands when I take a bash at you.' Shifting his grip to the ferrule, he suited action to the words.

As Piper ducked, twisting aside, he turned his face away from the swinging umbrella. Alec stopped the swing just before the handle caught the Detective Constable a whack on the side of his head, towards the upper rear.

'That's it!'

A stern voice came from behind him. '*Aw*right, awright, awright! *Nah* then,' the bobby continued for a change as they all turned to face him, 'what's goin' on 'ere?'

He regarded with equal suspicion their hastily produced Metropolitan Police warrant cards – fortunately Alec carried his both on and off duty – and Alec's explanation of his experiment. His face cleared, however, when Alec thought to mention Horace Bott. Miss Hopgood's landlady's house was on his beat, he said.

'I'll see 'em when they comes back, sir, never you fear. But I'd take it kindly, sir, not meanin' no offence, if you'd do your 'speriments off the street. Gives people ideas, it does, sir. That's what it does, gives people ideas.'

Properly abashed, Alec apologised. Appeased, the constable saluted and watched them pile into the Austin, which tilted under Tring's weight.

'Listen,' said Alec, turning right on the Reading Road, which confusingly became Duke Street, then Bell Street as they drove through the town, and then Northfield End just before meeting the Marlow Road. By that time he had given the others a swift résumé of the case.

'Cor, Chief,' said Piper admiringly from the back seat, 'it doesn't sound like you need us. You've got it taped already.'

'As a matter of fact,' Alec admitted, his cheeks growing warm, 'a great deal of my information comes only from Miss Dalrymple. I haven't had a chance yet to confirm what she's told me.'

'Ah,' said Tom meaningfully. Alec knew without looking that beneath his moustache was a grin.

'If Miss Dalrymple told you, Chief, it's as good as seeing it with your own eyes.' Piper's belief in Daisy was boundless.

'What's first, Chief?' Tom asked.

'I think I'll drop in on Lord DeLancey, as we have to pass the gates of Crowswood, where he's staying. He can confirm quite a number of points, and he wouldn't take kindly to being summoned to Bulawayo.'

After a short, stunned silence, Tom said cautiously, 'Bulawayo? Isn't that in Africa?'

It was not easy to stun Tom Tring. Alec managed not to smile as he said, 'Oh, didn't I mention it? Miss Dalrymple's uncle was a colonial administrator. He calls his house "Bulawayo."'

Piper breathed an audible sigh of relief.

'Ernie, you'll come in with me to take notes. Tom, I want you to drive on to the Cheringhams' – it's a mile and a half or so – and search the boat-house, inside and out.

It shouldn't take too long. If you have time, take a look at Basil DeLancey's bedroom.'

'Fosdyke's the name of the young chappie he shared with? The one Miss Dalrymple said put him to bed?'

'That's right. I can't see the lad taking a weapon to a supposedly drunken crew-mate, however obstreperous, but if it was done there, it couldn't have been anyone but Fosdyke. You needn't bother with fingerprints in the bedroom, unless you find something which might have been used as a weapon.'

Tom was a stickler where fingerprints were concerned. 'I'll get DeLancey's dabs off a hairbrush or summat, for elimination,' he said firmly.

'Yes, do. I'll telephone when I want you to come and pick us up. My questions won't take all that long, but his lordship will probably keep us waiting as a matter of principle.'

'That sort, eh?' said Tom.

'I suspect so. I may be maligning the man. When I spoke to him, he was in shock over his brother's death.'

They came to the gates Daisy had pointed out and Alec turned in. Driving along the winding avenue through the wooded park, he elaborated on Tring's instructions. 'You know what to do,' he finished as they emerged from the woods and drew up before the pillared portico of a substantial mansion.

'Right, Chief.' Tom came round the car, as

always surprisingly light on his feet for a man of such bulk. The Chummy tilted the other way as he took his place behind the wheel. 'Back in an hour.'

He drove off. Alec and Piper gratefully entered shade of the portico and rang the bell.

The butler who answered the door looked thoroughly affronted when Alec presented his warrant card and asked for Lord De-Lancey.

'Is his lordship expecting you?' he enquired frostily.

'His lordship is aware that I wish to speak to him.'

'Indeed. I shall send a footman to inform his lordship of your arrival, but it will take some time, even should he decide to receive you. Naturally, his lordship is down by the river observing the boat races. You may wait in here.' He opened a door and ushered them into a small anteroom, sparsely and uncomfortably furnished.

On a hot summer day it was pleasantly cool. In winter, Alec thought, it would be icy. 'This is where they put unwanted callers,' he said as soon as the door closed behind the butler, 'hoping they'll go away. Well, Ernie, what do you make of it?'

'Watching the races!' The youthful Detective Constable bubbled with indignation. 'And his brother a few hours dead!'

'What do you make of it?'

Piper simmered down and thought. 'He hasn't told anybody. Right, Chief? The rest of the nobs'd think it pretty queer if they knew, wouldn't they? Though you never can tell with nobs.'

'A good point,' Alec said encouragingly, then frowned. He went over to the window, which looked out on the porch under the portico, the view obstructed by pillars. Not that a better view would have helped. They were facing the wrong way.

'I can't tell just where we are in relation to the river,' he said, sitting down on a cane-bottomed chair with a singularly uncomfortably shaped back, and waving Ernie to a similar seat. 'I wonder how far upstream this is from the top of Temple Island, the point where Basil DeLancey died? Less than a mile, I'd guess, but possibly too far for anyone to make out details of what was happening to whom, even with first-rate binoculars.'

'But would he risk it, Chief? I mean, s'posing someone did see what was going on, and Lord DeLancey came back and never said a word, that'd look even queerer.'

'I gather the last thing he would risk is causing talk. Perhaps he knew none of the people here went down to the bank to watch until this afternoon. The morning races were just a few odd heats, I understand. Today's finals didn't begin until well past noon.'

'They'd be bound to find out, though, Chief, sooner or later. Maybe he'll tell 'em he only just found out himself. But why would he want to keep it under his hat? Just because he wants to watch the rest of the Regatta?'

Alec shook his head. 'I doubt it. I suspect it's all due to his morbid fear of being the subject of gossip which might stir up an old scandal. If he's not thinking very clearly – and when we met he didn't strike me as a particularly clear thinker, at least not under pressure – he may simply want to postpone as long as possible the tattle his brother's death is bound to arouse.'

'D'you know what the scandal is, Chief?'

'Miss Dalrymple didn't specify. She said it wasn't relevant, and I dare say it's not.'

'If she says not,' Piper agreed, loyal but disappointed.

Amused, Alec reverted to more relevant matters, giving Piper a bit more detail on the three chief suspects than there had been time for in the car.

'So that's Bott, Frieth, and Cheringham,' he ended. 'Then there's Fosdyke, whom I think unlikely. Not much more likely than the other four, that is.'

'Leigh, Meredith, Poindexter, and Wells.' Ernie Piper's memory for numbers was extraordinary, and with experience as a detective his memory for names was rapidly becoming almost as good.

'As far as we know, none of the five had any specific reason to detest DeLancey. They were annoyed that his teasing of Bott made them lose the race, and disgusted with his treatment of Bott afterwards. Any of them might have gone down to the boat-house to check the fours boat, but only Fosdyke was personally concerned with the fours race.'

'So he's more likely to've gone, Chief, as well as sharing DeLancey's room and putting him to bed when he was in a state.'

'Yes. The others shared two bedrooms, so if one went out in the middle of the night, the other might have heard.' But Alec recalled that Daisy had crept out without disturbing her cousin. No squeaky floors or door-hinges in that well-conducted house. 'Dammit, I need to talk to them all. Where the dickens is Lord DeLancey?'

'I 'spect the butler took his time,' Piper suggested. 'Sent the slowest footman, I bet. He didn't approve of us.'

'Butlers never approve of police in the house,' Alec said dryly.

Lord DeLancey came in a few minutes later. He was red-faced, apparently from heat and hurry as drops of perspiration glistened on his brow, less extensive than Tring's but equally bedewed.

'Sorry to keep you waiting, Chief

Inspector,' he said somewhat breathlessly as the two detectives rose to their feet. 'The river is a quarter-mile or so from the house.'

For a moment, Alec wondered why his lordship had decided to be affable, but of course he must be anxious to see his brother's killer caught. He had been in a state of shock at their last encounter, Alec reminded himself.

'We've not been here long, sir.' he said. 'This is Detective Constable Piper, who will take notes. As I told you, I have a number of questions to ask you. My apologies for disrupting your afternoon.'

Lord DeLancey, whose colour had receded somewhat, reddened again. 'You must think it odd that I should attend the Regatta when Basil... The fact is, I have told no one. I didn't wish to ruin the occasion for my host and hostess and the other guests.'

'Most understandable, sir. Most considerate. Won't you take a seat?'

They all sat down. Ernie produced his notebook and one of the pocketful of well-sharpened pencils he always carried, even now after his hurried departure from home. Proud of the shorthand which had helped him become a detective, he had never yet been caught unprepared.

Alec asked when Lord DeLancey had last seen his brother alive.

'Yesterday, around noon.'

‘And was his conduct then in any way out of the ordinary?’

‘You may have heard ... something of a contretemps ... a lamentable show of temper, I’m afraid.’

‘So I understand. We’ll get to that in a minute. He didn’t seem confused or incoherent, didn’t complain of a headache, weakness, dizziness, or anything of the sort?’

Lord DeLancey shook his head. ‘No. He had just rowed a race – if you can call it that when the cox was taken ill in the middle. Since the result was a foregone conclusion, the crew didn’t force the pace and Basil wasn’t even winded when they came in, as they usually are. He was the picture of health when we parted.’

‘I realize it will be painful, sir, but please describe the scene when the Ambrose College boat came in.’

‘You can find plenty of witnesses.’ his lordship said testily.

True enough. Alec decided to let it pass. Before he had formulated a tactful way to phrase his next question, Lord DeLancey continued, ‘Basil was in a filthy temper and he behaved like a fool. I stopped him as soon as I reached him.’

‘Did Mr. DeLancey often – er – fly off the handle like that?’

‘Is this really necessary, Chief Inspector?’

‘The character of a victim is often extremely significant in explaining the motive of the murderer, which frequently points to who he is. I'm sure you can see that in this case…'

'Yes, yes, I see. I'm sorry to say my brother was abominably overindulged. Basil is – was – the baby of the family, the youngest by several years, the darling of the mater and our sisters,' Lord DeLancey said sourly.

Once again Daisy had hit the nail on the head! 'And Lord Bicester?' Alec asked.

'The pater always spent a great deal of time in London as a member of the Government or an active member of the Opposition. He brought business home with him as often as not, and I'm afraid he did little to correct the faults in my brother's upbringing.'

'In other words, Mr. DeLancey tended to be governed by his impulses?'

'He never learnt to control them.'

'So he would act with little or no consideration of the feelings of others.'

'None!' Lord DeLancey's bitterness suggested this was not the first time he had suffered from his brother's shortcomings.

'And he would be unlikely to heed advice?'

'He always did exactly as he pleased.'

'Then it would not surprise you,' Alec suggested, 'if he kept vigil in the boat-house at Bulawayo last night in spite of your prohibition?'

Lord DeLancey suddenly turned wary. 'I've no reason to suppose he did. Is that' – he moistened his lips – 'Is that where you think he was struck down?'

'It's possible. You confirm that he proposed to spend the night there?'

'Yes. He said something to that effect. I didn't take it very seriously. Basil liked his comforts and a night in a boat-house hardly qualifies.'

'Far from it,' Alec agreed. 'I assume you knew why he considered keeping guard over the boat. Were you present when the threat was made against it?'

'Yes, it was just as I persuaded him to leave that the cox swore to get his own back. But he threatened Basil, not the boat. I can't imagine why Basil decided the fellow was likely to damage the boat. I'd have expected him – Basil, that is – to think better of it pretty quickly since it meant an uncomfortable night.'

'But when you last spoke to him, he was still intending to keep guard?'

'When I spoke to him on the…' DeLancey stopped and swallowed, perhaps recalling his last contact with his living brother. He pulled himself together and started again. 'When I spoke to him on the telephone?'

Alec pricked up his ears. 'When was that?'

'Oh, yesterday evening.'

'What time?'

'About a quarter to eleven. I was playing bridge. When I was dealt the dummy, I realised I wasn't sure what time Ambrose's race was this morning, so I called him up. Neither of us mentioned his ridiculous plan.'

'How did he sound? Normal?'

'His voice was a bit slurred. I assumed he'd had a whisky or two. You don't suppose he had already been hit?'

'I've no idea at present, sir. Did your brother answer the phone himself?'

DeLancey gave him a condescending look. 'Lady Cheringham's butler answered, naturally.'

'Did you receive an impression as to whether anyone else was still up and about?'

'I couldn't tell you. I believe the crew generally go to bed quite early during the races, but of course four of them – five with the cox – had no race today. Was it the cox who did it?'

'I haven't enough information to begin to decide, sir. As far as you know, did anyone else have reason to bear him a grudge?'

'A great many people, I dare say. Basil had a damned nasty tongue and he wasn't shy of using it. It must have been one of the crew, though, don't you think?'

'They certainly had the best opportunity,' Alec said cautiously. He stood up. 'Well, thank you for your cooperation, Lord De-

Lancey. I mustn't keep you from your friends any longer.'

With a grimace, his lordship said, 'I suppose I'd better tell them about Basil.'

'It's bound to be in the evening papers, I'm afraid.'

'The papers!' Groaning, Cedric DeLancey buried his head in his hands. 'Somehow I'd managed to put the press out of my mind. Trust Basil to make as much trouble dead as alive!'

CHAPTER 11

'Lord DeLancey confirmed a good part of what Miss Dalrymple told me, Tom,' said Alec, stepping out of the shade of the portico into the boiling sun.

''Course!' Piper said indignantly as he climbed into the Austin's back seat.

'He agreed his brother talked about spending the night in the boat-house?' Tom asked.

'Yes, though he made light of it.' Alec sat down in the passenger seat and closed the door. 'He said he didn't think Basil would go through with it.'

'Looks like he did,' said Tom laconically, engaging the clutch. He drove well and carefully, or Alec wouldn't have trusted him with the precious Chummy.

'What did you find?'

Squinting as he negotiated the alternating shadow and brightness of the avenue, Tom said, 'Looks like a smear of blood, Chief, and a few dark hairs on the floor. A cushion hidden away in a back corner, where you wouldn't notice it, or anyone sitting on it, as you was coming in the door. And one o' the young gents told me there was an oar found damaged when they went to put the boat in the water this morning.'

'Damaged?' Alec frowned. 'I'd be surprised if a blow with the flat of the blade, which didn't do much external damage to DeLancey's head, had left a visible mark on the oar.'

'The dent was on the edge of the blade. Like Mr. Cheringham said, it looked like it'd been dropped, which made Mr. Frieth pretty "browned off," he said, him being the captain.'

Daisy would have noticed an oar lying on the floor, even if she missed a cushion in a back corner. Yet if DeLancey was struck in the boat-house, it must surely have been before he burst into her bedroom.

'Did they find the oar on the floor in the morning?' Alec asked.

'No, it'd been put back in the rack, Chief. Could be whoever hit him dropped it in shock, like, then picked it up again and put it away. I expect it wouldn't be natural for one of these rowing blokes to just leave an oar lying about.'

'Very likely. Dabs?'

'Loads. Seems the oars are all pretty near identical, so anyone might've rowed with it. Then there's the young ladies, Miss Cheringham and Miss Carrick. They often helped carry 'em, Mr. Cheringham said.'

'Mr. Cheringham seems to have been very helpful.'

'Said he was by way of being host, his uncle having buzzed off. He's not Miss Dalrymple's cousin, right, Chief?'

'Right, but he's as close as a brother to Miss Cheringham, who is.' Alec sighed. As Tring and Piper knew very well, Daisy had a tendency to take one or more suspects under her wing. Who more likely than Cherry?

'Ah!' Tom ruminated for a moment. 'He told me his dabs are on the oar, him having picked it off the rack to row with this morning afore anyone noticed it'd been bashed.'

'Covering his traces, do you think? If there are so many fingerprints, they won't help much anyway.'

The sergeant disagreed. 'Some of them's on top of others. Once I've identified all of 'em, I might be able to tell who touched it last, besides Mr. Cheringham, or at least who didn't.'

'True. You'd better get on to that as soon as we get back, Tom. The place is locked up?'

'I got a padlock from Bister, the gardener-handyman chappie. Here's the key, Chief. Seems they don't bother keeping it locked in the summer,' Tom said disapprovingly. 'Now, is it likely anyone's going to pinch a boat in the winter, I ask you?'

Alec laughed. 'Probably not. You've packed up a sample of the blood smear to send for analysis?'

'Done.'

'Good man. One of the local bobbies can take it into town. No handy footprints outside, I suppose? It's been too dry, and in any case the same applies as with fingerprints – everyone's been there.'

'No handy footprints, Chief, but me and the constable found plenty of snails and earwigs and...'

'Tom!'

'Spiders,' said Tom innocently, 'and an old ducks' nest, and cigarette ends, and a tent-peg.'

'A tent-peg?' Why did that sound significant?

'Not polished wood like the oar, so no dabs. No dead leaves on top, so at a guess it hadn't been there long, but tent-pegs being used outside and stuck in the ground, it's dirty and weathered.'

'DeLancey wasn't bashed with a tent-peg, Sarge,' Ernie Piper pointed out.

'No,' Alec agreed, as the Austin turned into the Cheringhams' drive, 'but I have a feeling it means something. Don't lose it, Tom.'

'Me lose evidence!' Tom fulminated. 'Have a heart, Chief, when did I ever lose a bit of evidence?'

'Just getting my own back for the earwigs,' said Alec. Piper snickered. 'Did you manage to get a look at DeLancey and Fosdyke's bedroom?'

'Just a glimpse, no time for more. I got DeLancey's dabs off his shaving kit. Everything else polished within an inch of its life, including that electric torch on the landing. They took on a couple of extra girls, just tempor'y, what with having the house full to busting, and the housekeeper kept a smart eye on 'em.'

'Talk to the maid who did that room. If there was anything to see, *you'll* get it out of her.'

Alec grinned as Tom, stopping the Austin at the front door, preened his moustache. For all his bulk and his devotion to his wife, the sergeant had a way with female servants in particular, as well as servants in general. He didn't have to be told what to ask when he got around to interviewing the staff – one of the reasons Alec had sent for him.

'But that can wait.' Alec continued. 'It looks as if the boat-house was the scene of the crime…'

'Just like Miss Dalrymple said.' Piper put in.

'So your first order of business, Tom, is to take everyone's fingerprints and check against the dabs on that oar. More interviews for us, Ernie. Got enough sharp pencils?'

''Course, Chief,' the young Detective Constable assured him.

Although the front door still stood open and he was returning after quite a short absence, Alec rang the doorbell. He doubted that the easygoing Lady Cheringham would be affronted if he just walked in, but the butler might, and the butler might have been the last person to see DeLancey before he was hit. His cooperation could be vital.

Not to mention that a butler's cooperation always smoothed the path of the law, on the rare occasions when it could be won.

Lady Cheringham's butler was quite different from the supercilious individual employed at Crowswood. For a start, his face was black. Alec had not encountered him before, since Daisy had taken him into the house, and later ensconced him with the telephone in the library, and a maid had brought his lunch. He was momentarily startled, but when he considered that the Cheringhams had lived so long in Africa, it wasn't really surprising that they had brought a competent servant home with them.

Tom had already met him. 'This is Mr. Gladstone, sir,' he introduced the tall African to Alec. 'Detective Chief Inspector Fletcher, Mr. Gladstone, and Detective Constable Piper.'

Gladstone bowed with a gravity suited to the occasion and the deference due to Alec as the fiancé of the niece of Sir Rupert and Lady Cheringham, of which he was undoubtedly aware. 'How may I be of assistance, Chief Inspector?' he enquired in a deep, accentless voice, benignly courteous.

'I shall need a room in which to interview people.' Alec told him. 'The library will serve very well, if we shan't disrupt the household?'

'Not at all, sir. The gentlemen and Miss Carrick are all in the drawing-room or on the lawn under the chestnut tree, I believe, the terrace being without shade.'

'Miss Cheringham hasn't come down yet?'

'I understand Miss Cheringham intends to join her guests for tea, which will be served shortly. I am sure her ladyship would wish me to offer refreshments to you gentlemen.'

'Tea will be very welcome,' Alec assured him.

'Something cold for me, if you please, Mr. Gladstone,' said Tom, blotting his forehead with the spotted handkerchief.

'Certainly, Mr. Tring.'

'And if you've got a scullery I could use for the taking of fingerprints, it'd make things easier. It's a bit of a messy business.'

'The downstairs cloakroom would be more convenient for the gentlemen,' the butler suggested.

'Right you are, and we'll worry about the ladies when we get to 'em. Strictly for elimination.' Tom added hastily as Gladstone gave him a shocked look. 'So's we know which ones to disregard.'

'Of course,' said the butler, relieved. 'You know your way to the library, Chief Inspector? If you'll come with me, Mr. Tring, I'll show you where to go.'

'I'll take Mr. Leigh first, Sergeant,' Alec said. 'Take your pick of the rest. Piper, that's the library there, and that's the drawing-room, with French doors to the terrace and lawn. Fetch Mr. Leigh, please.' He usually started with the least likely suspects. Often he could cross them from his list, and they gave him background for questioning the more likely.

'Yes, Sir.'

'And you can send me a couple of the others, laddie,' said Tom.

Alec proceeded to the library. By each of the open windows stood a pair of armchairs. One of these he shifted so that its occupant's face would be well lit, but not in the sun – squinting made the expression hard to read. Sitting slightly sideways at the big desk, Alec would be in a dominant position with an excellent view of his victims. To one side and a little behind the armchair, he set a chair for Piper – suspects often dried up if they could actually observe their every word being written down.

Piper brought Leigh in. The young oarsman seemed to have recovered from the shock of his crewmate's demise and to be unintimidated by facing a police interrogation.

'Sorry about the shirtsleeves, sir,' he said cheerfully. 'It's devilish hot today, even with a bit of a breeze off the river. I suppose you want to know about Delaney's dust-up with Bott.'

'Among other things, Mr. Leigh.' Alec waved him to the chair and sat down at the desk. 'Your Christian name, please, for the record. Detective Constable Piper will be taking notes.'

'Donald. Among other things? You mean you don't think it was Bott who socked him?' Leigh was incredulous. Obviously he, and probably most of the others, considered the case closed.

'I haven't anywhere near enough evidence to decide.'

'But Bott's the only one who scarpered, besides being the one DeLancey bullied and the one who threatened...'

'Hold on!' Sometimes it paid to let a witness or suspect ramble on in his own way, but this was leading nowhere. 'I'd like to ask you a few questions.'

'Yes, of course, sir. Sorry. My hat, you mean we're all of us under...? Sorry! Not another word, except answers, of course.'

'Thank you.' Alec smiled at him. 'What makes you say Horace Bott has decamped?'

Leigh flushed. 'Actually, that's what we've all been saying, but it isn't true, is it? I rowed him across myself, this morning, long before DeLancey snuffed out. He was going to spend the day with his girl.'

'Did he take anything with him?'

'Just what he had in his pockets. No bag, or anything like that, if that's what you mean. He was talking of taking a picnic up the river. I suppose he wanted to get well away from the scene of his humiliation, poor chap. Come to think of it, he quite likely wouldn't even hear what happened, would he?'

'No,' said Alec absently. As Leigh spoke he had been half listening, half putting odds and ends together, his memory jogged by his own question and choice of the word 'decamped.' 'Did he mention his plans for after the Regatta?'

'He was going on a walking tour.' Leigh said promptly. 'Camping at night. I don't suppose he could afford to stay in country pubs even.'

'Excuse me a moment. I'll be right back. Piper!' Alec led the way out of the library. In the hall, he said, 'Go and find Bott's bedroom.'

'Tent-peg,' said Piper.

'Exactly. There should be a bagful. Take one and match it against Tom's find. Don't let anyone see what you're doing, Ernie.

They're already convinced Bott did it, and even if the tent-peg's his, it's no proof.'

'Right, Chief.'

Alec returned to the library. As he opened a desk drawer to look for paper and a pencil to make notes – he would not attempt a verbatim report – Leigh watched nervously.

'If it wasn't Bott,' he burst out, 'who was it? I didn't hit him. He never bothered me much.'

'But you didn't like him?'

'Oh, well, not exactly. He was a rotter. Not an out-and-out bad hat, you know, but a bit of a cad. If you ask me,' Leigh said earnestly, 'he'd have done better at the House – that's Christ Church College – where they're used to dukes and such. He'd have had to pull his socks up. As it is, he went from being the blue-eyed boy of the family to being a big fish in a small pond.'

'Oh?'

'Ambrose is a small college, and its mostly plain gentry, not the nobility. My people are County, not a title in the family. So what with his pater being the Earl of Bicester, and his allowance being double anyone else's, and good at sports on top of it, and sailing through his exams without ever swotting ... well, he just went on being cock of the walk. He's never had to consider anyone else's feelings. Sorry, there I go blethering on again!'

'Not at all. An understanding of the victim's character is often a great help in our investigations. So Basil DeLancey was accustomed to riding roughshod over all and sundry?'

'Yes, but he was especially offensive to people he despised, like Bott, and Miss Carrick. He didn't think women belong at the university, and she's – er – no Helen of Troy,' Leigh said, delicately tactful. 'He was pretty brutal to her. Verbally, I mean – I heard him more than once. Never laid a hand on her, of course. Miss Cheringham was the one he'd have liked to lay a hand on, if you'll pardon the expression.'

'In the way of love-making, I take it? Did she respond favourably to his overtures?'

'Lord, no. Stony-faced. Of course, he managed to make even a compliment insulting, saying she was wasting her time with education.'

'She and Miss Carrick must have been pretty upset.'

'Not half as upset as Cheringham and Frieth. But I shouldn't be gossiping about people like this,' said Leigh uneasily.

'It's not gossip.' Alec reassured him. 'You're helping the police to find a murderer.'

'It's not really murder, is it? I mean, Bott – whoever hit DeLancey could have finished him off on the spot if he'd wanted to. My hat, you don't think it was Frieth or Cheringham, do you?'

'I haven't enough evidence to be certain of anything.' Alec cast his mind back over what had been said by whom and when. Leigh and the others were presumably unaware that DeLancey had been hit on the back of the head with a weapon. 'What do you think?'

'Frieth wouldn't have hit him before the race.' Leigh looked and sounded positive. 'Not while there was still a chance of Ambrose winning a cup. I still think it must have been Bott, even if he doesn't know yet that DeLancey's dead. He's shorter and lighter, and DeLancey's boxed for Oxford, but Bott plays racquets. He's quick on his feet. He might have popped one over DeLancey's guard.'

Without any visible damage to himself? Alec didn't bother to voice his doubt, since it was irrelevant. He had noted Leigh's evasion with regard to Cheringham. Daisy's cousin's cousin had double Frieth's motive for anger, being protective of both his cousin and his fiancée. Also, the possible effect on the race of striking the stroke was probably less important to him than to Frieth, since he was of an intellectual bent.

On the other hand, since winning a trophy was more important to Frieth, he was more likely than Cheringham to have gone to the boat-house to check on the boat. He might have quarrelled with DeLancey, perhaps over his treatment of the cox and its results for the Ambrose eight, perhaps over Tish. In hot blood, he could well overlook the consequences for the next morning's race.

But would either of them have struck out with anything but his fists? Improbable, Alec thought, but certainly not impossible.

'Tell me about Bott and DeLancey,' he requested.

Apart from a penitent acknowledgement that he and his friends had rather egged DeLancey on in the whisky affair, Leigh's account differed only in minor particulars from Daisy's. 'Bott's rather a pill,' he said frankly, 'but he had every right to be mad as fire. DeLancey went too far. I'd have said he deserved to get his comeuppance, if he hadn't died of it.'

'It sounds as if he knew how to make himself unpopular. Had he a reputation as a womanizer?'

'There was a story making the rounds. But that was a shop-girl, not a respectable young lady like Miss Cheringham,' Leigh added hastily. 'The usual thing: got the girl into trouble and deserted her. I heard his brother came down quite handsomely to hush it up. No question of breach of promise, mind you, just her mother threatening to make a song and dance about it.'

'No father or brother out for his head?'

'Not that I know of,' Leigh said with regret, sorry to dismiss a hypothetical suspect who was a complete outsider. 'A widow with an only child, I believe. Anyway, it was last year people were talking about it. It's rather a long time to wait for vengeance unless you're planning something a bit more sophisticated than a biff on the noddle.'

Alec was relieved not to have to call on the Oxford city police to run to earth an unnamed and possibly mythical malefactor. He made a note, though, to check Leigh's information with the others.

'Was he biffed in the boat-house?' Leigh asked. 'I saw your man rooting around there.'

'To your knowledge, was DeLancey at the boat-house last night?'

'I didn't see him go, but he kept blethering on about Bott making threats and how the boat ought to be guarded. Said he didn't see why his brother should care if he chose to spend an uncomfortable night down there.'

'This was yesterday evening?'

'Yes, after dinner?'

'Who was there?'

'Lady Cheringham, Miss Dalrymple, Fosdyke for a while, but he's an early-to-bed-and-early-to-riser, Poindexter, Wells, Meredith.' Leigh stopped to think. 'Cheringham and Frieth were out on the terrace most of the time, with Miss Cheringham and Miss Carrick. Or vice versa, if you see what I mean. Miss Dalrymple went out to take a telephone call, then came back and said she was ready for bed. About half ten, I should say. That was when Lady Cheringham called the other girls in and they all went up together. Cheringham and Frieth came in a few minutes later, and went straight up.'

'They didn't stop to hear DeLancey holding forth?'

'Not that I remember.'

'And Bott wasn't there?'

'No, he didn't come in to dinner. With his girl, I expect, and went straight up when he got back. Can't blame him after what happened the night before and that morning. If he'd turned up, DeLancey hadn't the sense to leave him be. He had a couple of whiskies and was starting on a third when he got a telephone call. While he was gone, the rest of us buzzed off to bed. We were pretty fed up with his grousing.'

'All the rest went up?'

Leigh pondered. 'Yes, I think so. I'm pretty sure, actually. Meredith came out of the drawing-room right after me, and he was the last.'

'And you didn't see or hear DeLancey come up later?'

'Not a whisper. We were in and out to the

bathroom and so on, but I, for one, dropped off pretty quick and slept like a baby till morning. DeLancey wouldn't necessarily have made a lot of noise. He could put away three whiskies without bursting into song or falling over his shoelaces.'

It dawned on Alec that he did not know what DeLancey had been wearing when he was struck down. Daisy hadn't mentioned how he was dressed when he invaded her room, and Tom hadn't had time to investigate the contents of his wardrobe.

'Do you dress for dinner here?' he asked.

Leigh looked taken aback. 'Good Lord, yes. We rowers may expose our knobbly knees to the world at times, and sit on the lawn in our shirtsleeves on a hot day, but in general we're quite civilized.'

Alec had never given much credence to the tales of British gentlemen changing for dinner in the depths of the jungle, but perhaps they were true. Would Daisy expect him to dress every evening when they were married?

He dragged his mind back to the present. Heat and thirst made it difficult to concentrate. The admirable Gladstone wouldn't bring the tea in the middle of an interview.

Alec looked round as the door opened. Not Gladstone with the tea, but Piper, looking pleased with himself.

'That's all for now, thank you,' Alec said to

Leigh. 'You've been very helpful. Sergeant Tring will take your fingerprints, for elimination purposes, and I may have a few more questions for you later. Were you meaning to leave Henley today?'

'No, I'll stick it out. Don't want to leave the others in the lurch. Is it all right if I go up the river to watch the rest of the races?'

'By all means. Wait half an hour and some of the others will be free to go with you. Please don't talk about what we have been discussing.'

'Right-oh, sir.'

Leigh went out and Alec turned to Piper. 'Any luck?'

'Got it, Chief. Perfick match. I reckon Bott was going to hole the boat with it.'

'Possibly,' said Alec. 'The question is, why the dickens should he throw it away in the shrubbery?'

CHAPTER 12

A discussion of the tent-peg had to wait. The door opened again and Lady Cheringham came in, bearing a vase of pink and white phlox and followed by Gladstone with a tray.

'Gladstone told me you are interviewing in here, Mr. Fletcher. I thought a few flowers would brighten the place up for you.' She set the vase on the desk, while Gladstone silently deposited the tray on the long table and withdrew. 'Rupert never lets me put any in the library,' she continued. 'They make him sneeze, poor dear.'

'Lovely, Lady Cheringham. This is Detective Constable Piper, one of my assistants.'

'How do you do, Mr. Piper. I've met Mr. Tring, a charming man. My dear Mr. Fletcher, do you want to ask me any questions? You mustn't be shy, you know. After all, you'll soon be my nephew-in-law.'

'That's hardly a qualification for interrogating you,' Alec said with a smile. In fact, while shy was not the word, the relationship definitely made things more difficult. 'There is one question only you can answer: Do you know of anyone leaving the house last night after you went to bed?'

Lady Cheringham shook her head. 'I sleep very well after pottering in the garden all day. I wouldn't hear unless someone made enough noise to wake me, say by starting a car under my window. Is that all?' she asked, slightly disappointed.

'For now. How is Patricia?'

'She insists on coming down for tea,' said her ladyship, frowning, 'but she's still in a state of shock, if you ask me. I'd never have guessed she was so oversensitive.'

'Witnessing sudden death, even of a stranger and without the shadow of violence, is a severe shock to many people.' Alec said. 'When it's an acquaintance, and there's a suspicion of murder, it's naturally much worse.' He gathered neither Tish nor Daisy had informed Lady Cheringham of DeLancey's incursion and their consequent feelings of guilt.

'I suppose so. I can't decide whether it's just as well we didn't take her to Africa, considering the delicacy of her nerves, or whether it would have done her good, braced her backbone, so to speak. Still, it's too late now. Are you going to have to interview her?'

'Yes, I'm afraid so.'

'I'm sure I don't need to ask you to be gentle with her.'

'Great Scott, no! After all, she will soon be my cousin-in-law.' Which would make him nearly Cheringham's cousin, Alec realised, dismayed. Should he ask to be taken off the case?

'You are so nearly a relative.' Lady Cheringham reflected, 'it doesn't seem right that you are staying in town. The house is practically bursting at the seams, so I can't offer you a proper bedroom of your own. There's Mr. DeLancey's bed, sharing a room with Mr. Fosdyke, but I wonder if you would prefer to sleep on the sofa in Rupert's dressing-room? Would the convenience outweigh the discomfort?'

'As a matter of fact, it most definitely would,' said Alec, whose bed at the Old White Hart had felt almost as ancient as the fifteenth-century inn. Without a qualm he consigned Tom Tring's well-padded bones to its torturous embrace. 'I've been wondering what to do with Tring and Piper tonight. They can have my room at the White Hart, if you're sure I shan't be in the way?'

'Not at all.'

'Sir Rupert isn't coming back?'

'I haven't tried to get in touch. He was an excellent administrator, but since retiring, he has been obsessed with that blessed book of his. He wouldn't be the least help to you, to me, or to poor Patricia. I'll have the bed made up in the dressing-room, and you must come and stay again, some time when we don't have a murder in the house. Such a disconcerting business!'

'I'm afraid it tends to be,' Alec apologized, thinking he'd seldom seen anyone less disconcerted. Life in Africa must have inured her to shock.

She patted his arm. 'I'm so glad it's dear Daisy's young man who's in charge, not a stranger. Well, I'll leave you to your tea and your business.' With a smiling nod to Piper, who had tactfully withdrawn to the far end of the room, she departed.

'Nice lady,' said Piper, with a depth of admiration he usually reserved for Daisy.

Alec agreed, especially when he recalled the daunting disapproval of her sister, the Dowager Lady Dalrymple, Daisy's mother.

Used to hurried meals, Piper managed to devour two Gentleman's Relish sandwiches, three biscuits, a slice of Dundee cake, and half a cup of tea before Alec sent him running again.

'I'll see Poindexter next.' he said, pouring himself a second cup. Daisy was having tea – or perhaps champagne and strawberries – in the Stewards' Enclosure with her friends, Lord and Lady Fitzsimmons, and His Royal Highness Prince Henry, Duke of Gloucester. How old was the Prince? Twenty-two or three, Alec thought, not so much younger than Daisy.

Of course, she actually expected just to be presented to him, not to take tea with him.

And it was all in the way of business, Alec consoled himself.

He'd better return to his own business. Glancing at his brief notes of the interview with Leigh, he pondered the significance of what DeLancey had been wearing when he fell. His jacket at least, and probably his trousers, should show some signs of the fall. A dinner jacket smirched or damaged would not indicate where he fell. But if he had worn some other article of clothing, then he had changed after dinner, and why should he do so if not for a vigil? It would be another piece of evidence pointing to the boat-house as the scene of the crime.

Bott hadn't come in for dinner. Even if he came back earlier in the day to change out of his rowing shorts, no one would tell him of DeLancey's intention to guard the boat, would they? He had no reason to suppose the coast would not be clear when he crept down to the boat-house in the middle of the night.

Tent-peg in hand? How much damage could he do to a racing boat with a tent-peg? Why toss it aside, outside the boat-house? Why not plan to use a boat hook in the first place?

'Ah, Mr. Poindexter. Take a seat.'

Poindexter confirmed much of Leigh's report, but added little. The same was true of Wells and Meredith. Each claimed to have slept soundly, not leaving his room after going to bed, and not hearing his roommate stir until morning. They all agreed that no rowing man worth his salt would leave an oar lying about on the ground.

They also agreed that the annual 'bumping' races at Oxford proved the boats were pretty sturdy. Holing one with a tent-peg would not be easy, at least not without a mallet.

Tom could hardly have missed a mallet lying in the bushes. Why not hit out with a mallet one was carrying instead of putting it down to pick up an oar? Perhaps the tent-peg was nothing to do with Bott. It matched his, but tent-pegs were much of a muchness, after all. Analysis of the wood might prove something. No good counting to see if one of Bott's was missing – anyone in his right mind would take extras in case some split.

Where was Bott?

Alec dismissed Meredith and sent for Fosdyke.

The surgeon's son was higher on the list of suspects than the four already interviewed, but not by much. As a member of the fours crew, he had a reason to check the boat in the night, but no one had suggested he had any particular reason to quarrel with DeLancey. The possibility remained of DeLancey having become obstreperous when Fosdyke was putting him to bed, but the evidence all pointed to the boat-house, not a bedroom.

'What was DeLancey wearing when you went to his assistance last night?' Alec rapped out as Fosdyke entered the library.

'His sweater, and flannels. I was glad, because I'd have had a job getting him out of a dinner-jacket.'

'He was being difficult?'

'Just limp.' The eyes that met Alec's were as guileless as Daisy's. He reminded himself that he would never describe Daisy as guileless. 'As it was, I didn't even bother to undress him.' Fosdyke continued, sitting down as Alec waved him to the chair. 'But it wasn't him, it was Miss Cheringham whose assistance I went to, and Miss Dalrymple. She's a brick, isn't she? I thought DeLancey was drunk. The pater says it was a natural mistake, but I still feel bad about it.'

'DeLancey was a friend? You chose to share a room with him?'

'Crikey, no! I don't think he had any real friends, just a few toadies. The others all teamed up, and I got stuck with him. I kept pretty much out of his way, getting up early and going to bed early. He didn't pick on me much, anyway, because I took no notice. People like that soon quit if you ignore them.'

'Very true.'

'The pater taught me that before I went

away to prep school. The pater's a good egg,' Fosdyke said defensively, with an air of embarrassment. Perhaps in his circles fathers were generally regarded as antediluvian antiques.

Alec decided the young man was probably just as ingenuous as he seemed. What had Daisy said about him? A nice, obliging boy who lived to run, row, eat, and sleep.

'Were you awake, or did you wake up, when DeLancey came up to change his clothes?'

'He woke me. That was typical – he turned on the overhead light and didn't attempt to be quiet. Though I think he really was a bit tipsy then.'

'What time was that?'

'I don't know. I didn't want him to know he'd woken me. When he went off again, I had to get up to turn off the light, but I didn't look at the time.'

'Where did you suppose he was going?'

'To the boat-house, I assumed. He'd been talking about it earlier, though I didn't believe he'd do it.'

'Were you concerned about Mr. Bott's threats against the boat?' Alec asked.

'He didn't threaten the boat, he threatened DeLancey. The boat business was all DeLancey's imagination.' Fosdyke paused, forehead wrinkling. 'At least, I suppose he was right, wasn't he? I mean, Bott hit him down there, and why was Bott there if not to bash in the boat?'

'We have absolutely no evidence of Bott's presence in the boat-house last night,' Alec said repressively, as he had already stated four times in various ways. He asked a few more questions, but he was inclined to give young Fosdyke the benefit of the doubt.

'I told Father I'd go and find him when you had finished with me.'

'You're free to go, but please telephone if for any reason you don't come back here for the night. Piper, I'll see Miss Cheringham next, in case she wants to retire to bed again.'

As Fosdyke and Piper left, Tom came in. 'Didn't want to interrupt, Chief, case you was getting a confession.'

'No such luck. What about you?'

'I been talking to Mr. Gladstone. DeLancey barely noticed the servants existed, so there's no motive there. He had a telephone call from his brother about quarter to eleven.'

'Yes, Lord DeLancey told us. What did Gladstone have to say about it?'

'All the rest went upstairs while Basil DeLancey was talking on the telephone. Gladstone went into the drawing room to tidy and lock up. DeLancey was angry when he came in, 'cause he'd been deserted, I s'pose. He told Gladstone not to lock the French doors as he was going to step out for a cigar. Said he'd lock 'em himself, then rushed off upstairs. Gladstone finished tidying and was just leaving when DeLancey came back dressed in a jersey. Looks like the boat-house is it, don't it, Chief?'

'Oh yes, we can be pretty certain of that. Have you checked the dabs on that oar?'

Tom's reply was forestalled by the sound of an argument just outside in the hall. Piper came in.

'Mr. Frieth and Mr. Cheringham want to come in with Miss Cheringham Chief, but she…'

Tish burst in, turning on the threshold to say vehemently, 'Do go away, the two of you. I don't need you to hold my hands. I don't *want* you to hold my hands.'

From the hall came Miss Carrick's musical tones, unruffled. 'Cherry, come along, do. Mr. Fletcher doesn't bite, you chump.'

'Little does she know,' came sotto voce from Piper as Alec strode towards the door.

Turning as he approached, Tish shut the door firmly behind her. Pale and wan, she looked up at him apprehensively, as if Piper's words were closer to her expectations than Miss Carrick's.

'I don't bite.' Alec reassured her. 'Come and sit down. I imagine you don't want them here when we talk about DeLancey being in your bedroom last night.'

'No,' she said with a little gasp. 'They

know now, but talking about it… It was too awful…' And she started to cry.

Dearly wishing Daisy was there, Alec took her hand and led her to the chair. He had coped with many a weeping woman in his time, and more than a few weeping men, but never one who was shortly to become a close relative.

At that inopportune moment, the telephone bell rang. Of course, it might be for anyone in the house, but it was about time Bott turned up. Alec glanced at Tom, who nodded and trod silently from the room.

Sitting on the arm of Tish's chair, Alec handed her his handkerchief. 'Have a good blow.' he said. 'At least, that's what I say to my daughter. Perhaps it's not quite proper to a young lady.'

'It's what Cherry used to say when I was little.' A tentative smile hovering on her lips, she looked up at him with tear-drenched eyes. 'I didn't know you had a daughter. Daisy did mention that you had been married before.'

'Yes.' He moved to the desk. Not sure whether he was putting a prospective witness at ease or improving his acquaintance with his fiancée's cousin, he went on, 'Joan died in the influenza epidemic in nineteen, like Daisy's father. Belinda's nine. She adores Daisy.'

'Daisy's wonderful, isn't she?' Behind her,

Ernie Piper nodded vigorously – Alec was relieved to see he hadn't started taking notes yet. 'One feels one can tell her *anything* I wish I'd known her better growing up. I don't know what I'd have done last night if she hadn't been there.'

'Do you feel able to talk about it now? I haven't had much chance to get the details from Daisy. In any case, it helps to have two witnesses. One often notices what the other misses.'

'Wh-when do you want me to start?' Tish asked tremulously.

'Let's go back to the riverbank yesterday. I've plenty of witnesses to DeLancey's ducking Bott, but none of them was there when he first took it into his head that Bott might damage the fours boat. Daisy just mentioned it in passing. Were you there?'

'Oh yes. It was later, in the general Enclosure. Dottie and Cherry and Rollo and I were having something to drink – it was beastly hot. Daisy was with us. She had gone off with Bott and his girl, and we'd been a bit worried about where she'd got to. I remember... Oh!'

'What?'

Tish blushed. 'Oh, just that Dottie told her we nearly called in the police but weren't sure whether to get the local chaps or Scotland Yard. Just joking, you know. Daisy said you'd have wrung her neck.'

'I might have,' Alec agreed, laughing. 'Did Bott and his girl turn up with her?'

'No, thank heaven. Because just then the DeLanceys came up, looking as if they'd been squabbling ever since we last saw them. Mr. DeLancey apologised for the scene with Bott, but not as if he meant it. It was obvious Lord DeLancey made him say it. That was when Basil DeLancey started to worry about the boat.'

'Were Frieth and Cheringham worried?'

'Not a bit,' Tish said quickly. Too quickly? 'Cherry said, "Bosh" – no, "What rot!" and Rollo said they wouldn't share guard duty with him. Then Lord DeLancey told Basil not to be an ass, he'd make himself a laughingstock sitting in the boat house all night. So that was the end of that.'

'You didn't hear any more about it? Your cousin and Frieth didn't discuss it?'

'After the DeLanceys had gone, Rollo said something like that was the last we'd hear of that. Cherry said if Lord DeLancey was capable of making Basil apologize, it was a pity he didn't exercise his authority more often. Then we went to watch a race.'

'What about in the evening? At dinner and after?'

'At dinner no one talked about any of the business with Bott. Even Basil DeLancey behaved himself pretty well when my mother was there.' Again the quick colour flooded

Tish's cheeks. After dinner, we were out on the terrace, and the rest were inside. Did DeLancey say he was going to the boat-house after all?'

'Not in so many words, I gather.'

It sounded as if Cheringham and Frieth expected Basil DeLancey to be ruled by his brother. Tish did not seem to grasp that they therefore had a motive for checking on the boat themselves – though a quick check would hardly do much good unless Bott happened to be caught sneaking down there, Alec realized.

He blamed the heat for his slowness to reach that conclusion. Frieth and Cheringham were intelligent men who would surely have worked it out for themselves. On the other hand, DeLancey and Bott were supposedly highly intelligent, and look at their idiotic behaviour. Intelligence was no guarantee of common sense.

Or common sense could be overborne by emotion, Alec thought, regarding Tish's tear-stained face. However, that would be more to the point if Frieth or Cheringham had known DeLancey was in the boat-house and had deliberately gone to confront him.

Which seemed unlikely, since they had no lack of opportunity for a confrontation. Only intentional murder would require the cloak of night, and Basil DeLancey had not been intentionally murdered.

Alec saw that his long pause was making Tish apprehensive. 'All right,' he said, 'tell me about DeLancey coming to your room.'

She looked relieved. 'Daisy heard him and turned on the bedside light. I was scared to death. Someone must have told you how he kept ... badgering me, and wouldn't take no for an answer?'

'Yes.'

'I thought he'd come to ... to...'

'To seduce – or perhaps assault – you?' Alec said gently

Tish nodded. 'He was ... he seemed to be drunk. He could have forgotten Daisy was sharing my room. Did she tell you I was sleeping on a camp-bed? He staggered in and fell over it, and it collapsed.' A slightly hysterical giggle escaped her. 'I'm sure it was funny, if I hadn't been terrified. He just lay there, though. Daisy thought he was probably just drunk enough to have turned the wrong way at the top of the stairs. She sent me to wake Nick Fosdyke. She said she didn't mind being alone with DeLancey. She's so brave!'

'Foolhardy,' Alec muttered, then said aloud, 'Fosdyke was asleep?'

'Fast asleep. I didn't dare knock very hard on the door, in case I woke the whole house, so I went in and called to him. He didn't stir. I had to shake him awake, and then he was still half-asleep until he actually saw

DeLancey in our room. He was an absolute angel.'

'Yes, I don't believe I've properly expressed my appreciation.'

'He thought DeLancey was drunk, too.'

'Mr. Fosdyke Senior and Dr. Dewhurst, the police surgeon, both assure me you couldn't possibly have guessed he was injured. You really must stop blaming yourself, Tish.'

The only result of his reassurance was that she started crying again. Alec began to feel a bit impatient. Why couldn't she pull herself together, like Daisy? Admittedly, she had known DeLancey better, and many people felt guilty when someone died whom they had detested, as if ancient superstitions about ill-wishing lingered in the modern unconscious.

He didn't think Tish bore the additional burden of fear that Cherry or Rollo was responsible for DeLancey's death. Those two young men looked less and less likely as suspects. Alec could only hope something decisive would come out in his interviews with them.

If they didn't decide to sock him in the jaw first for making Tish cry.

'Shall I send Piper for your mother?' he asked.

Mopping her eyes with his handkerchief, she shook her head. 'No, I'll be all right, honestly. I'm just rather tired. I think I'll go back to bed. It's awful of me after inviting everyone, but I just don't feel up to...'

'Don't cry! I'm sure no one expects you to be the perfect hostess after such a shock. Off you go, now. Nothing will seem quite so bad in the morning. I promise you.'

As Tish left, Tom returned. 'That was Henley Police rang up, Chief,' he reported. 'Bott's back at Miss Hopgood's lodgings. They've got a man watching, but they can't spare him for long. Things are starting to get lively in town.'

'You'd better take the Austin and bring Bott along.'

'Right, Chief. D'you want Miss Hopgood too?'

'I'd forgotten her. No, I'll see her tomorrow if I need to. Oh, you'd better stop at the White Hart on the way and pick up my things, would you? But first tell me about the dabs on the oar.'

'All accounted for, Chief. Mr. Cheringham's freshest, like he said; Miss Cheringham's – he told me the young ladies often help put 'em away, remember; the deceased; Mr. Meredith; Mr. Wells; and a whole lot of old 'uns underneath. Then there's Mr. Frieth's on the blade, where you'd expect him to touch when he looked at the damage.'

'None of Bott's?'

'None as match what I got off his hairbrush, Chief.'

'And he'd hardly wear gloves for a bit of mischief-making on a warm summer night.'

'No gloves among his things, Chief.'

'Damn!' said Alec.

CHAPTER 13

Leigh, recalled, was pretty sure he'd have noticed if Bott had been wearing gloves with his flannels and college blazer when he crossed the river that morning.

'He does get things wrong, but not quite that wrong. He'd have looked abso-bally-lutely Victorian setting off for a picnic on a hot day in gloves. I'd remember.'

Thanking him grimly, Alec saw his likeliest suspect fading before his eyes. Was the oar a red herring? Was he on the wrong track altogether, unable to see the wood for the trees? Had Basil DeLancey in fact been drunk enough to fall down twice?

The abrasion on his head and the blood on the floor in the boat-house argued against it. A man might skid along the ground if he fell while running, but one doesn't run in a boat-house.

Alec decided he needed to inspect the boat-house and to consult Dr. Dewhurst. But first he'd finish the interviews. He had kept people waiting long enough.

'Fetch Miss Carrick, please, Piper.'

Dorothy Carrick had changed into a navy-blue linen skirt and pale blue blouse which suited her much better than her flowery dress. She wasn't over plump, just sturdily built, and Alec, who vastly preferred Daisy's curves to the fashionable boyish flatness, saw nothing much amiss with her figure. To be sure, her face would never launch a thousand ships, but she had a charming smile, with perfect teeth. Add intelligence, and the kindness she had shown to her distraught friend on the riverbank, and Cheringham's choice was not to be cavilled at.

And then there was that marvellous voice: 'I'm afraid your weekend has been ruined, Mr. Fletcher. Daisy was so thrilled that you'd escaped from Scotland Yard for a whole two days. Rotten luck!'

'Rather rotten luck for Basil DeLancey, too.' Alec said dryly.

'I shan't pretend I'm sorry he's gone. I'm only sorry the *Erinyes* caught up with him now, involving us. It was bound to happen some day.'

'The Furies were on his trail? Wouldn't you say death is too severe a punishment for what, as far as I can gather, was little more than a thoroughly unpleasant tongue?'

'He made Horace Bott ill, assaulted him, and publicly humiliated him. The Furies had worse punishments for what we might consider lesser sins. Daisy mentioned that you're a student of Georgian history. Wasn't the death penalty applied then to what we'd call misdemeanours?'

'For shoplifting goods worth five shillings.' Alec admitted. 'So you think Bott hit DeLancey?'

'Mr. Fletcher,' said Miss Carrick earnestly, 'Horace Bott has a brilliant mind. He's a mathematician and a scientist, which requires a logical mind. In the heat of the moment he threatened vengeance. Once he cooled down, he could not but come to his senses and see the illogic of damaging the boat, which would penalize Cherry and Rollo as much as DeLancey. He had no quarrel with them.'

According to Daisy, Bott's feelings towards his fellow collegians in general were none too kindly – though hadn't she said something about Rollo Frieth sticking up for him. Where was she? Shouldn't she be back by now? Alec wanted to talk to her.

She wouldn't make the mistake of believing Bott's brilliance at applying logic to numbers meant he would do the same to life. Alec reminded himself that, for all Dottie Carrick's knowledge of ancient Greece, she was very young, not more than twenty, with little experience of the world.

'What did Cheringham and Frieth make of Bott's threats?' he asked her.

'They both thought it was bravado. They have a rather low opinion of him, I'm afraid.'

'And what was their opinion of DeLancey's concern over the boat?'

'Sheer rubbish,' said Miss Carrick decidedly. 'Cherry said DeLancey didn't really believe it himself, he was just getting at Bott again, trying to turn everyone else against him.'

'They both disliked DeLancey.'

'Who didn't? But as Rollo said, we never had to see him again after this weekend, so why worry?'

'An eminently sane point of view.' Alec asked Miss Carrick a few more questions, but she merely confirmed what he had already learnt. He ushered her out, and Piper fetched Frieth.

As the crew's captain dropped wearily into the chair Alec indicated, Ernie Piper announced, 'Lord DeLancey's here, sir.'

Alec groaned. 'He'll have to wait.'

'He doesn't want to see you, sir. I asked. He said he came for his brother's stuff, and I told him he couldn't take it yet. Right?'

'Right.'

'He seems to want to talk about his brother,' said Frieth. He was more mature than the others Alec had interviewed, a combination of years and war experience. With the light from the window on his face, he looked anxious, discouraged, and just plain tired. 'Deucedly awkward, when no one has a good word for him except for his rowing. I'm afraid some of the fellows have been rather going on about Bott and the boat-house, for want of anything else to say.'

'It can't be helped, I suppose.' Alec said with a grimace. 'I thought they were going to watch the rest of the Regatta.'

They decided it was too much bother, what with the heat and ... everything. They're playing croquet on the front lawn. They'll have another chance to be part of the Regatta next year.'

'And you won't?'

'No. I didn't pass the final exams, and if I decide to go back and try again, I'll have to concentrate on swotting, not rowing.'

'So winning this year was important to you?'

'It would have been nice to have a trophy to take back to Ambrose, but it all seems pretty unimportant compared to a man's life, even a swine like DeLancey.' Frieth dropped his head in his hands. 'Oh God, why did I let him row?' he groaned.

'Why did you?' That was a question Alec ought to have explored with the others. With his war service, Frieth must have some understanding of head injuries. Hitting DeLancey was one thing, seeing his symptoms and still permitting him to exert himself was quite another.

Frieth raised his head. 'I never guessed for a moment it was anything but a hangover.'

'Weren't you afraid his rowing would be affected? You could have substituted one of the others.'

'DeLancey was both stroke and steersman, not just an oarsman. I could have taken his position and put Meredith or Wells in at bow, but DeLancey was absolutely determined to race. It would have meant a hell of a row if I'd kicked him out. Besides, he'd turned up with a bit of a head before and always been all right on the water. In fact, he had no trouble rowing up to the start this morning. He'd eaten well at breakfast, too. How could I guess anything was seriously wrong?'

Reasonable, and easy enough to check, Alec thought. 'You didn't hear his carrying on in the middle of the night?'

'Not a whisper. Poor Tish. I wish she'd come to me.'

'What would you have done?'

Frieth looked taken aback. 'Well, actually, I couldn't have done much that Fosdyke didn't do – making a big fuss of it, then or later, would only have upset Tish even more. She's just had too much to cope with, what with one thing and another. At least I could have comforted her, assured her I didn't for a moment suppose she'd given that bastard any encouragement, if I'd woken up.'

'You slept soundly throughout the night?'

'As a matter of fact, no. DeLancey can't

have made much noise or I would have heard, because I had a rotten night. Tossing and turning all night, or that's what it felt like. It's a good job Cherry insisted on taking the camp-bed. I'd have overturned it.'

'He didn't wake?'

'Didn't stir, and how I detested him for his oblivion!'

Frieth said wryly. 'You know how it is: misery loves company.'

If that was an attempt to provide his friend with an alibi, Frieth was a lot more subtle than he appeared. Alec was inclined to take his words at face value. 'What were you miserable about?' he enquired.

'Oh, well, miserable's a bit too strong. I was a bit pipped over DeLancey's mistreating Bott. As captain, I ought to have been able to put a stop to it, especially as it led to us being knocked out of the Thames Cup. And then there's general sort of worry about the future, trying to decide whether to stick out another year at Oxford or to try to get any old job paying enough to support Tish. I'm not getting any younger.'

'You're what, twenty-five?' Alec said with some asperity. 'You have thirty or forty working years ahead of you. Do you want to spend them in a job you don't care about?' Great Scott, sorting out peoples private lives was Daisy's forte – it must be catching! He shrugged. 'It's your choice. You weren't worrying over whether Bott would sabotage the boat?'

'That was DeLancey's fantasy,' Frieth snorted, 'whatever the others are saying now. As I told Tish, if Bott had done anything of the sort, everyone would have known exactly who was to blame. Admittedly he's not exactly popular, but his name would have been mud, and not only at Oxford. There are plenty of Cambridge crews at the Regatta.'

Making his public humiliation at DeLancey's hands that much bitterer, Alec reflected. 'What did you think of DeLancey's plan to guard the boat?' he asked.

'It looks as if he did, didn't he? When his brother laid down the law, we assumed that was the end of it. After all, Lord DeLancey had somehow forced Basil to apologize, to us if not to Bott. Come to that, I don't suppose the notion of begging Bott's pardon so much as crossed Lord DeLancey's mind.'

'I'd say it was highly unlikely,' Alec agreed. He found himself liking Frieth; just as well if they were to he cousins-in-law. Was it influencing his judgment? He could not see the young man as a liar, nor as quick to violence, let alone as a cold-blooded murderer. 'You fell asleep in the end, I imagine,' he said. 'Have you any idea what time?' Glancing at his wrist-watch, he was dismayed to see how late it was.

'The last time I remember checking, it was past three.'

'You're prepared to swear neither you nor Cheringham left your room before then?'

'Absolutely,' said Frieth with confidence. 'He couldn't possibly have left without my knowing. You see, our bedroom is pretty small. The only way he can get out of the camp-bed without tipping it up is to climb over my bed.'

His certainty was convincing. Alec decided to let him go. He could always get back to him later, and he wanted to see Cheringham before Tom returned with Bott.

As Frieth and Piper left the library, Daisy waltzed in. Though her curls were flattened by hat and heat, her blue eyes sparkled and she looked decidedly pleased with herself.

'Alec, darling.' She kissed his cheek. 'I've had a too, too marvellous interview with Prince Henry. He actually said it was a great pity "our American cousins" hadn't entered a crew this year, only two men in the single sculls. My editor will be thrilled to death.'

'Lucky man,' Alec grunted.

'Have you had a frightful afternoon? I would have come back earlier, but Betty's brother was rowing in the last race, the Stewards' Cup final, so I couldn't ask them to drive me home till it was over. It was too frightfully hot to walk. Would you believe, I only had one glass of champagne because it made me even hotter, so switched to lemonade.'

He smiled. 'You're bubbling as if you'd been drinking champagne all afternoon.'

'Well, it's been a most successful day, and if I'd been here, you'd only have said I was meddling. But you haven't heard all of it. The two Americans who rowed in the Diamond Sculls were presented to Prince Henry while I was there, and when he moved on I talked to them, getting their views on the Regatta. They're enjoying it, even though they were both beaten by the same Leander rower. Nice chaps, one from Boston and the other from somewhere called Duluth. Believe it or not, the Boston one's called Codman.'

'"Good old Boston, the home of the bean and the cod."' Alec quoted.

Daisy giggled. 'I didn't like to ask him about it. They've been invited to Phyllis Court this evening. You *will* be able to come with me, won't you?'

'I don't know, love. I don't seem to be getting anywhere.'

'Then it will do you good to get away from the investigation for a while,' Daisy said decisively. 'From a distance you'll be able to see the whole picture instead of getting bogged down in details.'

'I do feel as if I'm too close to the trees for a good view of the wood.' Alec admitted. A couple of hours away may help, and it'll give Ernie a chance to write up his notes so that we can study them. Also, dining here with the people I've been interrogating promises to be uncomfortable, to say the least.'

'Spiffing! I must go and wash my hair. It's positively glued to my head. We ought to leave here by twenty to eight at the very latest,' she added as Piper came in with Cheringham. 'Tom will bring the Chummy back by then, won't he? We passed him heading into town.'

'Yes, he's just gone to pick up Horace Bott.'

Cheringham perked up. 'You've found Bott? Then this whole ghastly business will be over soon.'

Daisy turned towards him, opening her mouth. Alec gave her a warning glare. She shut her mouth, wrinkled her freckled nose at him, and departed.

Alec invited Cheringham to sit down, ignoring the intrusive ring of the telephone. If it was for him, Gladstone would inform him. He was rather surprised it hadn't been ringing like billy-oh – somehow the press hadn't yet discovered where DeLancey had been staying.

'What makes you think finding Bott is the answer?'

'Because he's the one who hit DeLancey,' said Cheringham impatiently. 'Oh, I don't blame him, and I dare say it was self-defence, but after all he shouldn't have been anywhere near the boat-house. He must have been going to bash in the boat. I must say, I never would have thought he'd be such an idiot. Dottie's always going on about how brilliant he is.'

'Intelligence and common sense don't always go hand-in-hand.'

'Is that a dig at me? I'm not really jealous of her admiring Bott, you know. It's only his brain she respects. She has too much common sense to– Now, there you are, Dottie's both brainy *and* practical.'

'Miss Carrick doesn't believe Bott's our culprit?

Jealous or not, Cheringham flushed. 'What's more important is, do you?' he asked with a touch of truculence.

'My beliefs are unimportant. I need evidence.'

But all Alec's questions elicited nothing to change the picture. Though Cheringham was by no means so straightforward a character as Frieth, nor so tolerantly peaceable, his words rang true. He had not left their bedroom last night, could not have done so without disturbing his friend.

Neither Cheringham nor Frieth was so stupid as to lie about anything so easily disproved, though Alec would send Tom to check the room anyway.

He glanced at his watch. If Tom was not back yet with Bott, not to mention Alec's dinner jacket, Daisy would have to leave for Phyllis Court alone. He didn't like to think of her fraternizing with those two American rowers, without his escort.

Not that he was jealous.

'Piper, please go and see if Sergeant Tring is here,' he ordered. Turning to Cheringham, he said, 'In view of our future relationship, I hope you'll excuse my probing.'

'Lord, yes.' Cheringham stood up and offered his hand. 'No hard feelings. You're just doing your job, and if Rollo and I had done a better job of keeping DeLancey off Bott's back, you might have been able to enjoy a peaceful weekend. I hope you manage a bit of revelry tonight.'

'I'll try.' Alec shook his hand, breathing a silent sigh of relief. It didn't look as if he was going to have to arrest any of Daisy's relatives.

Cheringham left. Piper returned, followed by a short, slight young man with a fearsome scowl.

Tom brought up the rear. He introduced Alec with a mild courtesy obviously designed to give the cox nothing to complain about. 'Detective Chief Inspector Fletcher, sir. Sir, this is Mr. Bott.'

'What the...?' Bott started belligerently.

Alec interrupted him with a cordial, 'Do

sit down, won't you, Mr. Bott? Excuse me a moment. I have one or two instructions to give my sergeant.'

The wind taken out of his sails, Bott sulkily subsided into the chair. Alec moved away with Tom and in a low voice told him to give Cheringham and Frieth's room a look over. 'By the way, did any of the servants see Bott last night?' he added.

'Mr. Gladstone and the parlour-maid both saw him come in about twenty past eight, when they were serving dinner. No one saw him after. I fetched your bags, Chief. Mr. Gladstone said to tell you young Fosdyke telephoned. He'll stop at the Catherine Wheel tonight, with his pa. Lady Cheringham wants to know, do you want me and Ernie to stay the night in his room, the one he shared with Mr. DeLancey?'

'Yes, bless her!' Turning back to Bott, Alec caught an apprehensive look, quickly wiped away.

'What the hell's all this about?' Bott demanded. 'I suppose you think you can pick on me because I'm not one of the nobs.'

'Everyone in the house has been questioned, Mr. Bott. Basil DeLancey's dead.'

'Dead!' Was that a flicker of panic in his eyes, along with the astonishment?

Alec would swear he was genuinely astonished. 'He was hit in the boat-house last night and died this morning of the delayed effect of his injuries. We have reason to believe you went to the boat-house last night.'

'Reason to believe? What the hell does that mean? I had no reason to go anywhere near the boat-house, and I didn't.'

'We found one of your tent-pegs in the bushes.'

Again a flicker of dismay, then Bott became condescendingly logical. 'One tent-peg is very like another. Can you prove its mine? If so, that doesn't prove either that I was the one who put it there, or that it only got there last night.'

Inarguable, and just what Alec had already recognised. 'You threatened DeLancey.'

'I did. I had good cause. What has that to do with the boat-house?'

'DeLancey believed you intended to sabotage the boat to get your revenge on him.'

'I'm not responsible for DeLancey's beliefs. I repeat, I did not enter the boat-house last night.'

And Bott continued to reiterate his denial, even when Alec assured him the police would aim for a verdict of self-defence. Those moments of fear weren't evidence, nor even necessarily an indication of guilt. Bott was convinced the world had it in for him, and learning that one was suspected of murder was enough to frighten anyone. As he said, he was not responsible for DeLancey's notions. The odds against his happening to choose the method of revenge that DeLancey happened to suspect must be huge – unless he had heard talk of it.

Everyone, including the servants, should have been asked whether they had mentioned the matter to Bott, or seen him in a position to overhear others mention it. Now it would have to wait until tomorrow, Alec thought wearily.

So would his visit to the boat-house and inspection of the oar. He needed to discuss with Tom what he had learnt from the servants, and to go over Piper's reports of the interviews. He needed to step back and see the whole case in perspective.

He needed to go and change into evening clothes at once if he and Daisy were not to arrive late at Phyllis Court.

'I'll talk to you again tomorrow,' he said to Bott. 'Don't go anywhere, please, without informing my officers.'

Bott stalked out. That he had been evasive, Alec was certain. That he was DeLancey's assailant, Alec was more than half-convinced. That it could ever be proved, Alec doubted.

He needed a confession, and it seemed highly unlikely that Bott would oblige.

CHAPTER 14

'So you're pretty sure it was Horace Bott,' said Daisy, as Alec squeezed the little Austin in amongst the Rolls Royces, Napiers, Daimlers, Lanchesters, Hispano-Suizas, and Isotta-Fraschinis. During the short drive he had, at her insistence, given her a quick report of the results of his investigations.

'I didn't say so,' he protested.

'No, but you've just about ruled out everyone else.' Waiting for him to come around the car and open her door, she wondered whether he had deliberately misled her as to his interest in Cherry and Rollo. He might want to spare her feelings – or to forestall her interference.

'I haven't crossed anyone off my list,' he said, handing her out. 'You look stunning, love. Is that a new dress?'

'No, but Lucy helped me refurbish it. You know how good she is at clothes.' Pleased, but not to be distracted, Daisy went on, 'It couldn't have been Cherry because of being stuck in his camp-bed, and it couldn't have been Rollo because his fingerprints were only on the blade of the oar. Fosdyke's weren't on it at all, you said. Nor Bott's.'

'I also said I'm having my doubts of the oar as the weapon, but never mind that. If it wasn't Cheringham, Frieth, Fosdyke, or Bott, who was it?'

'One of the other four?' she proposed doubtfully.

'None of them appeared the least alarmed at being interrogated, which argues that they didn't consider themselves suspects. Not one was smug, either, as if he thought he was getting away with ... murder. I have far more reason to believe it was not one of the four than that it was.'

'What about an outsider, looking for a boat to steal perhaps?'

'The skiffs were outside, moored to the landing-stage.' Alec pointed out patiently. 'Besides, DeLancey would surely have spoken up, not to say yelled blue murder, if he'd been attacked by a stranger.'

'He'd have yelled blue murder if Bott hit him.'

'I think not. He wouldn't want to admit to having been bested by Bott, whom he despised.'

'Oh. Perhaps not. I still can't see that it was necessarily Bott.'

'Are you telling me his threats and DeLancey's demise aren't connected?'

'No, of course not. If he hadn't made those threats, DeLancey wouldn't have been in the boat-house. Then none of this would have happened, and we'd have had our weekend...'

'Let's at least have our evening, Daisy. I don't want to hear another word about the case until tomorrow. Please?'

'Right-oh, darling, my lips are sealed.' But her mind kept working as they entered the club, an attractive Georgian mansion presently far too full of people to be properly appreciated.

If the oar was not the weapon, then the lack of Bott's fingerprints meant nothing. The tent-peg was perplexing, but it pointed to Bott rather than to anyone else. Alec was right, he was the most likely of the suspects, Daisy thought despondently. Little as she liked him, she was sorry. DeLancey had tormented him brutally. Besides, it was going to be hard on Susan Hopgood, whom she did like.

A pre-dinner sherry in the lounge with her friends, and wine with the meal, effectively drove Bott's fate from her thoughts. After dinner, their host and hostess, of her father's generation, chose to sit on the terrace with coffee and liqueurs. However, they kindly assured Daisy she must not feel herself tied to their apron-strings.

There was dancing, but Daisy, who was convinced she had two left feet, had no difficulty persuading Alec to stroll about the pleasant riverside grounds. They ended up on the croquet lawn, teaching the game to Mr. Codman from Boston, Mr. Hoover from Duluth, and a Swiss, a Norwegian, and a Canadian who had also rowed in the Diamond Sculls.

They had a hilarious time. Daisy had never seen Alec so carefree. Their weekend was not a total disaster after all.

At last it grew too dark to play. Everyone moved down to the riverbank to watch the firework show. Amidst booms, cracks, and whistles, rockets soared in showers of red and green sparks, golden rain fountained, Catherine wheels whirled, Roman candles glittered – all reflected shimmering in the river.

Alec put his arm around Daisy's shoulders. She slipped hers around his waist, under his dinner-jacket, and pressed close to his side.

Daisy clung to the last shreds of her dream. Alec was kissing her in the middle of a fountain of sparkling light every colour of the rainbow, while a heavenly choir sang a song of love.

The song resolved itself into a thrush outside the open window, through which a ray of the rising sun alighted on Daisy's face. She blinked and sat up. It was still very early. Sunday hadn't really quite begun. Maybe she and Alec could steal a few more moments and memories before the rest of the world awoke.

Tish was fast asleep. With hasty stealth,

Daisy flung on her dressing gown and went to tap on the door of Uncle Rupert's dressing room.

She held her breath. Would being woken at daybreak make him furious?

The door opened. 'Daisy, what's wrong?' he mumbled, eyes half-shut.

'Nothing.' She reached out to smooth a tuft of hair sticking up by his ear. He was wearing blue and pale grey striped cotton pyjamas, his feet bare. The sight of his bare feet was oddly intimate, disturbing – Daisy suddenly understood why a poet would write an ode to his mistress's earlobe. 'It's a simply glorious morning,' she said hurriedly. 'Let's go out in the garden before anyone else gets up.'

Already alert, his grey eyes smiled at her. 'Good idea.' He felt his dark-bristled chin.

'Don't bother with shaving, and I shan't powder my nose. Ten minutes?'

'Ten minutes.'

Ten minutes later, they sneaked down through the quiet house. With a deliberate effort, Daisy dismissed from her mind the memory of her previous surreptitious expedition. It returned vividly, however, when they found the drawing-room French windows unlocked.

'Someone's beaten us to it,' she said, disappointed.

'Never mind. If we see them, we'll head in

the opposite direction.'

The air was fresh, and cool enough for Daisy to be glad of her cardigan. Dewdrops twinkled on the roses and the lawn. Wraiths of mist curled up from the river as they descended the steps and strolled down the path, hand-in-hand.

In the shadow of the boat-house, a figure moved. Daisy gasped.

The sinister shape emerged into sunlight and turned into Cherry, in flannels and his rowing shirt. He came towards them. 'I woke up and thought I'd take a skiff out while it's cool and peaceful,' he said, 'but the sculls are in the boat-house and it's padlocked. Your doing, I take it, Mr. Fletcher.'

'Sergeant Tring's.'

'An estimable fellow. Oh, in case you're wondering, Rollo cursed me, turned over, and went back to sleep.'

'I have the key. Can you get the skiff's sculls without disturbing anything else? They're different from your racing oars?'

'As chalk from cheese – to a rowing man. We've been putting them on the floor behind the rack while it's occupied with racing oars. Let me at 'em and I'll take the two of you out, if you like. I want the exercise as much as the peace.'

Alec consulted Daisy with a glance. It wasn't quite what she'd planned, but floating on the water as the sun dispersed the golden mists sounded too good to turn down. True, Cherry would be there as well as Alec, but that meant neither he nor she would have to row.

'Let's.'

'I'll get the sculls,' Alec said, taking a key-ring from his trouser pocket.

Suspicious, Daisy warned him sternly, 'No investigating.'

'Not till we come back,' he promised, laughing.

'Better bring a boat-hook if *we're* steering, and get a couple of cushions, darling.'

'There's a boat-hook in the boat already,' Cherry said.

Daisy turned to the river as Alec unlocked the padlock. 'One of the skiffs is missing!' she exclaimed.

'Yes.' Cherry knelt down on the landing-stage to slot the unshipped rudder into place. 'Someone else must have had the same idea, but earlier. I suppose a pair of sculls and the boat-hook got left out yesterday, hardly surprising in the circs.'

Daisy shuddered, recalling the return to Bulawayo with DeLancey's body. There had been great confusion on the crossing. Cherry, soaked after his rescue attempt, had already rowed one skiff across with Tish and Dottie, so much ferrying back and forth had taken place. Small wonder if oars had been forgotten.

Alec handed her two cushions and went back for the sculls, which he passed to Cherry, before replacing the padlock and clicking it shut.

'We'll go upstream, if that's all right with you,' said Cherry. 'That way I can take it easy coming back. Anyway, you can't go far downstream before you get to the Hambleden lock and weir.'

They set off, Daisy and Alec together in the stern seat. No other boat was visible on the river, but the water-birds were making the most of the quiet. Swans, removed for the Regatta, had already returned. A pair sailed by, giving the intruders a haughtily disgruntled glare. Moorhens bobbed about near the reeds, and a grey heron rose from the bank, its huge wings flapping so slowly it seemed impossible it should stay aloft.

In the absence of traffic, Alec was perfectly confident and competent with the tiller-lines. Cherry rowed with long, leisurely strokes. The banks moved steadily past and Temple Island approached ahead.

'We'll go to the left of the island,' Cherry said. 'Incorrect, but we're unlikely to meet anyone and the current's not so strong as the other side. I'm going to be good and ready for breakfast.'

'You make it look easy,' said Daisy. 'I'd like to take a turn at the oars – sculls – on the way back, when we're going with the current.'

'Have you ever rowed?'

'Not since before the war. We used to take a dory out at Upton-upon-Severn or Severn Stoke, and Gervaise and his friend Phillip usually made me row because they wanted to fish.'

Cherry and Alec laughed. 'Right-oh,' Cherry agreed, 'I'm prepared to put my life in your hands. Keep over to the island side of the channel, Fletcher, as we're going the wrong way. The current's pretty feeble close in, too – easier rowing. Turn around at the head of the island.'

They came to the place where the Regatta course had started. The booms had been moved over to the bank already, out of the way of the boat traffic which would soon begin to move homeward. Still no one was about. The only sounds were the lap of water against the hull, the creak of oars in the rowlocks, the twitters and warbles of birds in the trees on the island.

Daisy kept an eye out for the first glimpse of the temple. Before she saw it, she heard a shout. A moment later the tranquillity shattered at the crack of a gunshot.

For a moment Daisy was taken back to yesterday's race and the starting pistol. Then another shot rang out, followed by a splash.

'Look! There!' Daisy cried, and pointed to where something came bobbing down the stream from the head of the island, moving with the current out towards mid-channel. Something maroon. Ambrose maroon? 'Oh my gosh! It's a man!'

Cherry had already twisted his head to look. Now he swung his sculls in-board, stood up, and dived into the river.

The skiff rocked. It was still making headway from the momentum of his last stroke, but any moment it would start to drift backwards. With cautious haste, Daisy scrambled forward to the rowing bench. Turning to sit down, she saw Alec, his jacket stripped off, leaning over the back of the stern bench to pull the rudder from its slot.

'Daisy, can you manage?' he demanded. 'Cheringham needs help.'

'I'll manage.' She swung the sculls out, glad Cherry had left them in the rowlocks.

Alec slipped over the gunwale, rocking the skiff again. Daisy saw him set off after Cherry with a dogged breaststroke, then rowing demanded all her attention.

Somehow she managed not to catch a crab with her first two clumsy strokes. The rhythm returned – like riding a bicycle: once learned, never quite forgotten. Steering was another matter. She was facing backwards. Gervaise was not there to shout at her to back water with the right nor Phillip to fend off if she ran into the bank.

The bank was awfully close. The left scull

brushed through the drooping fronds of a leaning willow. Daisy quickly corrected her course, pleased to see that at least she was moving upstream in the quiet water close to the island.

But where was she going?

She remembered the landing-stage in front of the temple. If she could just get beyond it, the current would move her towards it, and it would be easier to get ashore than amongst the trees and bushes. Only that was where the shots had come from. Was a man with a gun standing there, listening, waiting?

Daisy rested on her oars for a moment. The birds were still silent after the shock of the shots. She forced herself not to look for Cherry and Alec, to concentrate on listening.

From beyond the top of the island came the creak of oars, the splashing of an inexpert oarsman.

He was escaping! Daisy bent with redoubled energy to the sculls. Slowly, so slowly, the trees crept by. She glanced round and saw between the leaves a patch of white wall, before a dark evergreen blocked the view again. Nearly there.

Drawing level with the temple, she glanced round again. His back to her, a man was rowing clumsily forwards, away from her, towards the Bucks bank.

Clumsy or not, he was pulling away.

Daisy's shoulders ached, her arms felt like lead, and she was getting a crick in her neck from trying to see behind her. As she cleared the tip of the island, the current caught her. She couldn't fight it.

One more glance back. Dark hair, white shirt – a fat lot of help that was. She turned her attention to reaching the island without sinking the skiff.

Stick the left scull in the water and make a strong stroke with the right. Obediently, the skiff turned broadside to the stream. Daisy shipped her oars and snatched up the boat-hook as the river carried her, drifting like thistledown in still air, towards the landing-stage. Another skiff, the twin of hers, was moored there. Kneeling, she reached for it with the boat-hook, caught the bow, and pulled herself in to shore.

'Daisy! Hullo! Daisy, where the dickens are you?'

An echo in her mind told her Alec had called before, when she was too busy to pay any heed. 'Over here!' she shouted, trying to hang on to the boat-hook while grabbing the painter. 'Here, at the temple. He got away!'

'All right, stay there, we'll be right there.'

What spoke to Daisy next, as she stepped ashore, was a painful memory from summer days on the Severn: 'Don't end up with one foot on the bank and the other in the boat unless someone's holding it.'

Too late. Daisy's frantic effort not to do the splits failed dismally. She toppled into the river.

Coming up spluttering, she found her feet in three feet of water, the end of the painter clutched in a death-grip (Gervaise had not been pleased that time he'd had to swim after the dory). Daisy eyed the landing-stage, a good eighteen inches above the river's surface. She'd have to wait for help.

In the meantime, fending off the skiff as the current kept bumping it against her, she gazed after the presumed villain of the piece. Though the wisps of mist were dispersing, too tenuous to block her view, he was too far off to be clearly visible. Close to the Bucks bank, he had turned upstream. As Daisy, shivering, watched, he came to what looked like a boat-house, nosed in, and climbed ashore. To her disappointment, he didn't fall in.

'Daisy? Where...? Great Scott, darling, how did you manage to land in the river?' Alec's face was carefully expressionless, but there was amusement in his voice.

'I decided to take a swim,' she said crossly. '*You* try getting out of a boat on your own.'

'It takes practice.' Cherry, behind Alec, was openly grinning.

He quickly sobered as Alec said, 'Here, put him down, Cheringham. Gently does it.'

Between them, Daisy realised, they carried

a limp body. 'Who is it?' she asked in dread. 'Is he...?'

'He's alive. Unconscious, with a head wound.' Alec knelt to give her his hands.

She handed him the painter and he tied it to an iron mooring-ring set in the landing-stage. Of course he was dripping wet too, as were Cherry and... 'Bott?'

'Bott,' Alec confirmed, hauling her out. 'He's been half-drowned and creased by a bullet. We have to get him to a doctor, fast. Cheringham thinks it'll be quickest to row back downstream to Bulawayo, telephone the local hospital from there, and run him into Henley by car.'

'Fletcher!' Cherry had tactfully turned his back as Daisy emerged from the Thames with her skirt clinging to her legs. He was stooping over something on the ground near the other skiff. 'Here's a pistol. A Mauser.'

'Don't touch! Good find, well done. I'll get the handkerchief from my jacket pocket to wrap it in.'

Alec sat down on the edge of the landing-stage with his legs in the skiff to retrieve his jacket from the stern seat. Daisy went over to Bott.

'Alec, this hankie round his head is soaked through with blood, and it started out sodden with riverwater, which I bet isn't any too clean. If you've got a clean, dry one, Bott's head needs it more than the gun. The pistol, I mean. Gervaise always insisted that a pistol is not a gun, though why… Never mind. Here, you use my hankie.' She felt in the sleeve of her sodden cardigan and produced a soggy wad.

Alec reluctantly gave her the clean one. He took hers, wrung it out, and unfolded it. 'This isn't big enough to wrap the pistol.' he complained.

'Make do.'

Taking off the cardigan, now a source more of discomfort than warmth, she watched as he gingerly picked up the Mauser with the handkerchief. He sniffed the barrel.

'It's been fired, of course. I hope there are fingerprints to help us find the owner, because it must be a War souvenir and it's probably not licensed.' He sighed. 'I suppose I'll have to use my jacket to wrap it in. Let's go.'

'There's a pair of sculls in this other skiff,' Cherry reported. 'Two of us can row.'

He and Alec lifted Bott again and, with Daisy steadying the skiff, laid him on the nearer arm of the V-shaped forward seat, his head on a cushion from the stern seat. Daisy sat right at the bow, at the point of the V, pressing Alec's folded handkerchief to the long, mercifully shallow furrow in Bott's scalp. If she lifted the pad, blood slowly welled up and trickled down. She couldn't guess how much he had lost, but his face was very white and he lay very still.

Shivering, she could only hope he wasn't going to die while under her care.

Cherry, in command, directed Alec to the sternward rower's bench. 'If I can see you.' he explained, 'there's more hope of co-ordinating our strokes.'

Untying the painter, he threaded the loose end through the ring and handed it to Daisy. With her holding it and Alec wielding the boat-hook, there was no fear of Cherry landing in the drink as he stepped into the skiff.

'Right-oh, Daisy, let go and pull the painter in.' He smiled at her over his shoulder as he sat down on the nearer bench. 'I'll show you how to do the whole thing solo when we're not in a rush.'

'After this weekend, I don't think I'll ever want anything to do with boats again,' Daisy muttered.

'Fletcher, shove off, please. Leave the sculling to me until we're clear.'

Once out in the channel, with the current bearing them downstream, Cherry had Alec take a couple of strokes, then fell into rhythm with him. Daisy waited till it looked as if Alec knew what he was doing before she addressed the back of his head, beyond Cherry.

'Alec, I saw the man who shot Bott.'

'You didn't recognise him?' Alec asked a trifle breathlessly.

'He was facing away from me, even though it meant rowing backwards. Or forwards, depending on how you look at it. All I could see was that he had dark hair, so I couldn't identify him by his looks, but he went ashore on the Bucks bank, at a boat-house, and I think that must be Crowswood land. There's no public towpath along that side, is there, Cherry?'

'That's right. You can walk through the meadows from Bulawayo to Crowswood, I think, but it's all private property. The boat-house over there belongs to Crowswood Place.'

'And only one person connected with the case is staying at Crowswood,' Daisy pointed out.

'Lord DeLancey,' said Alec, a world of perplexity in his voice.

CHAPTER 15

Distracted by Daisy's revelation, Alec caught a crab. The resultant shower hit the empty stern seat, not that, wet as they were, anyone would have cared about getting splashed. Alec rocked back but just managed not to topple into Cherry's lap.

In spite of this lapse, the banks slid by infinitely faster on the way back to Bulawayo than they had on the outward voyage. The men were silent, their breath needed for rowing, and Daisy stayed mum so as not to disturb Alec's concentration again. Her mind seethed with speculation, though.

What on earth was Lord DeLancey doing on Temple Island at dawn with Horace Bott? Apart from shooting him, of course. If DeLancey believed Bott responsible for his brother's death, the shooting must be revenge. But what on earth was Horace Bott doing at dawn on Temple Island with Lord DeLancey?

One thing was certain: they couldn't possibly have met by chance. If the encounter was proposed by DeLancey, Bott would have had to be crazy to turn up – unless he was both innocent and unaware that he was the prime suspect.

On the other hand, why should Bott want to meet DeLancey? In the hope of convincing him of his innocence? Proving it to Alec was more to the point.

A rendezvous with pistols at dawn sounded like a duel, but the custom of duelling had died out in England more than half a century ago. Anyway, duels were between gentlemen, and Lord DeLancey did not accord Bott that status.

Could it have been someone other than Lord DeLancey? That seemed even less likely than a duel.

None of the affair made any sort of sense that Daisy could see.

They were approaching the Cheringhams'. Cherry's frequent glances over his shoulder and consequent adjustments to his stroke had kept the skiff on a roughly straight course. Given the bend in the river, this brought them close to their destination before further manoeuvres became necessary.

'Right-oh, Fletcher, ship oars and man the boat-hook,' he instructed, and with apparent ease brought the skiff gently alongside the landing-stage.

Manfully, Alec manned the boat-hook. However, exhausted by his exertions, he sagged as soon as Cherry had stepped ashore and the skiff was safely moored.

'My arms ... won't work any more,' he gasped. 'I don't dare risk ... lifting Bott in case I drop him.'

'You did a good job,' Cherry said kindly. 'Rowing uses just about every muscle in your body, including some most people never know they have. I'll buzz on up to the house and get help. One or two of those sluggards must be up by now.'

'Don't ... tell...' Alec panted.

Daisy guessed: 'Don't mention Lord DeLancey, Cherry. Nor the shots or the gun,' she added, as Alec gestured weakly at his bundled jacket. 'The pistol.'

'Right-oh.' Cherry set off up the lawn at an insufferably energetic run. Alec summoned up just enough energy to glare after him.

'He's made a point of developing all the right muscles.' Daisy consoled Alec, tactfully steering clear of the ten years difference in age. 'I was fagged out after fifty yards. Alec, do you have any brilliant ideas about what they were doing there? Lord DeLancey and Bott? I can't make head or tail of it.'

'I haven't exactly had much leisure for thought.' He was regaining control of his breathing, at least. 'Tell me your conclusions, or what led to a lack of them. But first, how's Bott doing?'

'He hasn't stirred.' Daisy peeked under the pad of handkerchief, then removed and refolded it. 'The bleeding seems to have stopped.'

'How's his pulse? He still has one, I take it?'

'He's breathing, wheezing a bit.' She laid the hankie clean side down over the wound and grasped Bott's wrist. 'I'm not very good at pulses. It seems to me steady but rather weak.'

'I hope to heaven he recovers, or we may never find out what was going on back there.'

By the time Daisy finished explaining her reasoning and her failure to deduce any answers, help was on the way. Rollo, Leigh, and Meredith came galloping down the garden like the Charge of the Light Brigade, with Tom Tring and Ernie Piper bringing up the rear.

Hastily picking up the jacket-wrapped pistol, Alec stepped up onto the landing-stage and helped Daisy ashore. Fortunately, her light summer clothes had dried off enough not to be utterly indecent.

While Piper helped Rollo, Leigh, and Meredith to lift Bott from the skiff to the landing-stage, Alec surreptitiously passed the Mauser to Tom Tring. The sergeant enveloped it in his own spotted handkerchief and deposited it in the capacious pocket of his startling blue and white check suit jacket.

'Mr. Cheringham sent Mr. Gladstone to

rout out Bister to start up Lady Cheringham's motorcar, Chief. He's telephoning the hospital now so's they'll he prepared. He didn't say what happened, just that Mr. Bott's in a bad way.'

'I'll explain in the car, Tom.'

'Right, Chief. What about this here?' He patted his pocket.

'Bring it, and your kit.'

'I'll go get it.'

As Tom set off back to the house, Daisy said, 'Has he got Lord DeLancey's dabs to match it with.'

'No. We'll have to get them somehow.'

They turned to the others. Piper was stripping off his jacket, saying, 'You can make a stretcher with a couple of coats and two of them ... those oars.'

'Good thought,' said Rollo, and took off his blazer while Meredith and Leigh retrieved a pair of sculls.

Bott was gently transferred from the planks to the makeshift stretcher, and once again a stretcher-bearing procession tramped up the path. At least the body on the stretcher was alive this time. So far.

'What are his chances?' she asked Alec as they followed.

'With proper care he may be perfectly all right, but plenty of things can go wrong with near-drowning victims, not only their lungs but hearts and brains, too. I've dealt with a few in my time. On top of that, there's the loss of blood, and we've had a graphic demonstration of the possible results of head injuries.'

'Yes.' Daisy shivered, though the morning was already warm.

'You go and change at once,' Alec ordered. 'I don't want you risking pneumonia, as well as Bott.'

'I'm perfectly all right.' Daisy had no intention of wasting time changing her clothes if it might mean being left behind. 'Are you going to the hospital, or straight to see Lord DeLancey?'

'To the hospital. For a start, I must arrange for a guard.'

'He's in no condition to try running away.' She stopped, horrified, at the foot of the steps. 'Oh, you think Lord DeLancey may try again?'

'Little likelihood, I'd say, but not to be ignored. Also, I must talk to the doctor, get a prognosis. If I'm extraordinarily lucky, Bott may come round and give me something to go on when I see DeLancey.' Alec was planning as he spoke. 'If not, I'll leave Tom. He can take a statement if it becomes possible, and double as a guard.'

'Miss Hopgood will want to be with Bott.'

'Oh, the dickens, I'd forgotten her. A hysterical female is just what I need.'

'Susan Hopgood isn't at all the sort to

succumb to hysteria.'

'All the same, don't you think she'd be better off not knowing till he recovers consciousness?'

'Or dies? No.' Daisy said firmly. 'Bister can fetch her. There must be family, too, who ought to be informed.'

'Not until I have more idea of what's going on.' Alec said with equal firmness as they entered the house in the wake of the stretcher party. He raised his voice. 'Carry him into the hall, please, Frieth, ready to move on as soon as the car is brought round.'

Wells and Poindexter were in the hall, trying to get more from an uncommunicative Cherry than that Bott was hurt. They turned eagerly to Rollo in hopes of better information. Cherry handed a rolled bandage to Daisy and turned with relief to Alec.

'I've spoken to the Sister on duty at Townlands Hospital. She's getting hold of a doctor and having a bed prepared. Sergeant Tring said Bott should have a private room?'

'Yes, thanks. Lady Cheringham's car...'

'Is on the way. Bister was asleep when Gladstone rang through to him. There are other motor-cars available, of course, but I thought Bott would be less shaken about in the Humber, so...'

A sharp cry interrupted him. Along with everyone else, Daisy looked up at the stairs.

Tish and Dottie had stopped on their way

down. Tish was looking over the banisters at Bott, lying limp and ashen on the improvised stretcher on the floor. Turning almost as pale, she crumpled in a dead faint.

Somehow Dottie managed to catch Tish before she hit her head on a step and tumbled down the stairs. Rollo and Cherry bounded up to her assistance. At that moment, Gladstone came in through the open front door and announced in a voice which remained deferential while cutting through the hubbub, 'Mr. Fletcher, sir, the Humber is at the door.'

Daisy had to choose instantly whether to stay with Tish or go with Bott. It was an easy decision, and curiosity had nothing to do with it, she assured herself. Her cousin had Dottie and Aunt Cynthia to support her, not to mention Rollo and Cherry, whereas Susan Hopgood had no one.

Slipping out, Daisy was already ensconced in the back seat of the Humber when Bott was borne out by Wells and Poindexter, with Meredith and Leigh in attendance. Alec, following the stretcher with Piper and Tring, glowered at her.

She smiled sweetly back, reasonably confident that, with all the others there, he wouldn't attempt to make her stay behind. Her confidence proved justified, whether because of the audience or because he was beginning to learn the futility of trying to order her about.

Thus Horace Bott's bandaged head was cradled in Daisy's still slightly damp lap as the Humber rolled down the drive. Piper sat in front, beside Bister in the cap and uniform jacket appropriate to his chauffeur's role.

Alec followed in the yellow Austin Seven with Sergeant Tring. Daisy wished she could hear what they were saying. Between them, they might solve the mystery of what brought Bott and Lord DeLancey together on Temple Island at dawn. It was very unfair, she reflected, that Alec expected her to reveal her speculations to him, without any guarantee that he would reciprocate.

She sighed. As a detective's wife she'd have to get used to it, she supposed.

As they entered the town, a board outside a newsagent's caught Daisy's eye: STROKE STRICKEN – REGATTA DEATH. Admiring the clever headline, she hoped the press hadn't yet found out where Basil DeLancey had been staying before his dramatic demise.

Bott turned his head and moaned.

'Piper, he moved!'

The young detective twisted to look back. 'Is he coming round, miss?' he asked anxiously. 'D'you want me to come back there to give you a hand?'

'No, he's perfectly still again,' Daisy

reported with regret. 'But it must be a good sign, don't you think?'

''Spect so, miss. The chief'll be happy.'

She watched Bott carefully the rest of the way without observing so much as a twitching finger or flickering eyelash. By the time they reached the cottage hospital a couple of minutes later, she wondered if she had imagined Bott's all too brief signs of life. He remained horribly limp when he was lifted from the car.

'I'm almost certain he moved his head.' she told Alec. 'I was thinking about something else, but I felt it more than saw it, and heard him moan, too.'

'He didn't open his eyes?'

'Not that I noticed.'

'I'll tell the doctor about the movement. It sounds promising. Thank you for looking after him on the way here.'

That sounded to Daisy like the opening of a dismissal. 'I'll go to fetch Miss Hopgood,' she said quickly, not giving him a chance to tell her she wasn't wanted at the hospital. She had already decided not to go in yet. She couldn't very well horn in on getting Bott to bed and the medical examination, even if she wanted to, which she didn't. 'However versatile Bister may be,' she explained, 'I can't ask him to break the bad news.'

'No, it would be a bit much, and I'm sure

she'd rather hear it from you. I agree that she must be informed, but do try to persuade her not to come to the hospital.'

'I'll see how she feels,' Daisy said non-committally.

'Your aunt wouldn't mind if you took her back to Bulawayo, would she? Then you could keep her company and she'd be near a telephone in case there's any news.'

'Aunt Cynthia wouldn't mind, I'm sure, but I think Miss Hopgood will want to be with Bott. She's very fond of him.'

Alec frowned. 'I could – perhaps I should – bar her from his room.'

'You wouldn't be so beastly! He's the victim, not the villain, after all. Besides, he's a different person with her, not pugnacious because he's not constantly on the defensive. She's very sensible. She might be useful in getting him to talk when he comes round.'

'If he's difficult, I can always send for her.' Alec pointed out.

'I'll see how she feels,' Daisy repeated, getting back into the Humber.

She knew she had no chance of being present at the interview with Lord De-Lancey. No matter whether Susan Hopgood chose to rush to Bott's bedside or not, Daisy was going to be there.

'Victoria Road, Bister,' she ordered.

Lace curtains twitched all up and down

the street as the Humber pulled up before Miss Hopgood's digs. Aware of eyes on her, though Daisy didn't go so far as to send Bister to knock before she descended, she did wait for him to get out and open the car door for her. Let Miss Hopgood's kind landlady milk the arrival of a chauffeur-driven motor-car at her little house for all it was worth.

Before Daisy could knock for herself the front door opened and Susan Hopgood appeared on the doorstep, her pretty face alarmed.

'Miss Dalrymple! What's wrong?' She glanced at the open window of the next house and lowered her voice. 'Has Horace got himself into trouble? He hasn't gone and done something dreadful, has he? That tec who fetched him yesterday wouldn't say what was going on.'

'He hasn't been arrested or anything like that,' Daisy reassured her. 'But I'm afraid I do have bad news. May I come in?'

Susan paled. 'He's not dead, is he?'

'No, no. But he is in hospital.'

'Did you come to take me to him? Couldn't you tell me about it on the way?' She pulled herself together with a visible effort. 'It's awfully kind of you. Just let me get my handbag, I won't be a moment.'

So much for trying to persuade her not to go, Daisy thought, turning back to the car.

‘Miss Hopgood is coming with me to the hospital,’ she told Bister.

He saluted. ‘Right, miss, only was you wanting me to wait? Acos the taties wants lifting, see, if there’s to be any for lunch. Them young gents gets through a powerful lot o’ taties.’

‘No, you need not wait.’ Daisy would be only too pleased to let him go. Alec could not expect her to abandon Susan on the hospital’s doorstep. By the time she had gone with the girl to find Bott’s room, Bister would be well on his way home without her. Surely Alec wouldn’t want to waste time taking her back to Bulawayo before he interviewed Lord DeLancey.

If he did, she would remind him that Horace Bott had confided in her before, and might be persuaded to do so again, however reluctant to explain himself to Sergeant Tring.

Susan hurried out of the house and Bister handed her into the Humber beside Daisy, before returning to his seat behind the wheel. Though being assisted by a chauffeur into a smart motor-car was surely a new experience, she was far too worried to appreciate it.

‘I’m reelly glad it’s you who came, Miss Dalrymple, not a p’liceman,’ she said as the Humber moved off. ‘What’s happened to poor old Horace? Is he bad?’

'Not good, I'm afraid. He's been hurt – a head wound.' Remembering Alec's caution, Daisy didn't mention the pistol. 'I don't know how much blood he lost, but the scalp does tend to bleed a lot. Also, he fell into the river and was half-drowned. He may well be perfectly all right, but all sorts of beastly complications are possible. I didn't wait to hear what the doctor had to say.'

'Poor Horace.' Susan's lips quivered. She looked much younger than her straightforward common sense had made her seem before, and a bit frightened. Daisy took her hand. 'He must be feeling ever so poorly.'

'That's one thing you don't have to worry about. He's still unconscious, or was when I left.'

'Oh. That's ... that's not very good, is it? But he's reelly, reelly fit. That'll help, won't it?'

'Bound to,' Daisy assured her.

'How did it happen? I mean, did he hurt his head when he fell into the water, or what?'

Daisy hesitated. 'I'm sorry, I can't tell you.'

'You mean "mustn't," don't you? Are the coppers still after him? What's he done?'

'Probably nothing. Everything's very confused at the moment. Alec – my fiancé – you remember I told you he's a detective? – he hasn't the foggiest what's been going on,' Daisy said with a mental apology to Alec.

Susan seemed relieved. 'Your fella's in charge? He won't try to make out like it was Horace did something when it was one of the toffs, will he?'

'Certainly not!'

'No, *you* wouldn't be in love with him if he wasn't a good bloke. I'm glad it's him. Poor old Horace. I s'pose, seeing he's still unconscious, no one's told his mam and da yet. He's their only one. Auntie Flo'll want to come, and it takes ages by train.'

'Auntie? I didn't realise he's your cousin.'

'Horace? He isn't. Auntie Flo's just my mam's best friend. Lady Cheringham's your real auntie, isn't she?'

'Yes, my mother's sister.' With a flash of guilt, Daisy recalled the state in which she had left her cousin. She hadn't spared Tish a thought since. Seeing Bott's inanimate body lying on the floor had been one shock too many for the poor girl.

Perhaps she should have stayed. But no, her reasons held. Susan Hopgood clung to her hand like a drowning man– Ugh, another morbid cliché! She would telephone to ask about Tish as soon as Susan could spare her.

'Here we are,' she said as the Humber drew up before Townlands Hospital. 'Perhaps you'd better tell them you're his cousin, or his fiancée, in case they're fussy about who they let in to see him.'

'You'll come with me, won't you, Miss Dalrymple? It's an awful lot to ask, I know, but *please*.'

'Of course, if you want me,' said Daisy with aplomb, as if the thought had never crossed her mind.

A larger hospital might have questioned the credentials of two young ladies bent upon visiting a patient under police guard. The cottage hospital porter-cum-orderly simply directed them to the poor young man's room, shaking his head as he added gloomily, 'Sorry to say, miss, 'e's in a bad way. Doctor don't old out much 'ope.'

CHAPTER 16

Alec and Tom Tring stood in the passage with a stethoscope-garlanded doctor, the hospital's Matron, and the Sister on duty, with Piper hovering on the edge of the group. They all turned at the sound of Daisy and Susan's footsteps on the tile floor.

Matron, a short, thin, grey-haired woman with rather severe features, stepped forward to meet them. With one glance at Susan's now tear-stained face, she said kindly, 'My dear, did my wretched porter tell you to abandon hope? He says the same for everything from a broken leg to a bleeding ulcer.'

'Get rid of that Job's comforter,' grunted the doctor.

'As you know quite well, Doctor,' she said, giving him an exasperated look, 'the Chairman of the Board of Trustees... Well, never mind. There's no reason to suppose that your young man won't make a good recovery, child, given the best of care, which he will have, will he not, Sister?'

'Of course, Matron.' Sister was large, plump, and motherly-looking, though Daisy, having worked in a hospital office during the War, was sure she and Matron could both be frightful Tartars to their staff. 'It's Miss Hopgood, isn't it, dear? You'll want to see Mr. Bott, I expect. Is that all right, Chief Inspector?'

'Yes.' Alec said unenthusiastically. 'Detective Sergeant Tring will be in charge, Miss Hopgood. If he asks you to leave the room, please do so at once.'

'Oh yes, sir. Please, can Miss Dalrymple stay with me?'

Alec raised his eyes to heaven. 'I suppose so,' he said with even less enthusiasm, 'but the same goes for her as far as obeying Sergeant Tring is concerned.'

'Naturally, Chief Inspector,' Daisy said demurely, catching Tom's twinkling eye.

Sister ushered them into a small room, spotlessly white from walls to night-stand to bed to the patient in it, and his bandaged head. At least, Horace Bott spent too much time out of doors for his face to be white, strictly speaking, but beneath the suntan his pallor was obvious. Susan gasped in dismay.

Daisy tried to listen to both the nurse's account of Bott's condition and the murmur of voices beyond the door, left ajar.

'–pulse and heartbeat are both strong, and lungs…'

'Good idea, Sergeant. Do that, but don't forget…'

'–always a risk of pneumonia and…'

'Thank you, Doctor. I promise Sergeant

Tring will…'

'–head injury appears superficial, but they're always liable to…'

'Don't let her interfere, Tom, for pity's sake. She's…'

Incensed, Daisy transferred her attention to Sister.

'…haven't got an X-ray machine here in Henley. It would mean moving him to Reading and the doctor says it's more important to keep him still than to take pictures of his skull. It's a bit worrying that he hasn't come round yet. You sit yourself down here beside him, dear. Hold his hand if you want, but don't sit on the bed or try to fluff up his pillows or anything like that. And you can talk, but keep your voices down, please.'

'Oh yes, Sister. Thanks ever so.'

The nurse glanced around the room. 'I'll have Porter bring another chair for Sergeant Tring.'

'A large one,' said Daisy, and Susan managed a smile.

'Large and strong,' Sister agreed. 'And don't you go listening to a word Porter says, dear. I'll tell him to hold his tongue.'

She went out. Daisy heard her voice, and Tom Tring's bass in answer, as Susan said in a whisper, 'He's so awfully still! Oh, Miss Dalrymple, what'll I do about telling Auntie Flo ? They'll be ever so upset. I ought to go and send a telegram, but I don't want to leave Horace.'

'We'll ask Sergeant Tring to arrange something.'

'I wish he wasn't going to stay.'

'Don't worry, Tom Tring's really frightfully nice.'

'What do the police want with Horace, anyway? It's something to do with that man who died, isn't it? The man in his crew?

Before Daisy was forced to find an answer, Tring came in, carrying his own chair. 'Have you had your breakfast, Miss Hopgood?' he asked benevolently. 'I haven't, and I know Miss Dalrymple hasn't, so I asked Sister to see what she could send along.'

'Bless you, Mr. Tring!' said Daisy, suddenly aware of ravening hunger.

'I was just starting mine,' Susan said, 'when... But I couldn't eat, really.'

'Ah well, I dare say a cuppa'd do you good, though. The missus always says a nice hot cuppa's the best cure there is for the mopes. Gives you a good breakfast, does she, your landlady?'

'Oh yes, bacon and eggs and everything.'

'I bet she put up a nice picnic for you, too. Nothing like fresh air to give you an appetite, is there? Me and the missus take a picnic out to Epping Forest now and then. Ever been there? It's a pretty place, but I 'spect the riverbank's prettier. Have a good time, did you?' He gave Daisy a warning glance.

That was when she realized the soothing rumble had a purpose. No doubt the 'good idea' Alec had approved was to seize the chance to interrogate the unsuspecting Miss Hopgood.

'It was lovely,' said Susan. 'I told Horace straight out, I didn't want to hear any more grousing about how they all picked on him. Once he stopped talking about it, he stopped thinking about it, and he soon cheered up.'

'Not another word about his troubles, eh?'

'No, he was talking about what he's going to do at Cambridge next year. I didn't understand all the science stuff, but I don't mind just listening to him when he's happy. We had a lovely day.'

'Hot enough for you?' Tring asked, a trifle roguishly. Susan blushed. 'It was hot in the sun. Horace wished he was wearing his shorts, like the day before.'

'Blimey – if you'll pardon the expression, ladies – he went around in rowing shorts all day?'

'No one minds in Henley, do they, Miss Dalrymple?'

'Not in Regatta time, at least.'

'It would have taken hours if he'd walked back to change. He'd've had to go round by the road, seeing he couldn't be sure there'd be a boat to take him across. I must say, people looked at him kind of funny at the fair.'

'The fair?'

'There's a fun-fair by the river.' Daisy explained. 'Coconut shies and merry-go-rounds and a Ferris wheel, that sort of thing.'

'It doesn't start till after the racing's over for the day,' Susan said, ''cause of the noise.'

'You must've had a late night then, eh?'

'Oh no, we went early. We had tea at my digs – high tea, it was extra, like the picnic, but I told Horace it was my treat and no harm in splurging once in a while.'

'None at all,' Tring agreed heartily.

'So we went to the fair after tea, and we didn't stay late, what with Horace having to walk by the road all the way back to the Cheringhams' house.'

'How silly!' said Daisy. 'He could have come back with the rest of us. Why didn't he say something when we met at the fair?'

'He didn't want to ask any favours.' Susan said with dignity, 'besides wanting to see me home first. He was always very particular about walking me home. Oh Horace!' Tears welled in her eyes as she turned to the still figure on the bed.

'And many a time to come he'll be walking you home, miss,' Tom assured her, with more hope than certainty, Daisy felt.

The arrival of a nurse-probationer with

the breakfast-trolley came as a relief to both of them.

Meanwhile, Alec drove back towards Crowswood Place. He was beginning to resign himself to the way Daisy managed to make it impossible for him to object to her doing anything she was really determined to do. It was lucky he had a modern view of marriage as a partnership, he thought a trifle sourly. A Victorian paterfamilias faced with Daisy as a wife might have been driven to choose between lunacy and murder.

The truly maddening thing was that he had to admit she was occasionally helpful in the murder investigations she insisted on meddling in. Had she not kept her wits about her when abandoned by both her escorts in mid-river, he would not have had the first idea of where to look for Bott's assailant.

It was a pity she had not actually recognised Lord DeLancey. Still, the chances of anyone else at Crowswood being interested in Bott seemed minimal.

On the other hand, Daisy's reasoning about the dawn meeting was sound. DeLancey might want revenge, but why should Bott agree to a rendezvous? Bott might want to try to convince DeLancey of his innocence, but why on an island at dawn? Could cross purposes have brought them together?

The first order of business, Alec decided, was to persuade Lord DeLancey to admit to having been on Temple Island.

'Ernie, make sure your notes of this interview are very accurate.'

'They always are, Chief,' said Piper, injured.

'Take extra care. I want my exact words on paper so that no lawyer can accuse me of lying to Lord DeLancey. If he chooses to misinterpret what I say, that's his problem.'

Piper grinned. 'Like that, is it, Chief? Don't you worry about my notes. Even if you was to have a slip of the tongue, like, it wouldn't need to go down in my notebook.'

'Don't let's start fudging.' Alec said mildly. 'We'll play it straight and hope for other evidence if I can't get a confession. Here we are.'

The gates of Crowswood Place stood closed this morning. Alec had no difficulty identifying the two sinister characters lurking nearby as members of the Fourth Estate. In fact, he recognised one as a reporter for the *Daily Graphic*. Unfortunately, recognition was mutual.

Before the Austin had quite come to a halt, Dugden was there. 'Well, well, Chief Inspector Fletcher of the Yard,' he said cheerfully, snapping a photograph, as the other man hurried over to join him. 'Any progress to report, Chief Inspector? Come to tell his lordship who did his brother in, are you?'

'If so, his lordship will be the first to know. Be a good fellow, Dugden, and knock up the gatekeeper for... Ah, here she comes?'

The woman who came out of the lodge examined Alec's warrant card, which he had automatically dropped in his pocket when he hurriedly dressed to go out in the garden at dawn. She went to open the gates.

'Aw, have a heart, Chief Inspector,' Dugden begged. 'Give us a statement.'

'The investigation is proceeding according to plan,' Alec said blandly, and inaccurately. 'I'll speak to the gentlemen of the Press at Henley Police Station this afternoon, if I can find the time.'

'If you have time? No arrest then,' said the other man, disappointed, as the car began to move again.

Running alongside, Dugden pleaded, 'Just tell me where the Ambrose crew is putting up?

'Not likely. And no trespassing, or I'll have you inside in no time flat.'

'You're a hard man, Chief Inspector.' The reporters fell behind as the Austin picked up speed along the winding drive.

'Regular pests, those newspapermen.' Piper said disapprovingly.

'Just doing their job, Ernie. They can be useful to us sometimes, so the trick is to ward 'em off without offending them.'

'Like butlers,' the young detective observed.

'More or less.' Alec drew up before the imposing portico. 'Luckily we're too early in the day for the butler to be answering the door, if I'm not mistaken. On the other hand, I've been swimming in these trousers.'

Whether or not influenced by the wrinkled, still-damp flannels, the liveried footman who admitted them to the mansion ushered them into the same chilly antechamber. With a degree of frost quite equal to the butler's, he enquired, 'Is his lordship expecting you?'

Alec responded placidly, 'I believe Lord DeLancey will agree to see me.'

'I believe his lordship has not come down yet.'

'Go and find out, there's a good chap. And if not, let him know we've arrived, will you? Detective Chief Inspector Fletcher is the name, if you didn't catch it. From Scotland Yard. We don't mind waiting.'

The footman's outraged face intimated as plainly as words that they had not been invited to wait. However, a Chief-Inspector from Scotland Yard was a far cry from the easily intimidated local bobby. He was not sure of his ground, and a half-suppressed snicker from Piper decided him. Turning red, he left.

'That was unkind,' said Alec, grinning.

'Jumped-up Jack-in-office,' Piper snorted.

'He hasn't even made it out of the uniformed branch.'

Alec laughed. 'But if you wrote down what he said in your precious notebook and read it back, you'd find nothing to take exception to,' he pointed out. 'All right, set yourself down somewhere inconspicuous and get your pencils ready. Lord DeLancey may not be the brightest star in the galaxy, but I don't think he's stupid enough not to realise a refusal to see me might put ideas into my head.'

Piper settled on a chair against the wall by the door. Alec crossed to the window. Gazing out at the uninspiring prospect of pillars and yellowish gravel carriage sweep, he planned exactly what he had to say.

They did not have long to wait. The moment Lord DeLancey entered the room, Alec knew Daisy was right again. The man was pale, his eyes haunted, his face sheened with a film of sweat although the day had scarcely begun to warm up.

Lord DeLancey was afraid, his fear far too evident to be disguised by belligerence. 'What the devil do you want at this hour in the morning? Couldn't it wait? Can't you let a man eat his breakfast in peace?'

'Have I interrupted your meal, sir?' Alec spared a momentary regret for his own empty stomach. 'I beg your pardon. I'd have thought you'd had plenty of time for breakfast since you came in?'

'Came in? Dammit, what do you mean, came in?'

'From the river?'

'The river?' his lordship blustered. 'You've got the wrong DeLancey, my good man. My brother was the oarsman, not I. You wouldn't catch me messing about in a boat before breakfast.'

'No?' Alec said softly. He had not mentioned boats. The natural assumption would be that he referred to a stroll on the river-bank. 'It's an ... exciting experience. The river is singularly beautiful at daybreak, as I found out for myself this morning.'

'Y-you?' DeLancey's voice wavered, but he rallied. 'I'm surprised you were able to spare the time from investigating Basil's death. Since you did, I'm delighted to hear you enjoyed it, though this is hardly the moment for social chit-chat. Your river excursion is nothing to do with me. You didn't see me there.'

'True, I didn't. But there was a witness.'

Lord DeLancey licked his lips. 'W-who?'

'Someone who knows you well by sight.' Alec said with deliberation. 'Someone who went on in the boat after Cheringham and I dived into the Thames in the hope of rescuing Horace Bott. He hadn't been long in the water, but then it doesn't take long to drown, though that's not exactly relevant since he'd been shot in the head.'

'I can explain! It's not what you think. It was his own fault, entirely his own fault.'

'Lord DeLancey, it is my duty to advise you that you have the right to remain silent if you choose to speak, what you say will be taken down and may be used in evidence.'

'I didn't do anything,' DeLancey gabbled. 'I've nothing to hide. I just hoped to avoid being mixed up in a thoroughly unpleasant business. The newspapers – but I don't have to tell you how they ruin lives with unjustified insinuations!'

'No, sir,' Alec agreed stolidly. Given what Daisy had told him of DeLancey's fear of gossip, his earlier denial was understandable. 'So you did meet Horace Bott on Temple Island early this morning?'

'Yes, yes, I was there. You know I was. You said someone saw me there. If it wasn't you or Cheringham, who the deuce was it? What's his name, Cheringham's friend, the Ambrose crew captain?'

'I'm afraid I can't reveal that, sir. *Why* did you meet Bott on the island at dawn?'

'He asked me to.'

'Did he give a reason?'

'He said he had something to tell me.'

'That's all? What did you think he meant, that made you agree to a meeting at such an ... unusual time and place?'

'I hoped he had information about Basil's death.'

'That he had not given me?'

'To sell. People of that class have money-grubbing souls,' DeLancey said self-righteously. 'They are quite capable of seeking to make a profit from someone else's tragedy. Besides, they regard the police as their enemies.'

Alec did not bother to inform him that on the whole the police found small shop-keepers among the most supportive and cooperative of citizens. 'Did it not occur to you to suspect Bott of being your brother's assailant?' he asked.

'Of course it did! He had threatened Basil, as you know. The other Ambrose men are convinced of his guilt.'

'Didn't that make you think twice about going to meet him in such an isolated place?'

'I couldn't imagine any reason why he should wish to harm me, but I took pre-cautions. I took a pistol. Not licensed, I'm afraid, Chief inspector,' he admitted with a feeble attempt at a man-to-man grin. 'It's a Mauser "Bolo", a souvenir of the War. I'm sorry I took it with me, but I don't suppose it really made much difference. A man bent on suicide will find a way.'

Suicide! Alec made an effort to conceal his surprise. Bott had not seemed suicidal at their interview yesterday. Had an evening spent with those who believed him guilty driven him to try to take his own life?

'Perhaps you'd better tell me exactly what happened on Temple Island, sir.'

'Of course. It turned out that Bott wanted to see me in order to apologise for killing Basil – inadvertently, he claimed. He knew he'd be caught, and he'd decided to kill himself rather than face a trial and prison, or hanging. His life was pretty miserable anyway, since he'd tried to rise above his natural level. He said he was going to drown himself, but I suppose, seeing the Mauser in my hand, he decided shooting would be easier. He seized it from me, shot himself in the head, and fell into the river.'

'There were two shots, Lord DeLancey.'

'Oh yes. One shot went wild before he got it away from me. When he made his grab, I was afraid for a moment that he had changed his mind, that he meant to dispose of the only witness to his confession, so I had my finger on the trigger. It fired when he wrenched it from my hand. But that was not the shot which killed him. The pistol was wholly under his control when he actually put the bullet through his head.'

His lordship was going to be peeved when he discovered he had been misled about Bott's condition. Alec was in no hurry to disillusion him. 'I see,' he said. 'You tried to stop him, of course?'

'Of course. As he backed away with the

pistol, I rushed at him. I'm afraid that's why he moved far enough to fall into the water.'

'Taking your Mauser with him?'

'Yes. No!' Flustered, DeLancey turned red. 'Excuse me, Chief Inspector, it was a terrible experience and I don't like to think about it. Er, no, he dropped the pistol immediately after firing, as he staggered backwards into the river.'

'*Dropped* it? You're sure of that?'

'Dropped it. Let go of it. It fell from his hand,' his lordship said testily.

'Odd. Considering where the pistol was found, I'd have expected Bott to fall into a boat, not the water.'

'Oh. Yes. I can explain that. I told you I've been trying to forget the whole thing. You see, I picked up the pistol without thinking, in a state of shock. As soon as I realised what I'd done, I tossed it away. I didn't want anything to do with it! So you found it?' DeLancey made a half-hearted effort to summon up indignation. 'You gave me the impression you thought it had gone into the river.'

'Sorry, sir, just a bit of a misunderstanding.' Alec prevaricated. 'It's a pity you picked it up. Your fingerprints will be on top of Bott's.'

'No, they won't. I was wearing gloves. However hot the days are, its damned chilly at dawn.'

His smugness added to Alec's feeling that his story had been hastily concocted, just in case, despite his denial, he was somehow linked to the events on Temple Island. The gaps in his explanation he still more hastily filled in as they became apparent.

Yet he was not discomposed by the reference to Bott's fingerprints, which suggested there really had been a struggle for the weapon. Or else it had not yet dawned on him that the absence of Bott's fingerprints would give him the lie.

On the other hand, the whole tale could be true, his odd manner caused by shock and his fear of publicity. Either way, Alec was eager to hear Horace Bott's version of their encounter.

'That will be all for the moment, sir.' he said. 'I may have a few more points to clear up later. Let me know, please, if you leave Crowswood. You can contact me through the Henley police.'

'If you insist.' DeLancey preceded Alec and Piper from the anteroom into the hall. As they turned towards the front door, he caught Alec's sleeve. 'Look here, Chief Inspector, there surely isn't any need for my presence at the poor fellow's suicide to be mentioned? It's all over and done with, after all. Nothing will bring him back and it'll be deuced uncomfortable for me if the press gets hold of it'

'I'm afraid I can't keep you out of it, sir. The provenance of the Mauser will have to be explained.'

'Damn! Will I have to give evidence? There will be an inquest, I suppose.'

'I hope not, sir,' Alec said with a keen look. 'Though Bott is still unconscious, the doctor at Townlands Hospital seems to think he will make a full recovery.'

Lord DeLancey's jaw dropped and his face turned pasty. Stunned? Appalled? Or just furious at being misled? Fury was what would undoubtedly spring to his lips. Alec didn't wait to hear it. DeLancey was not likely to say anything he could not weasel his way out of, but he just might do something stupid if left to his own devices.

CHAPTER 17

On the way back towards Henley, Alec gave his constable a chance to shine. 'What do you reckon, Ernie?'

'You gave him something to think about all right, Chief.'

'What about his story?

'Sounded like a load of bumf to me, Chief, 'cepting I can't see why he'd try to kill Bott, and if he didn't, why lie?'

'You don't think revenge is a good enough motive?'

'Not for him,' Piper said cautiously, 'Seems to me, he'd be too afraid of getting caught.'

'He does seem a nervy type. So you think Bott shot himself, but for some reason DeLancey's lying about how it happened?'

'There's something fishy. Tell you what, Chief, for a start can't see a lord going out rowing that early just because a chap he don't think much of says he's got something to tell him.'

'It does seem improbable,' Alec agreed.

'But if he's lying, why didn't he stick to it that Bott got shot when they was struggling for the pistol, stead of making up all that stuff about suicide?'

'"Merely corroborative detail intended to add verisimilitude to an otherwise bald and unconvincing narrative."' Stopping the Austin while the lodge-woman opened the gates, Alec noticed Piper's blank expression and added, 'Sorry, Ernie, just my favourite quotation from *The Mikado.* What it adds up to is the irresistible urge some people feel to elaborate on a story in the belief that complexity equals credibility.'

'Ah,' said Ernie, making use of Tom Tring's favourite monosyllable while he attempted to digest Alec's polysyllables.

Driving on, Alec continued, 'But as DeLancey said, he hoped his name might be kept out of a suicide. There would be no chance of that if he admitted to having even partial control of the pistol when it fired. So that could be the extent of his lying – or he might he telling the truth.'

'Could be, Chief. If Bott confessed like Lord DeLancey claimed, he'd be more likely to tell us than to shoot him, wouldn't he? That way he wouldn't get into trouble himself, but he'd have his revenge when we arrested Bott.'

'Hearsay, Ernie. A reported confession is not admissible evidence. We'd have no grounds for arresting Bott unless he repeated his confession to us.'

'But it'd give us more to go on,' Ernie argued, 'even if we couldn't just take his lordship's word for it.'

'True. The trouble is, it looks as if it's going to end up that way: DeLancey's word against Bott's. Assuming Bott recovers and will talk.' Alec frowned. 'Suicide never crossed my mind, but I didn't notice, and the doctor didn't mention, any powder-burns on Bott's hand. I wonder what dabs, if any, Tom's found on that Mauser?'

Tom Tring came back into the hospital room with his catlike tread. During his absence, Daisy assumed, he had worked his fingerprint magic on the pistol. She nearly asked if he had found anything of interest, but remembered in time that she had not told Susan about the weapon.

'I rung up the Birmingham coppers, Miss Hopgood,' Tom said. 'They'll send someone round to break the news to Mr. and Mrs. Bott.'

'Thanks ever so, Mr. Tring. That's much nicer than getting a telegram.'

'Any sign of him waking up?'

'He hasn't moved or opened his eyes,' said Daisy, 'but he did start to mutter. We couldn't make out any words. Listen, there he goes again.'

Tom bent over the still figure on the bed, his ear close to the twitching mouth. The mumble ceased and he straightened, shaking his head. 'Dunno if he's making sense or not 'cause I can't tell what he's saying, like you said.'

'It could mean he's coming round, though, couldn't it?' Susan asked hopefully.

'That it could, miss. If you don't mind, I'd better sit next to him so's I can hear proper if he starts talking clearer.'

With reluctance, Susan gave up her place at the bedside. Tom sat down, took out his notebook, and laid it on a thigh like a tree-trunk.

'Ta, miss. Let's have a bit of hush, now. I wouldn't want to miss anything.'

They sat in silence for several minutes, Susan with her gaze fixed on Horace Bott's face. Daisy heard the cheerful voice of a nurse in a nearby room. Beyond the hospital's walls, the town was Sunday-quiet, until church bells began to peal for the morning service. Impossible – she felt as if a century had passed since she got up that morning!

An early stroll had seemed such a good idea, a half-hour snatched from the ruins of the weekend. If only she and Alec had not accepted Cherry's invitation to go out on the river! But Cherry might not have been able to rescue Bott on his own. Bott would probably have died, and no one would have guessed that Lord DeLancey was involved in his death.

Daisy wondered how Alec was getting on

with DeLancey. She had not been able to identify him positively, so all he had to do was deny being on the island and stick to his denial. Alec would be stymied.

In that case they would have to rely on Bott's story, always supposing he recovered his wits and his speech, and was willing to talk. Daisy was dying to know what had happened on Temple Island. Just five minutes sooner, and they might have witnessed the whole...

'No!' Bott jerked bolt upright, his eyes still shut. 'No! Don't! I can't swim.' he cried in a high, panic-stricken voice.

'Horace!' Susan sprang towards him.

Tom warded her off. 'Easy, miss. He's still asleep, see, and dreaming. You don't want to wake him sudden-like. Just you set yourself down again and let me deal with him.' Gently but irresistibly, he pressed Bott back against the pillows. 'It's all right, sonny, you're safe now.'

As he soothed Bott, Daisy soothed Susan. 'Now we know he's capable of moving and speaking clearly, so it looks as if his brain wasn't damaged by the injury or lack of oxygen. He's just having a nightmare.'

'I s'pose so. He must be dreaming about when that brute DeLancey pushed him into the river.'

For a moment, Daisy wondered how on earth Susan could possibly know about the events on Temple Island. Then she realised the girl was talking about Basil DeLancey's assault at the end of the Thames Cup heat.

Was that what Bott was dreaming of, or had a similar scene played itself out on the island? Why, why, *why* should Cedric DeLancey attack Bott? Could it have been self-defence – but why should Bott attack Lord DeLancey? Why had they met there and then in the first place?

Finding herself once more thinking in circles, Daisy was delighted when Tom said guardedly, 'I do believe he's waking up.'

As Bott's eyelids flickered, Susan darted to the side of the bed opposite the sergeant. She took Bott's hand and said in an unsteady voice, 'I'm here, Horace. It's Susan. I won't let them bully you.'

'Now, miss,' said Tom, his tone indulgent, 'no one's going to do any bullying. But if you want to stay, you'll have to keep mum once I start asking questions.'

Susan sent a glance of appeal to Daisy.

'*I* shan't let him be bullied,' Daisy promised, 'not that Mr. Tring is a bully.'

Tom's luxuriant grey moustache twitched as he grinned at her, his little eyes twinkling. 'Same goes for you, Miss Dalrymple. One word out of place and you're out. And I'm none so sure the chief'd let you stay in the first place.'

Having her own doubts, Daisy merely

smiled. She moved a chair over beside the nightstand for Susan, who sat down without letting go of Bott's hand or shifting her anxious gaze from his face.

He raised his other hand to the bandage and moaned. 'My head! It hurts like hell.'

'Horace!'

'Sorry, Susie.' His eyes opening fully at last, he gave her a feeble smile. 'Like blazes. What happened?'

'That's what we'd like to know,' said Tom Tring.

'Can't you remember?' Daisy asked in dismay, but Bott was staring at Tom.

'Police!' he groaned. 'Detective Sergeant Tring, isn't it? What's going on? Where am I?'

'You're in hospital, sir,' said Tom with a warning glance encompassing both Daisy and Susan. 'You were pulled out of the Thames half-drowned. What we want to know is how you got there.'

Bott closed his eyes. 'The Thames? I fell in?' he said slowly. What little was visible of his forehead furrowed and he winced, raising his hand to his head again. 'My foot, I remember now! DeLancey!'

'No, Horace, that was the day before yesterday.'

'Please, Miss Hopgood, no interruptions!'

'The other DeLancey, Susie. By jingo, I shan't let him get away with *this!*'

'You remember where you were, Mr. Bott?'

'On Temple Island, Sergeant. I remember every– Oh God, I'm going to be sick.'

As Susan reached for the basin on the night-stand, Tom helped Bott sit up. 'Swallowed a fair bit of the Thames, I dare say. There you go, you'll feel better for getting rid of it.'

Daisy, doing her best to close her ears to the distressing sounds, rang for a nurse. Sister herself came in. Briskly kind, she wiped Bott's face and gave him water to rinse his mouth, covered the basin and produced a clean one from inside the night-stand.

'How do you feel, young man?'

'I think ... my stomach's all right, but I'm a bit ... dizzy.'

'Down you go again. I suppose you'll have to stay, Sergeant, but no disturbing him with talk, if you please, and you young ladies..?'

'No!' Bott gripped Susan's hand as he subsided onto the pillows. 'I'll lie down, Sister, but don't make her leave. And I *want* to talk to Mr. Tring. I *must* talk to him. It will disturb me more not to, truly.'

Sister took his pulse, felt the unbandaged patch of forehead, and nodded. 'Very well, then, but if you start feeling dizzy again, or sick, or feverish, or achy, or if you start to cough, I want to know right away.'

'We'll call you, Sister,' Susan promised fervently.

'I'll be back in a few minutes to see how he's doing. Don't excite yourself now, Mr. Bott. Keep calm.'

Bott waited until the door closed behind her before bursting out, 'Keep calm! That's a tall order when you've just been the victim of attempted murder!'

'Horace, what *are* you talking about?' asked Susan in astonishment. 'Miss Dalrymple, d'you think he's wandering? Shall I call Sister back?'

'No, don't. He's not wandering, I'm afraid.'

'But you two young ladies'll be wandering right out of here.' Tom said sternly, 'if you can't keep your mouths closed. Tell you what, Miss Dalrymple, why don't you take notes for me?'

'The devil finds work...?' Daisy took the notebook and pencil he held out.

He twinkled at her, but spoke to Bott. 'Go on, sir.'

'He pulled out a gun and ordered me to jump in the river,' said Bert in a tone of remembered shock. 'I told him I can't swim, and he said he knew, he was there when his brother pushed me in. He wanted me dead! Well, I wasn't going to oblige, you can be sure. A ruddy fool I'd be to jump in and drown myself, when he couldn't shoot me.

At least, that's what I thought.'

'Why was that, sir?'

'As I pointed out to him, a bullet-riddled corpse would be impossible to explain away as an accident. He said no one would connect him with it, but he was obviously getting the wind up. I don't think he expected me to resist: his mighty lordship commands and the lower orders run to obey!' Bott sneered, and Daisy remembered the 'lower orders' who had died at Lord DeLancey's command in the war.

'He didn't want to shoot me,' Bott continued. 'He started gabbling about how being shot was a much more painful death than drowning. He was waving the gun around like a peashooter. I shouted at him to be careful, but he fired into the air. I still wouldn't jump into the river for him. Then he lost his head, I think. He aimed at me. I took a couple of steps backwards. I couldn't help myself, with that pistol pointing at me, though I still didn't really believe he'd shoot.

'He did, of course.' Gingerly, Bott felt the bandage. 'Either his hand was shaking or he's a rotten shot, or I wouldn't be here talking to you.'

'Oh Horace!'

'It's all right, Susie. I've come off with nothing worse than a headache.'

'But even if he nearly missed you, you could've drowned!'

'Maybe he meant to miss. Maybe he still hoped to frighten me into drowning myself and hitting me was the mistake. Either way, I'll see his nibs rot in jail!' Bott snarled.

Susan was on the point of speaking again but Tom held up his hand. 'How did you come to fall in, sir?' he asked. 'That is, did Lord DeLancey push you, or drop you in when you were unconscious?'

'I don't think so,' Bott said unwillingly, obviously reluctant to give DeLancey the benefit of the doubt. 'As far as I can remember, I was caught off balance, stepping back, when the bullet hit me, and I just staggered backwards into the river. But I couldn't swear to it. I was seeing stars. I don't remember hitting the water, so I suppose I was unconscious by then.'

To Daisy, his resisting the temptation to accuse DeLancey of pushing or throwing him into the Thames gave his story the final ring of truth. She was already inclined to believe him. He hadn't had time to make up a tale, and anyway he was clearly the victim.

What she was dying to know was *why* Lord DeLancey had wanted to kill Bott. She would have asked long ago, but she thought Tom Tring was quite capable of sending her out if she interrupted, even though he allowed Susan a certain leeway. The sergeant had his own way of doing things.

Susan was about to speak again but Tom

held up his hand to stop her. 'Right, sir,' he said, 'and just what was it took you to Temple Island at that hour of the morning to meet Lord DeLancey?'

'His request, Sergeant. After the chief Inspector and I had our little chat, Gladstone gave me a note he had found on the hall table, with my name on it. A leaf torn from a pocketbook, it appeared to be. It said, "I must talk to you," and proposed the time and place. That's all. None of the social amenities for *me*.'

'Signed?'

'No, but I guessed who it was from. Anyone in the house who wanted to speak to me had no need to write a note, nor to suggest such an inconvenient meeting place. And I heard Wells mention that DeLancey had turned up that afternoon. Not a difficult deduction.'

'And why would Lord DeLancey want to talk to you, sir?'

Tom's stolid enquiry was followed by silence. Daisy glanced up. Bott had a distinctly wary look in his eye.

'I don't know,' he said brusquely. 'I suppose because I wasn't there when he talked to the rest of the crew about his brother.'

'No need to go to Temple Island for that, was there, sir?' Tom's mild, placid manner remained unchanged. He seemed almost bovine, an impression Daisy knew to be grossly misleading. 'I'm sure you must've guessed, or *deduced*, something more, or you wouldn't've turned up.'

'I don't know, I tell you.' Bott was fretful now. 'Must you pester me? I was nearly killed a few hours ago. I'm not up to an interrogation.'

'Leave him alone!' said Susan. 'Can't you see he's not well? Are you achy, Horace, or feverish?' She laid her hand on his forehead. 'Shall I ring for Sister?'

'No! For heaven's sake, don't fuss, Susan.'

'Perhaps you'll feel better for a drink of water, sir. Your mouth's dry from talking, I expect.'

At Bott's grudging nod, Tom raised him a little and Susan gave him the glass of water from the night-stand. He drank thirstily, then complained, 'It tastes just like the Thames.'

'Comes straight out of the river, I dare say. Now, just one or two more questions, sir, and I'll leave you in peace. You must see we have to know why you agreed to meet Lord DeLancey. He wasn't by any chance blackmailing you?'

'Blackmailing *me?*' Bott snorted with an unamused laugh. 'What the deuce do I have that he might want? Besides, you've got it the wrong way round, haven't you? Blackmailers are supposed to be done in by their victims.'

'It's always possible.' Tom said weightily, 'that you attacked him, and he shot you in self-defence.'

'Here now, don't you try to make me into the villain of the piece!' cried Bott. 'If you want to know, he thought *I* was going to blackmail *him*. I went to Temple Island for the pleasure of laughing in his face when he tried to bribe me to keep quiet. Only he didn't try to bribe me, he tried to kill me.'

'And what, sir, do you know about Lord DeLancey that he'd rather you kept quiet about?'

There was a long silence. Daisy discovered she was holding her breath, and she thought Susan was, too. Tom waited with massive patience. The struggle in Horace Bott's mind was apparent on his face.

'I'll tell you!' he burst out at last. 'Cedric DeLancey killed his brother!'

CHAPTER 18

'Those were his exact words?' Alec demanded.

Daisy peered at her shorthand, her own peculiar brand of Pitman's. Since no one else could read it and Alec wanted a verbatim report, he had been forced to include her in his conference with his sergeant, in the nurses' sitting room. He couldn't object. Tom had not wanted to stem the flow of Bott's revelations while he wrote down every word, and Alec admitted he had not expected Bott to come round so soon or speak so readily.

'"Cedric DeLancey killed his brother,"' Daisy repeated. 'After that, Bott refused to say another word. Then Sister came in and shooed Sergeant Tring and me out. She let Susan stay, though, and I shouldn't be surprised if she persuaded him he simply has to back up a statement like that.'

'Not to mention explaining why he didn't tell me sooner.' Alec agreed grimly. 'Tom, what about the Mauser?'

'Nicely polished, Chief.' Tom's face was bland.

'Not even smears or smudges? There

couldn't have been a struggle for it?'

'Not unless both parties was wearing gloves.'

'DeLancey says he wore gloves. Bott did not, at least not when we pulled him out, and I doubt he was in the river long enough for them to wash off.'

'Lord DeLancey says they struggled for the pistol?' Daisy asked.

'He says Mr. Bott took the pistol and shot himself, miss,' Piper informed her.

'Suicide! I wouldn't have said he acted at all like someone who just failed to commit suicide, would you, Mr. Tring?'

'Can't say I would, miss. Did Lord DeLancey say why Mr. Bott wanted to kill himself, Chief?'

Alec frowned at him, looked at Daisy, and sighed. 'Guilt, and fear of hanging. I suppose you might as well hear the rest.' He gave one of his admirable nutshell summaries of his interview with DeLancey. 'Have I missed anything. Ernie?'

Piper had skimmed his orthodox-shorthand notes as Alec spoke. 'Not really, Chief, just that Lord DeLancey was in a state over getting written about in the newspapers, same as last time.'

'It seems to be all he cares about,' said Daisy. 'If you ask me, this whole affair came about because of Lord DeLancey's fear of gossip. That's what he quarrelled with Basil about after the Thames Cup heat, so if it's true that he killed him... There's only one way Bott could know, isn't there, Alec?'

'Only one I can think of. Unless his health would be seriously endangered, I have to try to get the rest of the story from him. I'd better consult Sister.'

'I'll have a word with Susan,' Daisy volunteered, and escaped from the room before Alec could stop her.

She tapped on the door of Bott's room. Opening it, Susan glanced past her, saw she was alone, and in a hushed voice invited her in.

'How is he?' Daisy whispered. Bott was lying flat, eyes shut, but his cheeks now had a tinge of colour, not feverish, just enough so he no longer appeared to be at death's door. It stuck her how frightfully lucky he had been not to be killed, or at least seriously injured, by the bullet, and to have someone at hand to pull him out of the Thames.

Did he know who had rescued him? Neither she nor Tom Tring had told him, and she had not told Susan. Perhaps gratitude might persuade him to talk to Alec.

'His head hurts,' said Susan. 'Sister gave him some tablets, phenatecin, I think.'

Phenacetin, presumably – a pain-killer, not sleep-inducing, as far as Daisy knew. She raised her voice a bit. 'Good, he must be feeling better. He'll be able to talk to Chief Inspector Fletcher.' From the corner of her eye, she saw Bott's eyelids flicker.

'I told him he's going to have to, but he won't.'

'No? Well, you know him much better than I do, but I should have thought he'd want to thank the man who saved his life.'

'Saved his life?' Susan exclaimed.

'Yes, didn't you know? Maybe I didn't mention it. We were on the river this morning when he fell in, and Mr. Fletcher jumped in to pull him out.' No need to confuse matters with Cherry's part in the drama. A solo rescue was more impressive.

'Really?'

'Yes, so don't you think he'll want to express his gratitude? Or – oh dear! – perhaps he isn't grateful. Perhaps it's true, as Lord DeLancey claims, that Mr. Bott was trying to commit suicide.'

'I was not!' shouted Bott.

Daisy turned and gave him a hard look. 'No? But why should anyone believe you rather than him, when you won't explain your claim that he killed Basil?'

'All right, I'll tell,' said Bott sulkily, just as Alec burst in. Behind him, Sister came to a halt on the threshold, with Tom and Piper peering over her shoulders.

'Someone cried out!' Alec's swift glance swept the room, far too small to conceal an intruder. His gaze came to rest on Daisy.

She gave him a smug smile. 'Nothing to worry about,' she said. 'You'll be pleased to hear that Mr. Bott has now recovered sufficiently to tell you the rest of his story.'

Sister pushed past Alec to lay a hand on Bott's forehead. 'You're rather flushed.' She clasped his wrist. 'Are you sure you feel well enough?'

'Yes,' he said curtly.

'Well, your pulse is quite strong and steady, I must say. Ten minutes, Chief Inspector.' She glanced at the watch pinned to her apron and bustled out, Tom and Piper parting before her like the Red Sea before Moses.

'All right,' said Alec, 'Piper, come in and take notes, please. Ladies…'

'I'm not leaving,' Susan said adamantly.

'Susie, I'll be…'

'Don't argue, Horace, I'm staying, and that's that.'

He held out a hand to her, and she went to take it.

'Mr. Fletcher,' he said with a meekness which astonished Daisy, 'what I've got to say is going to upset Miss Hopgood. I'd be glad if you'd let Miss Dalrymple stay with her.'

Alec closed his eyes, and his lips moved silently as if he were begging heaven for mercy, or counting very fast to ten. His eyes opened again. 'As you wish, Mr. Bott. Sergeant Tring–' He went to the door and said something softly to Tom, who left.

Shutting the door, Alec moved to stand at the foot of the bed. 'Horace Bott, I must warn you that what you say will be taken down in writing and may be used in evidence in a court of law.'

'*I* haven't done anything illegal. You can use it against Lord DeLancey.'

'Well?'

'First, I want to thank you,' Bott said, not very graciously. 'Miss Dalrymple says it was you who saved me from drowning.'

'I merely assisted Mr. Cheringham in getting you ashore.'

'Cheringham? Oh. Well, thank you anyway. I was *not* trying to kill myself.'

'I'm glad to hear it. You claim Lord DeLancey tried to kill you to keep you quiet?'

'That's right.'

'Because you witnessed his attack on his brother?'

'I heard them quarrelling in the Cheringhams' boat-house in the middle of the night,' Bott said with relish.

That had to be it, of course, Daisy thought. Alec's sharp nod showed that his mind had run on the same lines.

'Lord DeLancey saw you?' he asked.

'I don't think so. But everyone was so convinced I'd gone down there, I suppose he believed it.'

'You're prepared to swear it was the DeLancey brothers you heard?'

'I know – knew – Basil's voice all too well, and he called the man yelling at him "Ceddie."'

'This is a very serious charge, Mr. Bott. You'll understand that I need some more information to support it. Let's start with exactly what they said.'

'I can't remember the exact words. "Ceddie" said something about being lucky the Ambrose Thames Cup heat was the first of the day and not interesting enough to bring out the reporters. Otherwise, the newspapers would have been full of Basil's assault on me. But if I went to the boat-house and he assaulted me again, I'd be bound to sue and it couldn't possibly be kept from the press.'

'And what was Basil's response?' Alec prompted.

Bott flushed. 'It was extremely insulting to me. You can't expect me to repeat it. But then he told Cedric to keep his hair on and stop interfering in what was none of his business. Cedric shouted that it damn well was his business. He was head of the family in their father's absence and like it or not Basil would do what he was told. Basil said he bloody well wouldn't kowtow to a coward. He yelled at Cedric to get out or he'd regret it. I expected Cedric – if not both of them –

to come out, so that's when I left. But that must have been when they started fighting.'

'Why didn't you tell me this yesterday, Mr. Bott? Concealing information from the police is a serious offence.'

'I was sure you'd get onto Cedric DeLancey without my help, and until you caught up with him, I knew I'd be made the scapegoat if you found out I was anywhere neat the boat-house. You wouldn't even have hunted any further, would you?'

'It is not my practise to look for scapegoats.' Alec said coldly. 'What were you doing near the boat-house in the middle of the night?'

With a sullen glare, Bott said, 'I'm sure you can work that out for yourself, Chief inspector.'

'Oh Horace!' Susan's dismay escaped her.

He turned his head away from her.

'I might venture a guess.' Alec agreed. 'You went to sabotage the fours boat.'

'Oh Horace, you promised not to do it!' She pulled her hand from his clasp.

'Well, I didn't, did I?' he snarled, goaded.

'What put the idea into your head, Mr. Bott?' Alec asked. 'To take your revenge on Basil DeLancey in that particular way, I mean.'

'It was at the fair,' said Susan, when Bott seemed reluctant to answer. 'We were behind Miss Cheringham and Mr. Frieth in the queue for the Ferris wheel. They didn't see us. Miss Cheringham asked Mr. Frieth if he was really sure Horace wouldn't damage the boat.'

'Did you hear Mr. Frieth's answer, Miss Hopgood?'

'Yes, he said it was just a silly idea Mr. DeLancey had got into his head. He couldn't believe Horace would spoil things for him and Mr. Cheringham and Mr. Fosdyke just to get his own back on Mr. DeLancey. And Horace *promised* me he wouldn't.'

'I wasn't going to.' Bott growled.

'What changed your mind, Mr. Bott?'

'I don't suppose I would have gone through with it.' Bott closed his eyes and spoke in a dreary monotone. 'It was just – I went back to the house and up to my room. Everyone knew I'd been shoved in the river that morning and had a long walk back from Henley, but not one of the b... – not one of them came to see if I was all right, let alone to ask me to join them downstairs. I sat and seethed till I couldn't think straight, then I decided to show the lot of them. It was stupid. I don't suppose I'd have actually done it.'

In the brief silence that followed his confession, Susan took his hand again and squeezed it. Daisy, feeling fearfully guilty that she had not enquired after him, looked at Alec. The compassion in the gaze he fixed on Bott made her wonder how much he suffered from the slights of those who considered themselves his superiors.

She would make it all up to him when they were married, she vowed passionately.

His professional mask descended again. In a matter-of-fact voice, he said, 'Just to clear up a loose end, Mr. Bott, how did you intend to hole the boat?'

'I thought of using a boat-hook, but I couldn't be sure of finding one in the boat-house in the dark. The moon was shining, but I couldn't remember if there were any windows. With the door open, I reckoned there'd be just enough light to pick my way to the boat. So I took one of my tent-pegs and the mallet.'

'We didn't find the mallet.'

'No.' Opening his eyes, Bott gave him a sour grin. 'I tossed the peg into the bushes in a panic when I thought the DeLanceys were coming out and might catch me. But I had enough sense left to hang on to my one and only mallet.'

'Fair enough.'

'You believe me?' Bott asked incredulously. 'About everything?'

'I'm inclined to. It's a pity we have no concrete evidence of Lord DeLancey's involvement. He must have been wearing gloves that night, too.'

'Typical namby-pamby swell.'

'What about his note?' said Daisy. 'That would be proof the invitation to meet on Temple Island came from him.'

Alec swung round to stare at her, not with annoyance at her interruption but with grey eyes narrowed in thought. At that moment, the door opened and Sister stuck her head in.

'Time for my patient to rest, Chief Inspector. I really must insist.'

'One moment more, Sister. Mr. Bott, the note wasn't found in your pockets when we pulled you out. *What did you do with it?*'

'Chucked it in the waste-paper basket in my room.'

'Thank you for your cooperation, and yours, Miss Hopgood. He's all yours, Sister. Come along, Piper.' Alec strode from the room, Piper loping after him and Daisy trotting to keep up. She pulled the door shut behind her as he turned, saw her, and said, 'You're not staying to support Miss Hopgood, Daisy?'

'She doesn't need me any more. Bott's conscious and you've finished questioning him. Besides, I don't want to be stranded here if you're leaving. When I telephoned, Gladstone said Tish is all right, but I want to see her and tell her Bott is recovering.'

'What you mean is, you don't want to be left out of what happens next.'

'That too,' she said with a sunny smile.

His answering smile was rueful. 'Well, I

haven't time to argue. Ernie, I want you to stay here, standing guard outside Bott's door. A Henley constable should be on his way to join you – I sent Sergeant Tring to phone for one. I doubt Lord DeLancey will try again to kill Bott in such a public setting, but it's always possible.'

'Right Chief. Do I arrest him if he turns up?'

'Only if he somehow gets past you and you actually witness an attempt on Bott's life. Otherwise, try to stall him until I get back. If that fails, if he leaves, telephone me at the Cheringhams'.

'Right, chief.'

'Good man. Come along, Daisy.' He set off at a fast pace along the passage.

'Do you really think Lord DeLancey might try again to murder Bott?' she asked, scurrying at his side.

'Not if he has his wits about him, but he does seem prone to losing his head.'

'That's what caused his trouble in the war,' Daisy panted.

Regarding her with eyebrows raised, Alec slowed his pace. 'It was? I'd better have the rest of that story, now that he's under suspicion.'

'I only know what Tish told me. Cherry said Lord DeLancey panicked and led his men into a massacre, only he led it from behind and he was the only one to come out unscathed. There were just two or three other survivors, I think. It was hushed up because of his father's position, but that's why he's in a blue funk about gossip.'

'A coward, in fact, who goes off the rails in the face of danger.'

'He can't help being afraid,' Daisy argued, finding herself unexpectedly defending Cedric DeLancey. 'He didn't ask to be sent into battle. I mean, I expect he could have stayed at home if he'd tried, Lord Bicester being a member of the government, but the social pressure was enormous. Michael said it took far more courage to withstand public opinion than...'

'Michael?' Alec stopped and frowned down at her, his dark, bushy eyebrows meeting over his nose,

'The man I was engaged to. He was a conscientious objector. You needn't look so beastly contemptuous.' Daisy blinked back tears. 'He joined a Friends' Ambulance Unit and was blown up by a land-mine.'

Taking her hands, Alec said quietly, 'I'm sorry, I didn't mean to look contemptuous. You must explain to me ... but not now.'

'No, I'm sorry, I didn't mean to bring it up now.' She sniffed. 'Here comes Mr. Tring.'

A quick squeeze of the hands and Alec was all business again, striding to meet the sergeant.

'Just coming to see if Sister'd chucked you

out yet, Chief. What's next?'

'About turn, Tom. We're going back to Bulawayo.'

'Right, Chief. There's a Henley man on his way. Not to Crowswood Place?'

'No, if DeLancey's there, he'll keep.'

'You're going to look for his note to Bott?' Daisy asked, once more trotting to keep up.

'Yes, it may be the only concrete evidence we can find. I'm just afraid DeLancey may remember it and go to hunt for it. He can use the excuse that he's fetching his brother's stuff to get upstairs to search.'

'He doesn't know Bott bunged it in the WPB,' Daisy pointed out breathlessly.

'No, but he could hope to find it in Bott's room. Oh, the dickens! Would the maids have emptied the wastepaper baskets by now?'

'It's Sunday.' Daisy panted, emerging into hazy sunshine a step behind Alec, Tom on her heels. With relief she saw the yellow Chummy parked nearby. 'I don't expect the local girls will be in today, so the bedrooms will only get a sketchy going-over. I'll hop into the back seat, Mr. Tring.'

'P'raps you'd better, miss.'

The little Austin bounced beneath Tom's weight descending on the front passenger seat as Alec pressed the self-starter. The engine, tuned by Scotland Yard's motor mechanic, purred to life. They zipped away down the street.

'Since Ernie and I left DeLancey, he's had plenty of time to get to Bulawayo and destroy that note,' Alec said, swinging the car around a corner. Fortunately, the traffic was still Sunday-morning sparse after last night's celebrations. 'I can only hope he wasn't too swift on the uptake, or that he dithered about what to do.'

'I just hope we don't have to go through the dustbins,' said Tom.

They turned into the Marlow Road. Clear of the town, Alec stepped on the accelerator. Daisy half-expected to see Lord DeLancey speeding towards them on his way to Townlands Hospital to bump off Bott. However, they passed the gates of Crowswood Place without meeting any motor-cars.

'Here, Chief, we're not at Brooklands,' Tom protested as the Austin rocketed around a bend. 'It won't do us any good to arrive with broken necks.'

'Sorry.' Alec eased up the merest trifle. 'I'm busy kicking myself for not telephoning from the hospital. The house is full of hefty young men quite capable of stopping DeLancey.'

'Cherry knows Lord DeLancey's under suspicion.' Daisy reminded him, hanging onto the side of the car. 'I expect he'll be keeping an eye on him if he's turned up already. So if you're using your brake-pedal foot to kick yourself, kindly stop it.'

Alec and Tom both laughed, but there was no noticeable diminution in their speed until they reached Bulawayo and turned into the drive.

On the front lawn, Poindexter, Wells, Leigh, and Meredith were playing croquet. Alec pulled up nearby 'Have you seen Lord DeLancey?' he called.

'No, s-sir, not today.'

'We've been out here for an hour or so,' Leigh added.

'Thanks.' Alec waved and continued to the house. 'Tom, find a spot indoors where you can see him drive up, assuming he does. Let him get inside, well out of the way, then let the air out of his tyres. If he's not after the note, we'll explain later.'

'What are you going to do, Alec?' Daisy asked, climbing out from the backseat.

'Try to catch him red-handed, without giving him a chance to destroy the note.' Alec rang the doorbell as they all went into the house. The butler came through the baize door at the rear of the hall. 'Gladstone, I want to station Sergeant Tring at a window overlooking the drive.'

'The dining room, sir?' Imperturbable, Gladstone opened the dining-room door, and Tom went to take up his post.

'We're expecting Lord DeLancey,' Alec said.

'To fetch Mr. DeLancey's things, sir?'

'So he'll no doubt say. When you answer the door, please direct him upstairs, don't accompany him.'

'Very good, sir.'

'Which is Bott's room?'

'Last door on the left in the right wing, sir. Opposite the back stairs.'

'There's a door to the stairs?'

'Oh yes, sir. The usual swinging door padded against sound.'

'Perfect. Thank you.' Alec headed for the stairs. When Daisy followed, he turned to her and shook his head. 'You're to stay well out of this. Cedric DeLancey is unpredictable and therefore dangerous.'

'I know, darling. I shan't get in the way, I promise, but I simply must go up and change my clothes.'

He looked her up and down and his grey eyes lit with laughter. 'It might be a good idea, love,' he admitted.

'You're not in much better shape yourself.' Daisy retorted.

She pottered about in bedroom and bathroom, intending to keep her promise yet reluctant to go too far away. After all, Alec was in danger, too. She was in Tish's bedroom when she heard a motor-car drive up. Discreetly peering from the window, she saw Lord DeLancey step out of a dark green Bentley sports car.

Gladstone must have been watching with

Tom, because he admitted Lord DeLancey at once. A minute or two later, Tom came out and knelt by the Bentley to open the valve of the first tyre.

'Hi, what's up?' called one of the croquet-players, and they all abandoned their game to cluster around the sergeant.

Daisy did not wait to try to hear what Tom said. Crossing the room, she eased open the door, and peeped out. No sign of Lord DeLancey on the landing or in the opposite passage. Then Alec emerged from the back stairs, crept across the passage, and opened the door of Bott's room.

Footsteps thundered up the stairs. Meredith and Wells charged across the landing, Leigh and Poindexter close behind. Between them, Daisy caught a glimpse of Alec turning his head to glance at them, looking annoyed. Then he lurched as DeLancey shoved past him.

'View halloo!' cried Leigh.

DeLancey darted through the swinging door to the back stairs and disappeared. After him went the oarsmen, in full cry.

'Tally-ho!'

'Gone away!'

'Yoicks!'

'So-ho! So-ho!'

'Damn!' Alec glowered after the pack, then turned and headed for the main stairs. Seeing Daisy, he gestured back towards Bott's room.

'Daisy, take a look in there, would you?'

'Right-oh.' She sped to the linen-room. Bott's camp-bed practically filled the floor space, with a frightful Victorian plant-stand of painted papier-mâché for a night-table. A shelf had been cleared of linens for his things. These were in disarray, tent-pegs scattered over rumpled shirts and vests.

On the bed lay a coat-hanger, a jacket half inside-out, a wicker waste-paper basket, and a small heap of its contents: an empty Woodbines packet, dead matches, a tobacconist's receipt, a pass for the general enclosure, and a crumpled sheet of paper.

Lord DeLancey couldn't possibly have missed it. Alec must have interrupted him just as he emptied the WPB.

Snatching it up, Daisy paused just long enough to make sure it was indeed the invitation to the Temple Island rendezvous. Then she dashed after Alec.

Half-way down the stairs, she saw him at the front door with Tom Tring and Gladstone.

'Alec, I've got it!'

She waved the note as all three looked round. Alec took a step towards her but suddenly his gaze shifted to beyond her. On the next to bottom step, Daisy turned to peer over the banisters and saw the green baize service door at the rear of the hall swinging open.

Lord DeLancey rushed into the hall. As the door swung shut behind him, Daisy heard the baying of the hounds on his trail. His pale, drawn face and terrified eyes reminded her of why she had always refused to go fox-hunting.

Alec moved to meet him. 'Lord De-Lancey...'

With a cry of despair, he swerved and darted through the nearest door, into the library. Wells burst through the baize door just in time to spot him. View-hallooing triumphantly, he and his friends galumphed after their quarry.

But the fox was not yet brought to bay.

'He'll go through a window,' Alec cried, changing direction. 'Tom, we'll try to head him off.' He ran into the drawing-room, the sergeant close behind.

Hurrying after them, Daisy was no longer sure whose side she was on.

CHAPTER 19

From the top of the terrace steps, Daisy had a grandstand view of the action.

Halfway down the lawn the four Ambrose men, slowed when they all tried to climb through the same library window, caught up with Alec and Tom. Cherry and Rollo had a headstart, dashing in from the side – they had been sitting under the chestnut with Aunt Cynthia and the girls when the hunt veered their way.

They all closed in on the landing-stage, where Lord DeLancey, already kneeling in one of the skiffs, slashed frantically with a pocket-knife at the painter.

The line parted. Pushing off, DeLancey grabbed the sculls and slotted them into the rowlocks. He pulled out into the stream as Rollo and Cherry pounded along the landing-stage to the second skiff.

'No oars!' Rollo cried in dismay.

Cherry swung round. 'Fletcher!'

Alec altered course towards the boat-house, slowing as he fumbled for the pad-lock key in his trouser pocket.

Poindexter overtook him. 'I put a pair here when we fetched the missing s-skiff from

Temple island.' He retrieved two sculls from the bushes and made for the skiff.

By then, Cherry and Rollo were installed on the rowing benches and Meredith on the rear seat, while Wells slid the rudder into place. Alec unfastened the boat-house door anyway. Leigh plunged in and came out with another pair of sculls, which he and Poindexter passed at arms' length to Cherry across the already widening gap between hoar and shore.

Lord DeLancey was nearing the middle of the river, heading across and downstream. A small, noisy motor-launch and several other rowing craft were making their way down the river from Henley, keeping to the right against the Berkshire bank.

Daisy looked down towards Hambleden. Nothing was coming up the river at the moment, but at the bend a number of boats were hanging on to the piles and booms above the lock, waiting their turns to enter. The lock must be filling to the level of the upper river.

Did Lord DeLancey know about the lock? His pursuers were bound to catch him there. Or did he intend to land on the Remenham bank and take to his heels? He couldn't possibly get far. Most likely he was in such a panic he had no plans at all.

With Meredith steering to take best advantage of the faster stream flowing towards the weir, on the near side of the river, Cherry and Rollo were rapidly gaining on DeLancey.

'There's not much they can do,' said Alec, joining Daisy at her vantage point, 'until he goes ashore.'

'Or reaches the lock.'

'It's just round the bend?'

'Yes, on the right. Those boats are queuing to get in when the water level– Oh, the gates must have opened. Here comes a launch.'

Its well-tuned engine buzzing like a persistent bee, the launch came up fast, steering towards the middle of the river out of the way of the downstream traffic. Meredith spotted it a moment after Daisy. His yell reached her ears over the launch's hum. Rollo and Cherry backed their oars.

Lord DeLancey kept going, pulling on his sculls in a manic frenzy. The launch hooted at him and took evasive action – too late.

The skiff's bows splintered against the launch's side, an oblique blow that tipped DeLancey into the river.

He started to swim away from the launch, downstream on a long slant towards the Bucks bank. The current was swift, racing towards the weir. Meredith, Cherry, Rollo, the men in the launch, all shouted at DeLancey. Unhearing or unheeding, he made no effort to head directly for the bank.

From the height and distance of the garden

steps, the speeding water looked smooth as glass, the swirling undercurrents concealed beneath the sleek surface. DeLancey's dark head bobbed on it like a fisherman's float, then disappeared.

'Drowned,' Alec confirmed tiredly, dropping to the grass beside Daisy in the chestnut's shade.

Jaws and teaspoons stilled.

In the hush, a heron flapping its leisurely way up the river emitted a loud *grawk*. Someone turned a nervous snicker into a cough, but the tension broke. Well-bred voices murmured once more, and porcelain cups chinked against saucers.

'Tea, Mr. Fletcher?'

'Please, Lady Cheringham. And a sandwich or two, if I may. I seem to have missed both breakfast and lunch.'

Daisy jumped up and piled a plate with cucumber sandwiches, watercress sandwiches, and Gentleman's Relish sandwiches, topped with two buttered scones. 'You're in luck, darling?' she said, presenting it to Alec. 'Cook is still catering to oarsmen's appetites.'

'That reminds me.' The first scone stopped halfway to his mouth and he raised his voice. 'Gentlemen, you're free to leave now, of course. I want to thank you all for being quite the most helpful and cooperative group of suspects it's ever been my pleasure not to have to arrest.'

Everyone laughed. Daisy guessed that in the minds of four young men the drama and tragedy of the past few days was already metamorphosing into a splendid story for future telling and retelling.

Perhaps Alec saw the same thing, for he added, 'I'm counting on you to keep your mouths shut, for the present at least. This is still a police matter, not to mention the innocent people who might be hurt if rumours spread.'

There was a disappointed murmur of assent.

'Does Fosdyke know he's free to go?' Daisy asked Alec.

'I left Tom to phone the Catherine Wheel before he joins Gladstone for his tea, since he, I gather, had breakfast at the hospital.'

'Yes, they fed us, though I can't recommend their catering. Do you know how Bott's doing?'

'I dropped in to tell him what happened, and that he's no longer under suspicion. He's a bit feverish. They're keeping him in overnight, but the doctor doesn't think it's serious as he's too fit to succumb easily to an infection. Miss Hopgood's confident enough to be going home tonight so she won't miss work tomorrow.'

'Good. What about you?'

'I've got a few odds and ends to clear up here. I'm meeting the three Chief Constables at Henley Police Station.' He consulted his wristwatch. 'In half an hour, so let me eat in peace, woman.'

'Right-oh, darling.'

Leigh and Meredith, Poindexter and Wells, were already taking leave of their hostess, so Daisy went to say good-bye to them. Cherry, Rollo, and Dottie were staying on at Bulawayo for a few more days.

Rollo drew Daisy aside. 'I'm dashed worried about Tish,' he confided. 'All this ghastly business has hit her awfully hard.'

Daisy glanced at her cousin, sitting close beside her mother. She was pale and wan, and the effort she made to smile at the departing foursome was painfully obvious.

'She's not exactly used to people assaulting each other and expiring all over the place.' Daisy said. 'It's just been one thing after another, with no time to recover from the shock in between. I'm sure a few days of peace and quiet will buck her up. Just take extra good care of her.'

'I wish I had the right to take care of her!' Rollo burst out.

'Have you decided yet what to do about your degree?'

He winced. 'To tell the truth, I dread another year of lectures and essays and tutorials. I'm just not cut out for it.'

Daisy gave him a straight look. 'It all rather depends on whether you consider Tish is worth the slog, doesn't it?'

Rollo was taken aback, as if he'd never thought in quite those terms before. He flushed. 'Yes, well, when you put it like that...' He glanced at Tish, who sent him a tremulous smile. 'Confound it, I'll try,' he said with a reckless air. 'I'd slay dragons for her, so what's a few dons here or there?'

'Spiffing! Go and tell her. That will cheer her up.'

She watched as he went over to Tish and the two of them strolled down towards the river. Then Alec got up, so she joined him.

'I feel almost human again,' he said, setting his empty plate and cup on the tea-trolley, but I must run. Lady Cheringham, my men will be off to London by train this evening, but if I might trespass further on your hospitality, I'd like to stay till tomorrow. There's business I can't complete till the morning, and then I'll be able to drive Daisy up to town.'

'You're more than welcome, Mr. Fletcher,' Aunt Cynthia assured him.

'Spiffing!'

Alec grinned at Daisy. 'While I'm gone, you'll have time to type up your notes of Bott's statement. Regard it as the penalty for...'

'...Meddling,' said Daisy, wrinkling her

nose at him but dutifully accompanying him into the house.

With all the departures, there were enough bedrooms for everyone that night. Daisy was in bed and about to turn off her light when Tish tapped on the door and came in.

'Daisy, can I talk to you?'

'Of course.' Daisy patted the bed. 'Come and sit down.'

To her dismay, her cousin's eyes were red and swollen. Aunt Cynthia had sent her up to bed right after tea, saying she looked exhausted, and she had had her dinner on a tray, so Daisy had not seen her since her talk with Rollo. She certainly did not look as if she'd been crying from happiness.

Yet Daisy was quite sure Tish was in love with Rollo. Had he got cold feet at the last moment? He had been rather quiet all evening.

'What's the trouble?' she asked.

'Oh Daisy, I simply *must* tell someone! But it's all so dreadful, I can't bear...' A sob escaped her.

Reaching for the handkerchief on her bedside-table, Daisy leaned forward to put her arm round Tish's shaking shoulders. 'Here, darling. Is it something to do with Rollo?'

'Not really. Well, sort of, now. He's asked me to marry him – it'd have to be a long engagement, but what does it matter? I told him I'd have to think about it, because I couldn't bear to disappoint him, but I can't let him marry a murderer!'

Daisy's head swam. Trying to think, she leant back and clasped both Tish's hands. 'Basil DeLancey?'

Tish nodded, her eyes shut and her lips trembling in spite of being pressed tight together.

'Darling, how frightful! Tell me.'

'I woke up in the night, that night.' Now she had started, the words poured forth. 'I started to worry about Bott and the fours boat. It was Rollo's last chance to win a cup, and I thought if he didn't, he'd quit the university and that would be the end of *us*. You know how awful everything seems at two o'clock in the morning...'

'Beastly.' Daisy agreed.

'Things go round and round in one's head, and one simply can't think straight. Rollo and Cherry were both sure Bott wouldn't do it, but they were equally sure Basil DeLancey wouldn't stand guard. In the end, I knew I'd never fall asleep again until I had seen for myself. So I crept out and went down there.'

'And there was the Hon. Basil, lying in wait for Bott.'

'I didn't see him till he had got between me and the door. The moon was shining right in at the windows, but Mother's vines kept half the light out, and you know how eerie moonlight can be.'

Remembering her own foray, Daisy nodded. 'Did he mistake you for Bott?'

'Oh no. He called me "pretty Patsy." which is a name *I despise*, and he said he was glad I'd come to give him a bit of nookie, he'd much rather have me than Bott. He was advancing on me, saying all sorts of horrible things. I grabbed an oar from the rack and told him to let me pass or I'd hit him. But he kept coming and coming until I couldn't move any further back, so I did.'

Tish buried her face in her hands, and Daisy put an arm around her shoulders again. 'Gosh, darling, how absolutely frightful for you.'

'He ducked, but the blade caught him on the side of the head. I didn't think I'd be able to hit hard enough to really hurt him, but I suppose the length of the oar... He fell, and slid across the floor, and lay still. I dropped the oar, but then I thought how annoyed Rollo would be to find it on the floor, so I put it back in the rack. I was going to go back to DeLancey to see how badly hurt he was, but when I turned round, he was already getting up. A moonbeam shone on his face, and he looked so angry and positively *evil* that I just ran away.

'I don't blame you a bit. No wonder you were terrified he had come after you when he barged into our room.'

'You were wonderful then, Daisy! I was sure you must be right about his being drunk. He wouldn't have behaved so badly if he hadn't had too much to drink, and I didn't think he could have walked back to the house if he was badly hurt. I didn't know people sometimes collapse later.'

'Nor did I. We'll both just have to go on being sorry we didn't guess something more was wrong.'

'But I was responsible. I can't tell you how I felt when he died.' She shuddered. 'And then I was afraid Alec would work out that I'd done it; then I thought Bott was going to be arrested and I'd have to confess to save him.'

With considerable relief, Daisy said, 'I'm glad you wouldn't have let Bott carry the can.'

'Oh no. But it was like a nightmare that went on and on and I couldn't wake up, however hard I tried. When Bott was hurt, Cherry said Lord DeLancey attacked him because he killed Basil, so it was my fault again.'

'If Lord DeLancey didn't hit his brother after all, I suppose he might have believed Bott did, but according to Bott, he was just afraid of anyone finding out he'd been in the boat-house.' Daisy felt that there was a circular argument in there somewhere but she couldn't quite pin it down. She concentrated on comforting Tish. 'Bott heard the DeLanceys quarrelling, you know.'

'He did? I suppose Lord DeLancey was afraid he might have. But still, it really was my fault, because if Basil hadn't died, Lord DeLancey wouldn't have attacked Bott and wouldn't have drowned. So I'm a double murderer, triple if Bott dies…'

'He's not going to. Alec says he's doing well.'

'...so how can I possibly marry Rollo?' Tish wailed.

'Darling, you're *not* a murderer. You had no intention of killing Basil DeLancey, what the lawyers call "malice aforethought," and anyway it was self-defence. He threatened you. No one could possibly imagine you would have hit him if he had not attacked you first.'

Tish raised a tear-stained face. 'Do you think Rollo would believe it?'

'Of course!' Daisy assured her confidently. 'You had far better tell him, you know, than let it fester away in your mind and come between you.'

'Perhaps. I suppose so. But what about your Alec?'

Suddenly cautious, Daisy said, 'There's no need to tell Alec. He never even considered you as a suspect, nor Dottie, let alone Aunt Cynthia. Since Cedric DeLancey is dead anyway, why stir up trouble?'

'You think there would be trouble? I'd feel much better if I knew he considered it self-defence. Couldn't you put it to him as a hypothetical case?'

'Right-oh,' said Daisy, with the deepest of misgivings.

'So the whole thing will be hushed up?' Daisy asked, as Alec turned onto the Marlow Road.

'Not the DeLanceys' deaths, of course, but the fact that one brother killed the other. Since Bott has agreed to keep quiet about Cedric DeLancey's attack on him – in exchange for not being prosecuted for concealing evidence – both can be written off as tragic accidents. The chief Constables and the Assistant Commissioner see no need to cause the DeLancey family further grief. I'd like to think it's not because their father is the Earl of Bicester.'

'It seems reasonable, anyway,' Daisy said decidedly. The one thing which had been worrying her about protecting Tish was that the belief that Cedric DeLancey had caused the death of his brother would deeply distress their relatives.

Still, she had promised Tish to try to find out Alec's opinion. 'Darling, do you mind if I put a hypothetical case to you?' she asked with caution.

'A hypothetical case? What do you mean?'

'Just suppose a girl went down to the boathouse that night. Suppose Basil DeLancey cornered her and threatened to ... assault her. If she picked up an oar and warned him she'd hit him if he didn't stop, and he didn't and she did, would the verdict be self-defence?'

'Daisy, you didn't!' Alec exclaimed, turning to her a face appalled and furious.

'Of course not, idiot! I told you I didn't go down until after DeLancey was safe in bed.'

He gave her another quick glance, full of suspicion. He only took his eyes off the road for a moment, but in that moment they rounded a bend and found themselves radiator to noses with a herd of cows.

Alec slammed on the brakes. Though the Austin Seven was not a model noted for the adequacy of its brakes, they held. The nearest cow mooed with more curiosity than alarm and licked the bonnet. Chivvied by a pair of black and white farm dogs, the herd strolled onward with no further interest in the mechanical intruder in their midst. The stolid cowman bringing up the rear tipped his cap as he passed.

Restarting the engine, which had stalled, Alec said, 'Daisy…'

'A purely hypothetical case,' she interrupted hurriedly.

'Then yes, it would probably be ruled as self-defence, and I don't want to hear any more about it. What I was going to say is, do you know anyone living within, say, a dozen miles of Lyndhurst?'

'Hampshire?' Daisy enquired, puzzled.

'Yes, the New Forest.'

'No, not that I can think of.'

'I know a nice country inn in Lyndhurst. I'm going to book a couple of rooms there for next weekend, and we'll...'

'Next weekend is the engagement party Mr. Arbuckle's throwing for us at Claridge's.'

Alec groaned. 'Do we have to go? It sounds ghastly.'

'Yes, love,' Daisy said firmly, 'we have to go.'

'The weekend after, then, we're going to spend in the New Forest, miles from anyone you know *and* from county boundaries. And the local police will jolly well have to cope with any bodies you just happen to fall over!'

The publishers hope that this book has given you enjoyable reading. Large Print Books are especially designed to be as easy to see and hold as possible. If you wish a complete list of our books please ask at your local library or write directly to:

Magna Large Print Books
Magna House, Long Preston,
Skipton, North Yorkshire.
BD23 4ND